6/12

2

D0225911

POLITICS AND AMERICA
IN CRISIS

Other titles in Praeger's Reflections on the Civil War Era series:

The Confederacy by Paul D. Escott

Weary of War: Life on the Confederate Home Front by Joe A. Mobley
True Sons of the Republic: European Immigrants in the Union Army by Martin W. Öfele

The Civil War at Sea by Craig L. Symonds

Decision in the Heartland: The Civil War in the West by Steven E. Woodworth

POLITICS AND AMERICA IN CRISIS

THE COMING OF THE CIVIL WAR

‿‿‿

MICHAEL S. GREEN

Reflections on the Civil War Era
John David Smith, Series Editor

PRAEGER
An Imprint of ABC-CLIO, LLC

A B C CLIO

Santa Barbara, California • Denver, Colorado • Oxford, England

Library of Congress Cataloging-in-Publication Data

Green, Michael S.
  Politics and America in crisis : the coming of the Civil War / Michael S. Green.
    p. cm. — (Reflections on the Civil War era)
  Includes bibliographical references and index.
  ISBN 978-0-275-99095-4 (alk. paper) — ISBN 978-0-313-08174-3 (ebook) 1. United States—Politics and government—1849-1861. 2. United States—History—Civil War, 1861-1865—Causes. I. Title.
    E459.G793 2010
    973.7'11—dc22   2009046113

14 13 12 11 10   1 2 3 4 5

This book is also available on the World Wide Web as an eBook.
Visit www.abc-clio.com for details.

ABC-CLIO, LLC
130 Cremona Drive, P.O. Box 1911
Santa Barbara, California 93116-1911

This book is printed on acid-free paper ∞
Manufactured in the United States of America

To Eric Foner

CONTENTS

Series Foreword   ix
Acknowledgments   xi
Prologue: The Evolution of American Politics   xiii

Chapter One: Provisos and Spots: The Cracking of Old Coalitions   1

Chapter Two: The Compromise of 1850   19

Chapter Three: "A Hell of a Storm": The Aftermath of Compromise   45

Chapter Four: Bleeding Parties, Bleeding Kansas, Bleeding Sumner   73

Chapter Five: A New President, a New Party,
                a New Constitutional Clash   97

Chapter Six: Great Debates and Greater Debates   119

Chapter Seven: Purging the Land with Blood   139

Notes   161
Bibliographical Essay   175
Index   181

SERIES FOREWORD

"Like Ol' Man River," the distinguished Civil War historian Peter J. Parish wrote in 1998, "Civil War historiography just keeps rolling along. It changes course occasionally, leaving behind bayous of stagnant argument, while it carves out new lines of inquiry and debate."

Since Confederate General Robert E. Lee's men stacked their guns at Appomattox Court House in April 1865, historians and partisans have been fighting a war of words over the causes, battles, results, and broad meaning of the internecine conflict that cost more than 620,000 American lives. Writers have contributed between 50,000 and 60,000 books and pamphlets on the topic. Viewed in terms of defining American freedom and nationalism, western expansion and economic development, the Civil War quite literally launched modern America. "The Civil War," Kentucky poet, novelist, and literary critic Robert Penn Warren explained, "is for the American imagination, the great single event of our history. Without too much wrenching, it may, in fact, be said to *be* American history."

The books in Praeger's *Reflections on the Civil War Era* series examine pivotal aspects of the American Civil War. Topics range from examinations of military campaigns and local conditions, to analyses of institutional, intellectual, and social history. Questions of class, gender, and race run through each volume in the series. Authors, veteran experts in their respective fields, provide concise, informed, readable syntheses—fresh looks at familiar topics with new source material and original arguments.

"Like all great conflicts," Parish noted in 1999, "the American Civil War reflected the society and the age in which it was fought." Books in *Reflections on the Civil War Era* interpret the war as a salient event in the hammering out and understanding of American identity before, during, and after the secession crisis of 1860–1861. Readers will find the volumes valuable guides as they chart the troubled waters of mid-nineteenth-century American life.

John David Smith
Charles H. Stone Distinguished Professor of American History
The University of North Carolina at Charlotte

ACKNOWLEDGMENTS

This book is a synthesis of the politics of the decade-and-a-half before the Civil War. While I intend it for undergraduates and general readers, I hope it is thorough enough to be useful to graduate students and more advanced scholars. As such, it is based partly on past and present primary and archival research, but mostly on secondary works. The end notes reflect a sample of the works I have read since I began studying this period as an undergraduate more than—gasp!—a quarter of a century ago. As with any other book, then, this one is the product of more than its author, so I take great pleasure in thanking those who made this book better than it otherwise would have been and absolving them of its failings.

First, I must acknowledge my debt to a long list of scholars. Some I never met but have long admired, such as Allan Nevins and David Potter. Others I have had the pleasure of meeting and been able to express my admiration to, including Sean Wilentz, Daniel Walker Howe, and the late Don E. Fehrenbacher. Still others I would like to meet. Their works show up in the notes, some in the bibliography, while others, whose work goes unmentioned here, I have on my bookshelves or have read in libraries. Whether or not I have agreed with everything they have said, all of it has gone into the intellectual mix. I am grateful to them and have profited from them.

John David Smith is the ideal editor, gently prodding and thoroughly supportive, never revealing how much I taxed his patience—which I did. Michael Millman was wonderfully supportive as I completed the journey. Without Paul Cimbala of Fordham

University, I never would have found them and they never would have found me. I owe Paul a great deal for that and much more.

Many friends have enriched my life, personally and professionally. Xi Wang, Michael Vorenberg, and Heather Cox Richardson have been wonderful companions and sounding boards as we have researched and written about nineteenth-century politics and society. Discussing this period with Richard Etulain and DeAnna Beachley has helped me enormously. Andy Slap and Greg Borchard lent their considerable expertise to making this a better manuscript. Yanek Mieczkowski and I have been best friends since graduate school, and his reading of this book went above and beyond the call.

I wish that Eric McKitrick, John Y. Simon, Gary Elliott, and Chuck Adams had lived to hold this book in their hands. They held me to a high standard and made me better for it. Ralph Roske did a great deal to teach me about this era, including how to love learning about it and how to make sure I took it, but not myself, seriously in the process.

The dedication of this book acknowledges a tremendous debt that anyone familiar with its subject and the writing of history can understand. Eric Foner guided me through graduate classes and my Ph.D. at Columbia University. He helped me get a publisher for my dissertation, which eventually led to my invitation to be part of this series. Eric suggested this topic for a book and has provided much-needed friendship, encouragement, and well-placed (and badly needed) kicks in the pants for a long time, all with his trademark good humor. He offered his usual perspicacious advice on making this manuscript better. He continues to set a sterling, daunting example for one to try to emulate as a scholar, a teacher, a thinker, and an engaged member of society.

Many authors readily state they have no reason to thank their children, except for diverting their attention from their work. I have no children to thank, but Abigail and Kirby would fully expect to be mentioned. Their incessant demands for play and scratching, not to mention walking across my keyboard, may have led to some strange—or stranger—writing on my part. But they are cats while I am a mere human, so their behavior and lack of interest in encouraging me to work are understandable.

Family and friends sustain everyone, not just me. To list them all would be impossible. I would like to single out my father, Robert Green, for constant support and the memory of my mother, Marsha.

Saving the best for last, I want to thank Lenora and Bruce Young. Sadly for me, I never met Bruce. Lenora is fun and inspiring, and her marriage to Bruce produced a wonderful family who have become wonderful friends, too, but none more wonderful than Deborah. For that, I will always owe them more than I can ever repay.

PROLOGUE: THE EVOLUTION OF AMERICAN POLITICS

By the mid-1840s, the United States looked to be a vital, prosperous republic. In many ways, the reality matched the appearance. With the Panic of 1837 ending, the economy was emerging from its doldrums. The Louisiana Purchase, treaties with England and Spain, and the tragic removal of Native Americans from the Southeast to lands west of the Mississippi made plenty of land available for farming, industry, and migration. In 1845, newspaperman John L. O'Sullivan wrote of "our manifest destiny to overspread and to possess the whole of the continent which Providence has given us for the development of the great experiment of liberty and federated self-government entrusted to us." Few white Americans would have disputed him. The republican ideals that produced the Declaration of Independence, the Constitution, and the idea of self-government found their way into Latin America, where revolutions drove out the Spanish Empire in the 1810s and 1820s. At the same time, European countries like England and France extended voter participation in ways similar to the United States. For the nation and its beliefs to move beyond their existing boundaries seemed only logical.

But this series of successes did nothing to obscure the divisions in American society. In 1820 and 1833, compromises in Congress had settled disputes between the North and South that had reminded Americans of the tenuous quality of their Union. Since then, Texans had won independence from Mexico and wanted to join the United States, but the presence of slavery in their vast territory made their goal a hot-button issue that politicians were reluctant to press. Democrats and Whigs, and the regions from which they came, were divided not only against one another, but also among themselves. The threads that held each party together were thin and getting thinner. Northerners in both parties—especially the Whigs—had long since tired of acceding to the South's wishes over slavery. Both parties also worried whether Manifest Destiny meant spreading both republican ideals and the institution of slavery—and whether they could accept that contradiction.

BIRTH OF A GOVERNMENT, BIRTH OF A PARTY SYSTEM

The United States was the first successful modern attempt to create a large-scale republic, complete with the election of a president. But war in Europe in the late eighteenth and early nineteenth centuries caught the United States between more powerful foes and created divisions that made Americans fear for their republic's future. The new republic's reactions sometimes proved unwise; the Alien and Sedition Acts of 1798 responded to hysteria over possible war with France by curtailing free speech. At other times, things worked out better than planned: the War of 1812, a near-disaster militarily, enabled the United States to demonstrate that it would be treated like a sovereign nation.

In this atmosphere of newness and danger, the development of political parties proved controversial. Although the Founding Fathers understood that people and groups would disagree, they saw political parties as too divisive, if not downright treasonous, especially in a struggling young republic. Responding in the early 1790s to Alexander Hamilton's broad view of federal and executive power, Thomas Jefferson, James Madison, and their supporters began forming what became known as the Jeffersonian or Republican Party, committed to expanding democracy and emphasizing agriculture over manufacturing. Hamilton countered by organizing the Federalists, who cultivated a belief in wealth in paper and manufacturing more than land and tied the United States more closely to the British industrial colossus than Jeffersonians preferred. They viewed their battle not as a competition for power, but as a fight to the finish. When Jefferson declared in his inaugural address, "We are all republicans; we are all federalists," he suggested the need for unity. When he wrote more than a year into his presidency, "I shall . . . sink federalism into an abyss from which there shall be no resurrection for it," he made clear that in his mind, unity meant eliminating the opposition.[1]

Jefferson almost succeeded. The Louisiana Purchase nearly doubled the nation's size, and he hoped to fill it with yeoman farmers who presumably would be loyal Republicans. Hamilton's death in an 1804 duel with Aaron Burr deprived Federalists of their leader, and regional divisions and their disdain for Jefferson's democratic leanings hampered their national campaigns. Nor did the War of 1812 help them. When Federalists in New England, the last area where they enjoyed any degree of success, began discussing seceding from the union, they largely sealed their fate. During James Monroe's presidency, from 1817 to 1825, the first party system ended. In the fight to the finish, the Federalists were finished.

But the battle over slavery had only just begun. The Second Continental Congress had deleted Jefferson's attack on slavery in the Declaration of Independence, but the Northwest Ordinance of 1787 banned it in the states that eventually formed the Upper Midwest. The Constitution's authors avoided using the word "slavery," instead referring to "persons held to service" and prohibiting interference with the international slave trade until 1808. The leaders of the early republic clearly disliked slavery but grasped its importance to the South's politics, culture, society, and economy—and it seemed on the road to extinction. But in 1793, Congress passed, and Washington signed, the Fugitive Slave Law. A northern Federalist introduced the law, befitting his party's strong commitment to property rights and efforts in the early republic to tamp down sectional differences, and successive administrations barely enforced it. And the states' rights sentiments that helped fuel the Republican response to the Alien and Sedition Acts manifested themselves increasingly in defending slavery against federal interference.

THE ERA OF NOT-SO-GOOD FEELINGS

To call Monroe's tenure "the era of good feelings," as one editor named it at the time, ignores the reality. The Panic of 1819 led to business shutdowns and destroyed savings, breeding in rural Americans in particular a distrust for banking that affected future political developments. The lack of a party system did nothing to reduce political infighting. The Federalists died out, but their ideology survived: Chief Justice John Marshall made the Supreme Court a bastion for federal supremacy and the protection of property and contracts, both Federalist hallmarks, during his tenure from 1801 to 1835. In addition, the Jeffersonians overdosed on the fruits of their success and divided into three groups. One group morphed into the Whig party by the mid-1830s. This party included former Federalists such as John Quincy Adams as well as like-minded Republicans such as Henry Clay; these men were believers in the need for an activist federal government. Another group, consisting of largely states' rights Jeffersonian Republicans and those even more strongly opposed to activist government, especially at the federal level, coalesced around Andrew Jackson as Democrats. The third group, almost entirely southerners, found even Jackson too much in favor of federal power. They considered the Constitution little more than a compact between states that had the right to tell the federal government to keep out of their business. Most of these men eventually cast their lot with the Democrats.

The second party system that these groups created differed in striking ways from the first party system. Whereas Federalists and Republicans sought mutual destruction, Democrats and Whigs simply competed for supremacy—a difference that allowed for more compromises and coalitions than would have been possible in the days of Hamilton and Jefferson. The guiding force behind building the Jacksonian Democrats, Martin Van Buren, emerged from New York politics, where he had battled Jeffersonians who at times united with the Federalists. Although Van Buren had fought them, he understood the need for politicians to work together to produce policy. Also, whereas Adams and Hamilton had fought with each other and against Jefferson, the politics of the second party system proved even more personal. While the Whig party backed Clay and what he called the "American System" of federally supported road construction and banking, Jackson's strong stand against federal action and for presidential power helped unify Democrats behind him and Whigs against him. Campaign tactics continued to focus on the issues that separated the two major parties, but they also became more democratic and depended increasingly on the personalities of such candidates as "Old Hickory" Jackson and the two Whig generals elected president: William Henry Harrison, known as "Old Tippecanoe," and Zachary Taylor, "Old Rough and Ready."

While Americans responded to personalities, they also responded to the issues the parties raised—and tried to avoid. Many of the Founding Fathers had expected slavery to die, a victim of moral opposition and dwindling profits. But events proved them wrong. The Industrial Revolution increased demand for textile mills and broadened the appeal of such inventions as the cotton gin, which made cotton production much easier and more profitable. Slave rebellions such as Nat Turner's in 1831 could have convinced southerners that they should rid themselves of a troublesome institution, but instead their leaders cracked down, making slavery more oppressive. By the early nineteenth century, those who once defended slavery as a necessary evil increasingly spoke of it as acceptable or even worthwhile for both masters and slaves. And in the North, artisans felt the pinch as factories often replaced them as makers and suppliers of goods, changing the urban landscape and their relationship with their employers and customers, while southerners relying more on slavery resented the cost of the goods they needed to import from the North or from abroad.

As more southerners changed their views of slavery, northerners changed their views of the world. For much of the first half of the nineteenth century, the nation was in the midst of a religious revival movement, the Second Great Awakening. In addition to its spiritual effects, its political impact proved staggering, especially in the North. Ministers preached the virtues of trying to achieve moral perfection. For southerners, this usually meant maintaining what they saw as an ordered, civilized society—including keeping slaves under control and assuring that even nonslaveholding whites participated in that effort through slave patrols and the hope that they might earn enough to own slaves. By contrast, throughout the North a variety of social movements and reforms sprang up that were designed to make society better, from women's rights to temperance, dietary reform to utopian socialist or religious communities. Abolitionism had a long history in the North—all northern states had acted against slavery in their state constitutions after the Revolutionary War. But the reforms reenergized the antislavery movement.

The free labor ideology was both distinct and inseparable from these revivals. The idea of freedom had been the cornerstone for the English colonizing the New World, whether it meant the freedom to worship, the freedom to earn, or the freedom to govern themselves. In the minds of these colonists and those who came after them, achieving these goals usually required independence of some kind, and Jefferson and his followers had seen property ownership as the road to that independence; whoever owned his own land, they thought, owned himself. This suggested the right to the fruits of one's labors—the freedom to labor, to keep the earnings from those labors, and, if those earnings came from an employer, to use them to create a business or buy land and establish that independence. For growing numbers of northerners, the free labor ideology's appeal brought with it a disgust with the South. According to these northerners, the South was backward, offered no reward for initiative or incentive to improve existing processes, and depended on forcing others to do work from which they derived little or no benefit. In addition, slavery occasionally created an unfair advantage for southerners competing economically with northern capitalists whose workers had more control over their lives. Northerners reasoned that without slavery, or at least with less reliance upon it, southerners would prosper.

Northerners who felt this way did not necessarily occupy the moral high ground. Some of the northern states that approved emancipation had made it gradual, enabling slavery to survive in some areas. Several states passed laws limiting or outlawing black migration. African Americans lacked the right to serve on juries or in militias, and few benefited as states extended the franchise to non-property owners. Most northerners wanted only to limit slavery's growth. Few actually called for abolition, and those who did faced violence and intimidation: Bostonians dragged William Lloyd Garrison through their city's streets, and in Alton, Illinois, in 1837, abolitionist editor Elijah Lovejoy died at the hands of a mob. Also, northerners often proved willing to compromise with the South on slavery or issues linked to it— enough that some northerners began to feel they had made too many concessions, and enough that southerners viewed northerners as pliable, or at least disinclined to take a stand.

In 1819, after relative calm over slavery during the three decades after the Constitutional Convention, the first sectional crisis over slavery—and the first round of concessions between the North and the South—involved Missouri's admission as a state. With Maine about to enter the Union and break the tie between free and slave states in the Senate in the North's favor, a congressman from New York proposed to ban new slaves from entering Missouri and the gradual emancipation of those already there. Southerners responded angrily, especially the more rigid Jeffersonians. This was a harbinger of future divisions over slavery within the Democratic and Whig parties and of future arguments in which southerners pointed to states' rights and northerners claimed both that the Founding Fathers opposed slavery and that national progress demanded restrictions on the "peculiar institution." It also foreshadowed the difficulties in resolving future conflicts. As speaker of the House, Clay helped broker the Missouri Compromise, also known as the Compromise of 1820, admitting both Maine and Missouri and thereby maintaining the balance in the Senate. The Compromise permitted slavery in Missouri and banned it from all other areas within the Louisiana Purchase that lay north of latitude 36' 30". But it was, as Jefferson wrote, "a fire bell in the night."[2]

Other alarms followed. In 1828, President John Quincy Adams signed a tariff increase that southerners called the "tariff of abominations." Already upset with the Compromise of 1820 (a sign of northern power) and Denmark Vesey's rebellion in 1822 (a warning to control their slaves), South Carolinians rebelled. An anonymous commentary, *The South Carolina Exposition and Protest*, outlined the doctrine of nullification—the idea that a state could nullify a federal law to protect itself against a tyrannical majority. The author was John C. Calhoun, whose views had enough of an impact for historian David Potter to call him "the most majestic champion of error since Milton's Satan in *Paradise Lost*."[3] Originally a nationalist who shared many of the ideas in Clay's "American System," Calhoun was by then Adams's vice-president and a presidential hopeful. He saw that South Carolina politics had shifted toward the radical Jeffersonian, states' rights view, and that his electoral future depended upon retaining support in his state.[4]

Calhoun continued as vice president under Andrew Jackson, who shared many of his states' rights inclinations—but not at the expense of federal supremacy. In 1828, Jackson easily defeated Adams in a brutal campaign: Jackson's supporters accused Adams, once minister to Russia, of procuring prostitutes for the czar; the Adams campaign highlighted Jackson's duels and vigilantism. Facing protests from South Carolina, Jackson proposed a tariff reduction. But he tolerated no disunion sentiment, emphasized majority rule and federal supremacy, and prepared to use military force to secure the Union if necessary. It proved unnecessary. In 1833, Clay, Calhoun, and Senator Daniel Webster of Massachusetts, a onetime Federalist who would join Clay as a Whig party leader, fashioned a compromise tariff, a lower tax that Calhoun urged even more pro-nullification South Carolinians to support. But the controversy pushed southerners further toward a sense of themselves as victims of federal oppression and toward an absolute states' rights position—sentiments that hardened with time.

Otherwise, however, Jackson and his supporters often sympathized with the South's states' rights views. They defeated an effort by Clay and Webster to recharter the Second Bank of the United States, partly because Jackson believed that the federal government should steer clear of banking and other private enterprise—a heartening sign for slaveowners. Indian removal—including the Trail of Tears that sent the five "civilized tribes" of the Southeast west to what later became Oklahoma—opened southern lands to slavery and to white ownership and development. During Jackson's tenure, the federal government stopped delivering abolitionist literature to offended southerners—an act that put southern Whigs in a bind, given their opposition to all things Jacksonian and need to retain power at home by supporting slavery. Congress approved the infamous "Gag Rule," which referred abolitionist petitions to a House committee that would bury them, but even that failed to mollify southerners. They resented the compromise that led to its approval because the original legislation banned the petitions entirely, as well as Representative John

Quincy Adams's efforts to force the House into a procedural pretzel to circumvent and overturn it. Jackson also opposed nationalist policies that would have involved the federal government in building transportation networks—the kinds of programs that many southerners saw as the first step toward federal interference with a more local institution like slavery. That institution, and the issues surrounding it, were about to become even less local.

TYLER AND TROUBLE TOO

In 1840, the Whigs finally figured out how to win a presidential election: act like Jacksonian Democrats. In 1836, they had run four candidates, hoping to throw the election into the House of Representatives, and they won enough support against Martin Van Buren to give them hope for 1840. Four years later, expecting to benefit from public displeasure with the Panic of 1837 and Van Buren's response to it, they emphasized unity at the expense of their party's most famous and controversial leaders, Clay and Webster, both of whom hungered to be president. Singing, "Van, Van is a used-up man," and proclaiming "Tippecanoe and Tyler Too," they emphasized the personality of their candidate, William Henry Harrison. Harrison was known as "Old Tippecanoe" for winning a battle there as a general, but he was a far cry from "Old Hickory." Whigs also benefited from and contributed to the Second Great Awakening: their platform bulged with government support for the kinds of improvements and reforms that appealed to those caught up in the religious revival movement. They stressed their democratic leanings, which many Whigs had only recently discovered, and tried to skirt any controversial issues.

But controversy dogged the Whigs throughout what would have been Harrison's presidency. He died after a month in office, and Vice President John Tyler, nominated largely because he had abandoned the Jacksonians for the Whigs and therefore might attract non-Whig voters, became president. But when Tyler left the Democrats, he took his principles with him, making him a Democrat in Whig's clothing. He had little use for a federally run bank—a key provision in the Whig platform— or for Clay's belief that he should control policy from Capitol Hill, with the president as a figurehead. Within months after Tyler assumed the presidency, the only cabinet member left from Harrison's brief tenure was Webster, who remained secretary of state until he completed a treaty setting the boundary between the United States and Canada. That left Tyler without a party, although he hoped to retain the White House. The question was how.

The answer seemed to Tyler to lie with slavery. He looked to the southwest, to what was then called the Lone Star Republic. In the 1820s, soon after the fall of the Spanish Empire led to Mexico's independence, Americans had begun moving into one of its northern provinces, Texas. By the mid-1830s, upset with Mexican strictures on religion and slavery, Texans revolted. After suffering a smashing defeat at the

Alamo, American forces regrouped and defeated the Mexican army, winning independence for Texas in 1837. But not easily—Mexico refused to acknowledge the change. Worse yet, Jackson and the Texans worried that the British saw the small Lone Star Republic as a territorial opportunity to sandwich the United States between colonies in their empire; the British might even plan to incite uprisings by Native Americans and—worse still—to emancipate slaves in the area, just as Great Britain recently had done throughout its empire.

For the Texans, the logical solution was to become part of the United States. Whatever their logic, though, it was not so simple. Democrats may have preferred geographic expansion and Whigs economic expansion, but both parties—like both of the sections—also had to deal with divisions within. Admitting Maine and Missouri had maintained the sectional balance, giving the South enough power to block action in the Senate as the North's population growth increased its power in the House. Adding Texas might upset that balance, especially when its size might allow it to be divided into several states. That bolstered northern opposition to adding Texas. And Jackson and Van Buren feared, with good reason, that Mexico might declare war on the United States if it annexed the new republic.

While Tyler worked for slavery and the nomination outside of the two major parties, a third party worked against slavery. The Liberty Party had run abolitionist James Birney for president in 1840, and the support he received heartened antislavery northerners. They renominated him in 1844 and stayed on the attack against what they called the "Slave Power," southerners and their northern allies determined to protect the institution at all costs. The Liberty Party traced the origins of the Slave Power to the three-fifths compromise at the Constitutional Convention of 1787 and saw it as the basis for all federal policies that seemed to kowtow to the South. Party members advocated African American rights and involved themselves in local campaigns against Democrats or Whigs who seemed too close to proslavery interests, endearing themselves to neither of the major parties. Democrats and Whigs had occupied the middle ground to try to keep slavery out of national politics, but forces on both sides of the slavery issue had made it impossible. Although the Liberty Party and uncompromising supporters of slavery might have seemed to live on the political fringe, they were finding growing support within the party mainstreams.

The presidential election of 1844 became the catalyst for an explosion over slavery. Hoping to consolidate proslavery support, Tyler had appointed Calhoun secretary of state, and together they moved ahead on behalf of Texas and slavery. This forced politicians who preferred to avoid these issues to take positions on one side or the other. For the presumed front-runners for the party nominations, it was especially difficult. Democrat Van Buren, who hoped to regain the White House, and Whig Clay, trying for the fourth time to win it, had to try to mollify those who opposed slavery and the annexation of Texas, and those who wanted to spread slavery and saw Texas as a way to do it. Whereas some Democrats urged annexation because they thought it could help spread democracy, Van Buren saw the motivation for adding Texas as "lust for power, with fraud and violence in the train," and came out against it. Usually considered shifty and shrewd, Van Buren stood up for principle—and cost himself the nomination by losing the support of expansionist northern Democrats and the southern, increasingly proslavery wing.[5]

Instead, the Democrats nominated James K. Polk and sent a strong message to the country. Polk had been successful enough in Tennessee politics to enable him to use the nickname "Young Hickory." If he lacked Jackson's color and personality, he shared his forcefulness and his ideology: pro-states' rights, but not at the expense of national honor or federal supremacy. Not only did he support Texas annexation, he also wanted to acquire other territory. The United States and Great Britain had jointly held the Oregon Country—including the present-day states of Washington and Oregon—since 1821, and Democrats wanted it all for the United States. More important, Polk and the Democratic platform depicted this expansionism not as part of a proslavery plot—Oregon helped counter that idea—but as a heartfelt desire to help others enjoy the benefits of democracy. That argument helped Polk retain the support of Van Buren loyalists angry at their favorite's loss and fearful of the Slave Power.

Whereas Democrats tossed aside their front-runner, Whigs stuck with Clay—and paid for it. A Kentucky slave-owner and longtime advocate of colonization to solve the issues of slavery and emancipation, Clay realized that Polk's nomination would hurt him in the South, where Democrats questioned his fealty to the cause. By attacking the hedonistic Clay's morality in the North, they sliced into the support that moral and religious reformers had given to Harrison in 1840. Making matters worse for the Whigs, the Liberty Party nominated Birney again and targeted Clay, whose campaign described him to northern voters as "antislavery in his feelings." Antislavery forces wanted more than that, and may have cost him the presidency in the process. In New York, Birney and the Liberty Party received 15,800 votes, and if one-third of those had gone to Clay without the loss of other states, he would have won the state and with that, the Electoral College and the White House. When the votes came in, John Quincy Adams, no fan personally of Clay's, dispersed blame among "Irish Catholics, abolition societies, liberty party, the Pope of Rome, the Democracy of the sword, and the dotage of the ruffian," Jackson.[6]

When Polk took office, he determined despite the close election and divided party "to be *myself* President of the U.S." He pushed through changes in fiscal policy, including a tariff reduction. To the displeasure of Whigs, Van Buren backers, and Democrats who supported expansion but not necessarily its architects, he accepted the Texas annexation plan that Calhoun and Tyler worked out. A combination of threats and finesse led to an agreement with Great Britain that won Polk one of the prizes he desired: the Oregon Country. But Polk had an even bigger prize in mind: California. The result of his quest would be a war and new territory—and more war over more territory.[7]

CONCLUSION

In the 1830s, some politicians began using the term "Young America" to describe themselves and what they stood for. Young men representing what they considered the highest hopes of a young republic, they hoped to spread democracy within American borders by expanding suffrage, to new territories they hoped to acquire, and to foreign countries that had retained too much of their old monarchies and dictatorships. But whether they were part of Young America in the Democratic Party or the American System in the Whig party, Americans faced a contradiction: how could they claim to support such ideals as freedom and democracy when they limited the vote and held millions of Africans in bondage? Inside and outside of the public sphere, many Americans hoped to keep the issue of slavery under wraps. Then, when it emerged, they hoped that it would go away.

But slavery proved inescapable. It informed and affected the debates and positions on such hot topics as the tariff, construction of transportation networks, the federal government's role in everyday life, and what rights the states enjoyed. Its presence increasingly bothered northerners on moral grounds, or because it ran counter to the intertwined ideas of free labor and freedom, or because the Three-Fifths Compromise had given more power to the South than its population technically justified, or because southerners seemed so determined to protect the institution at all costs. Worse, not only would they try to protect it where it existed, but they also would seek to move it beyond those borders, first into Missouri, then Texas, and perhaps into other places. As the United States looked to expand its boundaries and fill in the land it already owned, slavery would be the central issue that drove the country to what Civil War historian Shelby Foote would call "the crossroads of our being."[8]

ONE

❧❧❧

PROVISOS AND SPOTS:
THE CRACKING OF
OLD COALITIONS

Late on the afternoon of August 8, 1846, David Wilmot rose to address the House of Representatives. Until that moment, he had been a little-known freshman congressman from western Pennsylvania usually concerned with locally important issues like the tariff. But exposure to antislavery colleagues hardened his feelings about the peculiar institution. President James Polk had just asked Congress for $2 million to pay Mexico for "any concessions which may be made" in negotiating a treaty to end the war that had only recently begun between the two countries. Suspicious, Wilmot said, "We claim the Rio Grande as our boundary—that was the main cause of the war. Are we now to purchase what we claim as a matter of right?" Wilmot welcomed new territory, especially California, but not with slavery. Therefore, he proposed an amendment:

> That, as an express and fundamental condition to the acquisition of any territory from the Republic of Mexico by the United States, by virtue of any treaty which may be negotiated between them, and to the use by the Executive of the moneys herein appropriated, neither slavery nor involuntary servitude shall ever exist in any part of said territory, except for crime, whereof the party shall first be duly convicted.[1]

On the day Wilmot introduced his amendment, another politician, also little-known—at least for the moment—had just won his race for a seat in Congress. He was Abraham Lincoln, a respected lawyer and highly partisan Whig whom the voters of Springfield and the surrounding Seventh District of Illinois chose over Democrat Peter Cartwright. The only major issue had been religion; Cartwright, a legendary Methodist preacher, suggested that his opponent was an infidel. His attacks prompted Lincoln's only public statement about his religion, which avoided stating his views but reassured voters that he never spoke "with any intentional disrespect of religion in general, or of any denomination of Christians in particular," nor would he "support a man for office, whom I knew to be an open enemy of, and scoffer at, religion."[2]

Wilmot and Lincoln reflected changing times and changing politics. A loyal Democrat, Wilmot had favored annexing Texas and declaring war on Mexico. Now he echoed other northerners increasingly convinced that southerners would stop at nothing to spread slavery and that Polk, a slave owner who had advocated acquiring Texas, was part of this scheme. Wilmot made himself and his views known only after coming to Congress, sharing a home with other northern congressmen, and working with antislavery Democrats worried about their party's future if it seemed in thrall to the South. For these Democrats, a contradiction loomed: their party's commitment to Jacksonian states' rights and expansion into the West increasingly depended on southern support, which they would lose if northerners kept inching toward outright opposition to the spread of slavery.

Lincoln felt as strongly about the Whig party as Wilmot did about the Democrats. A disciple of Henry Clay, Lincoln hoped to join a Whig majority in backing internal improvements—better roads and canals, especially in what was then the West (now considered the Midwest, including the states of Illinois, Indiana, and Ohio). Like Clay, who engaged in his share of political acrobatics, Lincoln appreciated the art of compromise. Upon reaching Congress, Lincoln bridged the gap with southerners, whom Whigs had to hold onto if they were to survive. He admired not only John Quincy Adams of Massachusetts and Joshua Giddings of Ohio, both of whom had waged war against slavery, but also Alexander Stephens, a Georgian whom events drove onto more proslavery ground. For Whigs like Lincoln, a contradiction loomed: a party founded in part on the ideals of the Second Great Awakening's impulses toward social reform and personal improvement, with leaders who often had little to do with religion, had to come to grips with slavery.

Little did they realize the grip that slavery would have on them and their time. Fifteen years after Wilmot introduced his proviso and the Whigs sent the Illinois lawyer to Congress, Lincoln became the first born and bred westerner elected president—as the candidate of a political party formed to combat the spread of slavery into the West. Wilmot, his fellow Republican, became a senator from Pennsylvania, known across the nation for his role in the antislavery movement, and for his role in the movement to stop slavery from spreading into the West.

GOING TO WAR—WITH MEXICO

In 1846, out to obtain California, Polk launched a war that many Americans considered a monstrous wrong, then and since. Polk had no doubts, then or later. Born in 1795, the oldest of 10 children in a prosperous family, he received a good education at the University of North Carolina and moved west to Tennessee, where he entered law and politics. He attached himself politically to Andrew Jackson, who migrated from South Carolina to Tennessee before Polk was born, and he earned the nickname "Young Hickory." One of Jackson's staunchest supporters in Tennessee and in the House of Representatives, Polk rose to chair key committees and serve as speaker, then went home and won election as governor. He succeeded politically by working tirelessly and with deep partisanship, and economically by expanding his inheritance from his father and adding to his slave holdings. Friends and foes alike knew what he was: a dedicated Democrat, a dedicated Jacksonian opposed to an expansive federal government, and a dedicated southerner.

While Polk tended to view issues such as Mexico and the territorial matters related to it as simple matters of right and wrong, Wilmot and Lincoln and their colleagues saw the Mexican-American War as more complex. Although a strong believer in slavery and its merits, Polk seemed most committed to territorial expansion for the sake of adding territory to the United States and spreading American ideals beyond the nation's borders. Wilmot and Lincoln believed in the need to perfect those ideals within the United States and acted accordingly. Their words and deeds revealed the divisions within their parties over slavery and the West—and made those divisions clearer when they differed over the related moral questions of whether the United States should have gone to war with Mexico, how the war began, and what to do with the territory the United States might acquire from it.

When Polk took office, two of the issues most important to him were close to resolution. Texas's annexation neared fruition, and the British were ready to end the Anglo-American joint occupation of Oregon. The combination proved telling. The United States and Great Britain negotiated an agreement dividing the Oregon Country at the 49th parallel, just north of Seattle. The deal provided Polk with less land than he wanted and displeased expansionists who had demanded more of Canada, up to the 54th parallel, and trumpeted, "Fifty-Four Forty or Fight." Although northerners debated the implications that Texas had for slavery, they welcomed Oregon for the control it gave the United States over additional territory in the West and access to the Pacific Ocean. They complained that the United States should have acquired even more land and chastised southerners like Polk for doing too little to add northern territory. Senator John J. Crittenden, a Kentucky Whig, said of Polk, "If he don't

[sic] settle and make peace at forty-nine or some other parallel of compromise, the one side curses him. If he yields an inch or stops a hair's breadth short of fifty-four forty degrees, the other side damns him without redemption." More significantly, Polk settled the Oregon question with fellow white, Anglo-Saxon Protestants from England without damaging himself politically or involving the United States in a war that would cost much in time, money, lives, and, if the United States had lost or fought to a draw, respectability.[3]

While Polk made clear his desire for Texas and Oregon during his presidential campaign, he said nothing about acquiring California. Americans had long since become aware of the area's physical beauty and economic potential. During the 1820s—long after Spain had conquered California, Mexico had taken it over, Great Britain had sent commercial ships and fur traders, and Russia had established a fort north of San Francisco—American fur trappers crossing the continent in search of beaver pelts reported on California's commercial and agricultural possibilities. They and other visitors from the United States increasingly resented the people in the borderlands of northern Mexico. Most American visitors belonged to Protestant faiths, whereas Mexican California was Catholic. To the Americans, Mexicans and the Native Americans in the area believed in the wrong religion and lived their lives the wrong way; they failed to live up to the Protestant work ethic. In the right hands, Americans believed, the lush land of California would prosper.

Americans began moving into the Oregon Country by the 1830s, and California was next; emigrant parties arrived in growing numbers during the 1840s. Americans who visited California played a large role in attracting interest to the area. One of those committed to expansion was a longtime senator from Missouri, Thomas Hart Benton. Benton was a Jacksonian who opposed the Second Bank of the United States in the 1830s and was a foe of slavery in his state. In 1843, his son-in-law, John C. Frémont, led a U.S. Army Topographical Corps mapmaking expedition to California. He returned to Washington, D.C., after more than a year and wrote a report of his explorations filled with accounts of adventure and natural beauty. It became a best-seller and, as Benton hoped, excited further interest in California.

Polk shared that interest. During and after his presidency, Jackson had feared the British would acquire—or ally with—an independent Texas, then turn their attention to California. Polk appeared to agree. Soon after his inauguration on March 4, 1845, he told his secretary of the navy, Massachusetts politician and historian George Bancroft, "the acquisition of California" would be one of his major goals. Later, Polk told Benton, "In reasserting Mr. Monroe's Doctrine," designed to keep European powers out of the Western Hemisphere, "I had California and the fine bay of San Francisco as much in view as Oregon." Polk teamed with Bancroft and Secretary of State James Buchanan to instruct diplomats, the army, and the navy to be ready if Great Britain interfered in California or if Californians rebelled against the Mexican government.[4]

The president also dispatched fellow expansionist John Slidell, a Louisiana Democrat, to Mexico. Polk instructed him to offer to buy the ports of San Francisco and Monterey—not the rest of California. Already facing political upheaval at home over losing Texas, Mexican leaders recoiled at the suggestion that they should sell part of their land—and their anger angered Polk. He wanted at least part of California and to settle two issues: the boundary between Texas and Mexico and the claims of American citizens against the Mexican government. Although he talked tough to Great Britain, he understood the British government's desire for a settlement. But his attitude toward Mexicans was different. He saw little reason to treat the darker-skinned Catholics who governed Mexico with the same respect he showed toward white, Protestant leaders of Great Britain.

So Polk provoked a war. He ordered General Zachary Taylor to move his troops to the edge of the area the United States claimed for Texas and Mexico claimed for itself, between the Rio Grande and Nueces River. Mexican leaders already blamed the United States for inciting the Texas revolution for independence as part of a conspiracy to acquire Texas, and they resented the American naval ships off the coast of Veracruz. Taylor's presence would be the match that lit the fire.

On Saturday, May 9, 1846, Polk met with his cabinet. Although "we had heard of no open act of aggression by the Mexican army," he wrote, "the danger was imminent that such acts would be committed. I said that in my opinion we had ample cause of war, and that it was impossible that we . . . could remain silent much longer." The cabinet agreed to ask Congress for a declaration of war if Mexico attacked Taylor's forces. Four hours after the meeting came Taylor's report of a skirmish with Mexican soldiers who had attacked his reconnaissance. Within 48 hours, Polk had sent a war message to Congress.[5]

Polk tried to avoid admitting that he essentially provoked a battle over one issue— the Texas boundary—for the sake of another: westward expansion. He claimed a "strong desire to establish peace with Mexico on liberal and honorable terms, and the readiness of this Government to regulate and adjust our boundary and other causes of difference with that power on such fair and equitable principles as would lead to permanent relations of the most friendly nature" had motivated him to send emissaries to meet with Mexican leaders. He also defined "liberal and honorable" as offering nearly $30 million for land belonging to Mexico that the United States wanted or claimed. But, he lamented, Mexico "refused to receive him or listen to his propositions." After trying "every effort at reconciliation," he said, "The cup of forbearance had been exhausted even before the recent information" about Taylor's skirmish with Mexican soldiers. "Mexico has passed the boundary of the United States, has invaded our territory and shed American blood upon the American soil. She has proclaimed that hostilities have commenced, and that the two nations are now at war."[6]

After claiming that Mexico had invaded American soil that may not have been American or invaded, Polk never asked Congress for a declaration of war. Rather, he sought only an acknowledgment that a state of war existed. That may seem like hair-splitting, but Polk had good reason for it. The United States had fought two wars in its history. The first had been for independence, and although John Adams exaggerated in estimating that one-third of Americans favored the war, one-third opposed it, and one-third were undecided, his comments captured how intensely divided the colonists were. The second war, in 1812, was the subject of bitter regional and party divisions. Aware that the war effectively killed his old party, Justin Butterfield of Illinois, a Federalist-turned-Whig, said of the Mexican-American War, "I opposed one war and it ruined me. From now on I am for war, pestilence, and famine." By framing the issue as an attack on the United States, Polk silenced most of those who might have opposed the war. With thousands of Americans marching and speaking with patriotic fervor, the senator or representative who chose to vote against Polk's resolution would have to be courageous, politically invulnerable, or suicidal—or some combination of the three.[7]

Indeed, both houses of Congress quickly passed the measure, but strains were evident. The House voted 174–14. The 14 Whig dissenters included John Quincy Adams of Massachusetts, an ardent expansionist still fighting the South over slavery and convinced that slavery was the motivation for the war, which he called "unrighteous." Abolitionist Joshua Giddings branded it a war of "invasion and conquest," adding, "We know, the country knows, and the civilized world is conscious that it has resulted from a desire to extend and sustain an institution on which the curse of the Almighty most visibly rests." The Senate slowed the rush to war with debate, but only briefly, then passed the resolution 40–2.[8]

From the beginning, both sides expressed concerns that foreshadowed debates to come. While antislavery leaders like Adams and Giddings opposed the war, so did South Carolina's Senator John C. Calhoun. As a nationalistic supporter of the War of 1812, a key architect of nullification and defender of slavery and states' rights, and a perennial presidential hopeful, Calhoun could be a contrarian on almost any issue—but not on a war that might add slave territory to the United States. Because he claimed to read the Constitution strictly, he remained consistent when he argued that Polk had skirted the rules for going to war. He also was consistent on expansion: he welcomed the settlement with Great Britain over Oregon because he saw no reason to go to war for territory that was unlikely to include slavery, and he doubted that slavery would benefit from any fight with Mexico. Nor did he welcome more nonwhites into the Union. Privately, he warned, "Mexico is to us the forbidden fruit; the penalty of eating it to subject our institutions to political death." That could happen in several ways: by adding territory in which slavery had been banned, as it was in this area of Mexico, ultimately enhancing the North's power and hemming in the South; and by providing a location to which southerners without slaves or with economic problems could migrate, reducing the population and power of such existing states as Calhoun's South Carolina.[9]

Not only were the war and its impact an issue, so was Polk. Representative Garrett Davis, a Kentucky Whig, said, "It is our own president who began this war," signaling that when Whigs went on the attack, they would concentrate their fire on Polk. Worse for the president, Democrats were suspicious. Senator John Dix of New York, not noted for antislavery radicalism, wrote, "I should not be surprised if the next accounts should show that there is no Mexican invasion of our soil," and groused that the war "was begun in fraud . . . and I think will end in disgrace." He told Martin Van Buren, "I fear the Texas fraud is carried out to its consummation by a violation of every just consideration of national dignity, duty and policy." A close friend of Jackson and Benton, Francis Blair, who lost a key patronage post under Polk and thus had personal reasons to be critical, observed that the president "has got to lying in public as well as in private."[10]

GOING TO WAR—POLITICALLY

Democratic divisions were greater than even the comments by Dix and Blair suggested. When Polk's support for annexation and southern antecedents carried him to the nomination in 1844, it was at Martin Van Buren's expense. Van Buren did all he could to appease southern Democrats for much of his career, but drew the line at Texas. Understandably, Democratic divisions were especially bad in Van Buren's New York. In addition to disputes between urban activists and rural conservatives, New York Democrats had been split between conservative Hunkers, named for a mispronunciation of those who "hankered" for office and were ambivalent about slavery, and antislavery Barnburners, their name and their reputation for zealotry based on the old tale about the farmer who burned down his barn to kill the rats infesting it. Van Buren tried to float above the fray but sympathized with the Barnburners; his son John was among their leaders, and their opponents did little to help Van Buren regain the presidency.

By 1846, Democratic displeasure with the South's grasping for territory spread beyond New York and into New England. In New Hampshire's Senate election, a month after Polk sent his war message to Congress, Democrats chose John P. Hale. Hale was an antislavery congressman read out of the party for opposing Texas annexation, but had become part of an alliance of the Liberty Party and antislavery Democrats and Whigs. The same legislature that elected Hale passed a resolution criticizing the war with Mexico and backing "every just and well-directed effort for the suppression and extermination of that terrible scourge of our race, human slavery." In Connecticut, Democratic editor-politician Gideon Welles pondered Polk's war and wrote to Van Buren, "The time has come, I think, when the Northern Democracy should make a stand. Every thing has taken a Southern shape and been controlled by Southern caprice for years. The Northern states are treated as provinces to the South. We have given in, too much."[11]

The war with Mexico seemed an unlikely basis for northern Democrats to make the stand that Welles wanted. Even before Polk took office, Van Buren surmised that in case of war, "the opposition shall be able to charge with plausibility, if not truth, that it is waged for the extension of slavery," forcing northern Democrats "to the sad alternative of turning their backs upon their friends" in the South "or of encountering political suicide with their eyes open." Polk was at the other end of the political spectrum, and his nomination showed that he could be as cunning as Van Buren. But this time, Van Buren was the wiser analyst. Polk remained convinced, as he wrote in his diary, that slavery "has, and can have no legitimate connection with the War with Mexico." He told Crittenden that "the question of slavery would probably never be a practical one if we acquired New Mexico and California, because there would be but a narrow ribbon of territory south of the Missouri Compromise line . . . and in it slavery would probably never exist."[12]

Perhaps, but to borrow a phrase from Polk's war message, the cup of northern Democratic forbearance had been exhausted. The problems went beyond slavery or personal rivalries. They resented Polk's patronage policies, which favored southerners as well as northerners called *doughfaces* because they were at least neutral on slavery. Northern Democrats may have wanted to annex Texas and acquire California, but they noticed that Polk had obtained less of Oregon—a northern territory—than he had sought. He had been willing to settle with Great Britain to get less territory than he supposedly wanted in the *north*west while going to war with Mexico for territory in the *south*west. Because they expected Polk to accept a compromise to admit Texas but limit the spread of slavery there, they felt betrayed when Polk accepted annexation of Texas as slave territory.

Polk's stand on two other great issues of the day, internal improvements and tariffs, also troubled northerners, even when he followed Democratic orthodoxy. When Polk vetoed a bill to improve rivers and harbors, they could understand the Jacksonian ideology behind his decision, but they knew the measure would have helped the North, especially such states as Illinois and Michigan. Polk and his treasury secretary, Mississippian Robert Walker, engineered a tariff reduction that upset northerners who saw the measure as another means of mollifying the South. Van Buren's point about Mexico could be applied elsewhere: whether or not Polk really favored the South over the North, his alleged favoritism was plausible to northern Democrats.

Indeed, a group of northern Democrats became convinced that it was reality and decided to act. Like many congressmen, they boarded at homes near Capitol Hill when they were in Washington, D.C., dining together and discussing politics. Their leader was Preston King, a representative from New York, devout antislavery advocate, and follower of another antislavery Democrat, Governor Silas Wright of New York. Both Wright and King had long since pledged their political loyalty to Van Buren. But whereas Van Buren avoided tipping too far toward the Barnburners, Wright and King backed them all the way. Not only did this incline them to feel even more strongly about Polk's actions, but Wright was up for reelection in 1846, and all three harbored hopes that victory that fall would prove to be a giant step toward Wright's nomination for president in 1848. That would require support from anti-slavery and doughfaced northerners as well as from southerners. Antagonizing south-erners could be politically dangerous, but so could blindly following Polk.

The congressmen shared several characteristics that proved important as American politics and life unfolded in the decade-and-a-half before the Civil War. Twelve of the northern antislavery Democrats opposing Polk's policies were born in the nineteenth century. All were less than 50 years old and came of age in a different era than party lead-ers like Van Buren, Clay, and Polk, who was born in 1795 but seemed older due to his ties to Jackson and his world-weary appearance. They matured politically after the Com-promise of 1820 sought to eject slavery from the center of the national debate, and they saw how that effort failed. Northerners were hardly unanimous in condemning slavery, but all of the congressmen represented districts in rural areas where farmers and artisans were less connected to the market forces that governed urban life. Unlike wealthier traders, manufacturers, and shippers, and even their employees, these congressmen's rural constituents saw no obvious profits or benefits from the products that slaves pro-duced. If anything, they were likelier to resent not just southerners for using black slaves to do the same kind of work they did, but also any northerners who encouraged it.

Thus, when Wilmot rose in August 1846 to address the House, Whigs had thrown down a gauntlet that northern Democrats were ready to accept. Two Whigs from New York had just opposed Polk's request for a $2 million appropriation, which they were debating, as "buying territory at the South." One of the Whigs suggested that if Democrats wanted to prove their good intentions, they should amend Polk's proposal and ban slavery from any territory the United States acquired from Mexico. Wilmot took the challenge. The House approved the Wilmot Proviso 83–64, and agreed to the amended bill by a closer margin, 85–79, with 52 northern Democrats for it and 4 joining all 50 southern Democrats to oppose it. As Eric Foner has writ-ten, "the westerners had not been willing to jeopardize territorial expansion by vot-ing against considering the requests for funds, but the Proviso gave them the perfect opportunity to express their resentments against the administration." This was no attack on the war and expansion, because northern Democrats voiced no opposition to adding western territory, nor was it an assault on the South and slavery, because Democrats hoped to strengthen their party, which would be likelier to protect south-ern interests than the Whigs. Slavery could continue where it was—but not where the United States might plant the flag in the future.[13]

WHIGS AT WAR, WHIGS AGAINST THE WAR

Like their Democratic counterparts, Whigs divided over slavery. Clay's defeat in 1844 had been an unpleasant reminder not to take antislavery northerners for granted. They had to find ways to assure that bloc's political loyalty. Their support for internal improvements and reform made them less interested in preserving the peculiar institution or in recognizing states' rights. They owed a great deal of their ideology to the Second Great Awakening, which helped reinvigorate the abolitionist and antislavery movements. Thus, they seemed less in thrall to the South than Democrats were. But, like Democrats, Whigs hoped to remain a national party, and that required them to accommodate the South.

The war gave them that opportunity. The two generals leading the army into Mexico were not only southerners, but also Whigs—nominally in Taylor's case, because he had remained aloof from politics, but strongly in Winfield Scott's case, because he even had expressed interest in seeking office. For Whigs back home, North and South, because it was Polk's war they could feel free to criticize how the administration conducted it—and take credit for any successes. Their most prominent newspaper, Horace Greeley's *New York Tribune,* even applauded "the brilliant Whig achievements of Taylor," as though Taylor's success in battle had something to do with his presumed Whiggery—presumed, because he had never voted. Whigs celebrated Scott's successes and claimed that Polk and his fellow Democrats started the war, "but they left it to the Whigs to get us out of it."[14]

As if those comments were not enough to vex Polk, he felt that both generals maneuvered as much politically as they did militarily. Inspired by a dispatch in which Taylor complained about War Department interference, Polk wrote late in 1846 that "General Taylor is very hostile to the administration and seeks a cause of quarrel with it. . . . He is evidently a weak man and has been made giddy with the idea of the Presidency. He is most ungrateful, for I have promoted him, as I now think, beyond his deserts [sic], and without reference to his politics. I am now satisfied that he is a narrow-minded, bigoted partisan." When critical letters from Taylor appeared in the press, Polk grew apoplectic, convinced that the general was divulging strategic and tactical plans to raise his political stock.[15]

Polk wanted to avoid creating a war hero and future president out of any Whig general, especially Taylor. Convinced of "the impossibility of conducting the war successfully when the General-in-chief of the army did not sympathize with the government," he tried to promote Thomas Hart Benton. But a delegation of House Democrats, including future speaker Howell Cobb and future senator Stephen Douglas, told him Benton could never win approval. Not only would Whigs oppose him, but southern Democrats also would do almost anything to get even with Benton for his forceful opposition to the spread of slavery.

Although Whigs could claim a powerful military role, they suffered political divisions over the war in ways akin to the problems that Democrats encountered. Whigs split over the question of whether land acquired from Mexico would include slavery. In New York, leading the more reformist, antislavery group was *Albany Evening Journal* editor Thurlow Weed, a political manager extraordinaire known for his love for good times, intrigue, and the occasional ethically questionable deal. He was maneuvering to win a Senate seat for his closest electoral ally, former governor William

Henry Seward, a short, hawk-nosed attorney known for principled stands against slavery and against anti-Catholic sentiment. They teamed with Greeley, a dedicated Seward and Weed supporter hungering for political office himself. Unfortunately, Greeley was also an unguided missile who opened the *Tribune*'s pages to a variety of reform movements that led critics—and at times friends—to doubt his sanity and loyalty. On the other side were the far more conservative Silver Greys, named for the hair color of one of their leaders, Francis Granger. The Silver Greys were less interested in battling slavery than in economic programs and controlling state politics.

In Massachusetts, a similar gulf—and similar interests—separated Conscience Whigs from Cotton Whigs. Long connected to commercial interests that might sympathize with southern suppliers, Cotton Whigs belonged to the state's history; legendary orator, politician, diplomat, and attorney Daniel Webster had battled textile manufacturer Abbott Lawrence for party control. In 1845, the antislavery wing threw the Senate race to Webster. But the "Young Whigs"—some youthful and some simply younger than the aged Webster, some of them abolitionists and some just strongly antislavery—found the annexation of Texas and war with Mexico immoral. Charles Sumner, Wendell Phillips, Charles Francis Adams, and their allies occasionally disagreed among themselves, with Adams muttering that the idealistic Sumner required "the guiding and superintendence of a man more worldly wise," but the war with Mexico brought them much wider support than they had ever enjoyed before. The Conscience Whigs took over a daily newspaper and began attacking Representative Robert Winthrop, who opposed slavery but had been one of only two congressmen from Massachusetts to back an appropriations bill that blamed the war on Mexican aggression. Their publication, *The Whig*, assailed Winthrop for voting for "an unjust war, and national falsehood, in the cause of slavery," as Sumner put it. Their efforts did no damage to Winthrop's reelection hopes, but the support they gained from younger Whigs and abolitionists foreshadowed future gains in Massachusetts for their cause and its leaders.[16]

In Illinois, Whigs labored in the minority. Their only congressman traditionally came from the Seventh District, around the state capital of Springfield. As the war wound down late in 1847, that district's representative arrived in Washington to start the session. Abraham Lincoln had no special reason to stand out, and because his state party believed in rotating its officeholders, he would have only one term to make an impression. Nonetheless, he made one. He introduced what became known as the "Spot Resolutions," demanding that Polk identify the "spot" on American soil on which American blood was shed, and then voted for a Whig resolution declaring the war "unnecessarily and unconstitutionally begun by the President." But Lincoln found even other Illinois Whigs lukewarm toward his efforts. They warned him against opposing territorial gains and absolving Mexico of any responsibility for what had happened. Even his abolitionist law partner, William Herndon, told him that "the whig men who have participated in the war" resented his opposition to it—and, indeed, Whigs lost that congressional seat in the next election.[17]

While Illinois Whigs debated their stand, Ohio's Whigs were less divided. Giddings, joined by other antislavery congressmen, continued his assault on the war. He also gained an unlikely ally: conservative Whig Thomas Corwin, who lamented, "The uneasy desire to augment our territory has depraved the moral sense, and blighted the otherwise keen sagacity, of our people." He reasoned that if the United States acquired no new territory, any debate over extension would become moot. As he told Crittenden—just across the Ohio River, yet in a slave state and thus far away, too—"The Whigs of the South will not sustain any man, in favor of the Proviso, & the Whigs of the North will not vote for *any* man who is opposed to it. . . . Hence arises the great *necessity* of taking early and strong ground against any further acquisition, settle on *that*, & the Wilmot Proviso dies." Corwin's actions may have been rooted less in principle than in trying to remove slavery from the sectional debate by ending the war and to block another Ohio Whig, the more antislavery Supreme Court Justice John McLean, from running for president. This may have reflected both the personal divisions that had hampered the party before and would do so again and a lack of principle on an increasingly divisive issue. But for a normally conservative Whig to speak and vote so strongly against the war due to its implications for slavery showed how overwhelming the interrelated issues of slavery and territorial expansion had become.[18]

Although Corwin managed to sound antislavery, his solution actually mirrored southern Whig thinking and became known as No Territory. Northern Whigs split between those who opposed slavery and those who hoped to avoid the subject, but southern Whigs divided differently. Obviously, they could not be antislavery. But they had to figure out how to be proslavery and remain in a party whose northern members seemed to be digging in on the issue at least as rigidly as Wilmot, the Barnburners, and other northern Democrats. Calhoun, still maneuvering between parties and angling to protect slavery and southern interests, proposed that the government pull back the soldiers and add no territory south of the Rio Grande. That would permit the acquisition of western territory where slavery might spread. Alexander Stephens, a younger Georgian with more Whiggery and party loyalty than Calhoun, sponsored amendments to war funding bills to stop any acquisition of territory. He reasoned that whatever the United States acquired from Mexico would be unlikely to lead to more slave states. Whether southerners backed Calhoun or Stephens, following either would block the growing southern Democratic movement to obtain all of Mexico, which would add too many nonwhites to the population for southern Whig taste, and give Polk the victory they thought he wanted.

While Calhoun and Stephens represented two sides of a similar coin, their ideas also gave southerners—Whig, Democratic, and nonpartisan—a chance to do unto Wilmot as he did unto them. Stephens called the Proviso a "humbug" and "an *insult* to the South." On that, southern Democrats and Whigs could agree. Governor Joseph Matthews of Mississippi saw the Proviso as raising the question of "whether citizens of the slave states are to be considered as equals." Wilmot and those who voted for his Proviso had told southerners that they had no right to expand slavery. Even Greeley understood that "thousands at the South resist and execrate the Wilmot Proviso . . . not because they really desire the Extension of Slavery, but because they view the proposition as needlessly offensive and invidious toward the Slave States." By opposing expansion, southerners could agree with a large number of northerners while making the point that the decision should be theirs, not the North's. The South was no monolith, split as it was between the Deep South and the Border South, plantation owners and small farmers, urban and rural. But on the Wilmot Proviso and the threat they saw the North as posing to the existence and expansion of slavery—and the two were inextricably linked in their minds—southerners united.[19]

WHIGS IN 1848: SLAVERY AND WESTWARD EXPANSION AT THE FORE

Agreement on the 1848 presidential election across and within the parties was hard to reach on one hand and easy to find on the other. The unifying issue was the expansion of slavery into the West. The divide was over whether expansion would happen and how the two major parties would address the issue. The Wilmot Proviso helped expose fissures among northern Democrats and provide grounds for Whigs to unify against the war and acquiring territory. But would Democrats overcome their differences and Whigs continue to ignore their differences? The answer to these questions helps explain why a Whig became president and suggests that party ties were weakening over the key issues of the era.

For Whigs, 1848 offered opportunity. Polk made clear that he would serve only one term. The economy, still recovering from the Panic of 1837, had taken a slight downturn. When its revival deprived the Whigs of the chance to use it as an issue, controversy surrounded the reasons for fighting the Mexican-American War. The divisions in the Democratic Party that the Wilmot Proviso exposed meant that Whigs might be able to take advantage of their opponents.

The problem for Whigs was that they had either too many leaders or too few. Their veteran leaders had left a 40-year paper trail that Democrats could cite to counter almost any position they took. Henry Clay claimed to be retired from politics, but quietly maneuvered for the nomination. As part of that effort, he and his supporters tried to paint him as more strongly antislavery than a slave owner reasonably could be. Daniel Webster remained as determined as ever to reach the presidency, but he was too willing to compromise on slavery to be able to win the trust of northerners and too much of a northerner to win the trust of southerners. Other candidates enjoyed brief boomlets, but carried excessive baggage or lacked support.

The solution to these problems presented still other problems. Harkening to their successful campaign in 1840 on behalf of General William Henry Harrison, the

Whigs looked to the war's two leading generals, Scott and Taylor. Scott's ambitions and persona worked against him, and Taylor had no political background; besides, were voters likelier to warm to "Old Fuss and Feathers" Scott or "Old Rough and Ready" Taylor? More important, Taylor tried, in the spirit of George Washington, to claim to be above party. He even accepted the endorsement of a nativist party, the Native Americans, that saw his popularity as their chance to break down the Democrats and Whigs. On the era's biggest issue, he seemed lacking: northern Whigs wanted an antislavery candidate, but Taylor owned a Louisiana plantation with about 100 slaves. But southerners, led by Calhoun, sought to create a regional, proslavery political party, and Taylor's southern heritage could help stall any Whig defections—especially with Clay trying to appeal to antislavery Whigs, drawing adoring crowds as he toured northern states, and believing that as the party's senior eminence he was entitled to lead the ticket.

Ultimately, Taylor won the nomination through a combination of factors. Hoping to head off the movement toward Taylor, Clay declared that he wanted to be president, surprising few with the fact but many with the act: presidential candidates were supposed to remain silent and let the nomination come to them. When Clay reversed that tradition, he reminded Whigs that his long, controversial career could haunt them in the general election. Forced by Clay's maneuvering to abandon his claims of belonging to no party, Taylor issued a public statement proclaiming himself "a Whig but not an ultra Whig" who would "act independent of party domination." He also made clear his belief in the Whig concept of the presidency: he would execute the decisions Congress made, rather than trying to influence legislation himself. That reassured the party.[20]

Most important, the Mexican-American War ended. The U.S. envoy to peace talks with the Mexican government, Nicholas Trist, squabbled with Polk and Scott, ignored instructions and his own recall, and sent home the Treaty of Guadalupe Hidalgo, which added more than 500,000 square miles to the United States, including California and, ultimately, six other states (Nevada, Utah, and Arizona, and parts of New Mexico, Colorado, and Wyoming). For Whigs, that was a help and a hindrance. If the war's end and acquiring so much land proved popular, the party might benefit even more with the heroic General Taylor atop the ticket.

The issue was complicated. Whigs assailed Polk for starting the war and did all they could to achieve peace—but still got new territory, which was the divisive issue that led to the Wilmot Proviso, the idea of No Territory, and growing sectional anxiety. Nor could Whigs duck the issue: the Senate would decide on the treaty and they could block it. If they did, their antiwar stance would look hypocritical. If they did not, their No Territory stance would look hypocritical. They allowed the treaty to pass, but that reopened the question the Wilmot Proviso raised: Could slavery enter the newly acquired territory? Whigs were almost back where they had been in 1844, with their leading figure, Clay, trying to balance the two sections—or, in his case, to do the undoable. The solution, one party loyalist wrote, was simple: "What is wanted & what we must have is a candidate that will receive other than strictly Whig votes." Not only was that beyond Clay's ability, but he faced a party revolt: southern Whigs claimed he "sold himself body and soul to the Northern Anti-Slavery Whigs," and— maddeningly for him and his supporters—northern antislavery Whigs saw him as "not anti-Territory or anti-Slavery enough to meet the inflammatory feeling of the North." As one Whig surmised, a military hero "gives us an answer in a word to all the clamor & humbug about the war."[21]

But which general? Scott's liabilities—earlier efforts to win political support, poor relations with the more popular Taylor, even his nickname—worked to Taylor's advantage. When Whigs met in Philadelphia in early June 1848, they chose Old Rough and Ready. Greeley called the convention "a slaughterhouse of Whig principles" for turning away from the party's ideological and political warhorses, Clay and Webster, to a candidate who claimed Whig principles but had never voted in a presidential election. Greeley's friend and ally Thurlow Weed provided crucial support to Taylor's candidacy, and the two antislavery editors hoped to install Seward as the vice-presidential candidate. But, reflecting the old-fashioned political battle for patronage, the newer debate over the importance of extending slavery, and their determination to keep Seward out of power, conservative New York Whigs backed one of their own, Millard Fillmore. His selection, they argued, would do enough to mollify northern antislavery Whigs upset with the party for nominating a southern slave owner for president without causing southern Whigs undue heartache. Little did they know that they were setting the stage for further divisions over the spread of slavery, inside and outside of the Whig Party.[22]

DEMOCRATS AND FREE-SOIL

While the extension of slavery into western territories heightened divisions among Whigs, the issue also reopened old Democratic wounds and created new ones. With Polk out of the race, Van Buren remained the party's leading figure. But his defeat for reelection in 1840 and the nomination in 1844 made him damaged goods. Worse, his leading political protégé, popular antislavery New Yorker Silas Wright, had looked like a strong possibility for the nomination in 1848, but he died of a heart attack the year before. Still worse, Wright's fellow antislavery New Yorkers, the Barnburners, walked out of the state convention when the Hunkers, who wished that the slavery issue would just go away, opposed the Wilmot Proviso and carried the vote for their slate of candidates. The Hunkers held their own convention in Herkimer, New York, in October 1847. While Whigs barely held together over the issue of slavery, Democrats seemed to come apart.

The drive toward the nomination showed that Democrats were conscious of the problem, but at loggerheads over what to do about it. In February, the Barnburners met and agreed to compromise with the Hunkers if necessary. But after two decades of acceding to slaveholding interests, Van Buren drafted what became known as the Barnburner Manifesto, which declared, "Free labor and slave labor . . . cannot flourish under the same laws. The wealthy capitalists who own slaves disdain manual labor, and the whites who are compelled to submit to it . . . cannot act on terms of equality with the masters." Barnburners went to the Democratic national convention that May ready to fight for power against the Hunkers, slavery, and its sympathizers. And antislavery leaders in other states were watching them.[23]

The convention was open enough to leave the nominee's identity in doubt and closed enough to make the Barnburner cause hopeless. While the Whig candidates were too controversial (Clay) or unknown quantities (Taylor), the Democratic field was boring. After a lackluster fight, the delegates chose Senator Lewis Cass of Michigan, a veteran of the War of 1812 and weathervane on slavery: he supported the Wilmot Proviso before turning against it and advocating what he called "squatter sovereignty." In what seemed like true democratic fashion, he proposed to let residents of each territory vote on whether they wanted slavery in their midst. In response, the Barnburners walked out. Then the party approved its platform, which assailed those who would "induce Congress to interfere with questions of slavery, or to take incipient steps in relation thereto." With no explicit protection for slavery in the platform, the Florida delegation and two Alabamans, led by proslavery absolutist William Lowndes Yancey, also walked out.[24]

Yancey's efforts proved fruitless. Alabama and even South Carolina gave the Democrat their electoral votes, proving that southerners had yet to catch secessionist fever. But the Barnburners were a different matter. In June, they met in Utica, New York, and put up Van Buren for president. They echoed the Democratic platform on issues unrelated to slavery, endorsed the Wilmot Proviso, and called slavery "a great moral, social, and political evil—a relic of barbarism which must necessarily be swept away in the progress of Christian civilization." Across the North, antislavery Democrats, Liberty Party members willing to compromise their previously uncompromising position on slavery, and Whigs disaffected with slavery or Taylor's nomination or both began to coalesce. They agreed to hold the National Free Soil Convention in Buffalo, New York, in August.[25]

The result was a third-party candidate running on a sectional issue. Ohio Liberty Party leader Salmon Chase teamed with Barnburners Benjamin Butler and Preston King to produce a platform calling for the abolition of slavery in the District of Columbia and the territories, anywhere the federal government had the authority to act—but ignoring the Fugitive Slave Act of 1793 and issues of racial equality. Like any party, the Free-Soilers understood the need to accommodate large numbers, some of whom opposed slavery due to its inherently unfair advantage over free labor. One Barnburner congressman said, "I speak not of the condition of the slave. I do not pretend to know, nor is it necessary that I should express an opinion in this place, whether the effect of slavery is beneficial or injurious to him. I am looking to its effect upon the white man, the free white man of this territory." They concluded, "We inscribe on our banner, 'Free Soil, Free Speech, Free Labor, and Free Men,' and under it will fight on, and fight ever, until a triumphant victory shall reward our exertions." While New Hampshire's Hale enjoyed considerable support, and had a longer history and deeper antislavery principles, the convention nominated Van Buren, with the devoutly antislavery Charles Francis Adams as his running-mate.[26]

The Free-Soilers seemed well positioned. Their ticket consisted of a veteran Democrat newer to the antislavery cause and a younger near-abolitionist with a Whiggish background. Both had name recognition and inspired nostalgia—Van Buren for his friend Jackson and Adams as the son of antislavery icon John Quincy Adams, who had died on Capitol Hill just that past February. Taylor drew interest as a military hero but barely belonged to his party. Cass was loyal to his party, but his party was divided and he inspired none of the affection that Democrats had had for Jackson or Whigs for Clay. His unimpressive military record, especially in comparison with Taylor's, gave Whigs and Free-Soilers alike ammunition. One ardent Whig campaigner, Abraham Lincoln, likened the Democrat's service to his own in the Black Hawk War of 1832: "If he saw any live, fighting Indians, it was more than I did; but I had a good many bloody struggles with mosquitoes, and, although I never fainted from loss of blood, I can truly say I was often very hungry."[27]

But instead, the Free-Soilers came away hungry. Taylor won the White House by an electoral college majority of 163–127 and Van Buren carried no electoral votes and only 10 percent of the popular vote. Unsurprisingly, Free-Soilers faced the difficulty of creating a campaign out of thin air and overcoming an entrenched two-party system. Although Lincoln enjoyed flaying Cass and made clear his distaste for slavery, he remained a loyal Whig, ranging into New England to campaign for Taylor. Surprisingly, given their Jacksonian antecedents, Taylor's opponents may not have reckoned with his popularity as a military man. Free-Soilers outpolled Cass in New York, Massachusetts, and Vermont, but Taylor carried each state, undoubtedly benefiting from the Democratic split. Yet Taylor also regained parts of the South for the Whigs, carrying Georgia, Florida, and Louisiana. He may have lost Whiggish or antislavery parts of Ohio and Indiana to the Free-Soilers, enabling Cass to carry those states.

MEANINGS OF POLITICAL CHANGE

The election of 1848 and the events leading up to it can easily be read backward: since the Civil War happened, the divisions of the mid- to late-1840s seem like an obvious fork in the road to the war and its results. Although that was less obvious at the time, something in American political life clearly had snapped. Expansion westward and slavery's place in it had become, if they were not already, the key issues confronting the country. These intertwined issues divided Democrats and Whigs, forcing them into responses that did nothing to eliminate their divisions. After the Mexican-American War and the 1848 election, Democrats remained split over how to reconcile their Jacksonian democratic and states' rights views, which would protect slavery, with their nationalism, which might not. Whigs retained a commitment to internal improvements, a more activist federal government, and a weaker president, with their northern branch divided over extending slavery while their southern wing still had to stave off both more radically states' rights southerners and the threat that northern Whigs might make their position untenable.

None of these events guaranteed the divisions that vexed the country in the years to come. But they guaranteed that the question of the expansion of slavery and how the parties would handle it would remain at the heart of American political life. Polk would not; he retired to his plantation and, exhausted from four years of overwork in the White House, died three months after leaving office. Wilmot had assured his presence at the center of things, even if in name only. Lincoln seemed finished with politics: he had agreed not to seek reelection when he first ran, Democrats gained the seat he vacated, and he returned to Illinois. But he would be back, for the genies that Polk, Wilmot, and their allies had let out of the bottle would not be put back in, and a Whig ticket that seemed proslavery and dull would prove to be anything but.

TWO

❧❧❧

THE COMPROMISE OF 1850

On the night of September 7, 1850, cheering crowds gathered outside the homes of cabinet members and congressional leaders in Washington, D.C. Secretary of State Daniel Webster emerged from a dinner party and, feeling no pain, tried to invoke Shakespeare and mangled the quotation. A naval surgeon told an interested observer—James Buchanan, former secretary of state and future president—"One thing is certain, that every face I meet is happy. All look upon the question as settled and no fears are felt in relation to the movements in either the South or North. I can scarcely realize that I am now surrounded and conversing with the same men I heard in warm and angry discussion but a few days ago. The successful are rejoicing, the neutrals have all joined the winning side, and the defeated are silent." Referring to a pair of senators, he reported, "Mr. Foote has diarrhoa [sic] from 'fruit' he ate—Douglas has headache from 'cold.' . . . No one is willing to attribute his illness to drinking or frolicking—Yet only last evg. all declared it was 'a night on which it was the duty of every patriot to get drunk.' I have never before known so much excitement upon the passage of any law."[1]

That law—more accurately, series of laws—was the Compromise of 1850. Its evolution has become storied in American history. It marked the last major appearance on the national stage for three legendary senators who did so much to shape nineteenth-century American politics: Henry Clay and Daniel Webster, two years from death, rising as they had before to preserve the Union, and John Calhoun, almost in the grave, warning northerners for one last time to protect southern interests. It also served as a national political coming-out party for those who would shape the next decade-and-a-half in unanticipated ways. Among the most important figures in the fight were Jefferson Davis, fresh from his heroic service in the Mexican-American War and now a senator from Mississippi; New Yorker William Henry Seward, always seeming more radical and corrupt than he was; and Stephen Douglas, bursting with ambition and shrewdness, and using both to win the battle for union that Clay started.

Their accomplishments also became the object of historians' scorn, their work dismissed by such eminent authors as David Potter as "the armistice of 1850" and Sean Wilentz as "a balancing act, a truce that delayed, but could not prevent, even greater crises over slavery." As Potter pointed out, "If a compromise is an agreement between adversaries, by which each consents to certain terms desired by the other, and if the majority vote of a section is necessary to register the consent of that section, then it must be said that North and South did not consent to each other's terms, and that there was really no compromise—a truce perhaps, an armistice, certainly a settlement, but not a true compromise."[2]

Yet several other points are critical to understanding what happened in 1850. First, whether historians think that the two sides actually compromised matters less than whether those involved thought they had compromised—and most thought that they had. Also, did previous agreements have the aura of permanence that seemed necessary for them to be described as compromises by this or any other standard, or did they simply seem more permanent than they were? Finally, the agreement made in 1850 proved more successful than many historians, benefiting from the hindsight they derive from knowing that the Civil War was fought, have realized. The Civil War proved that the compromise was temporary. But, clearly, the two issues at the heart of the compromise, truce, or armistice passed in 1850 were American westward expansion and the spread of slavery into newly acquired territories. Northern and southern leaders alike revealed the importance of these issues and how they became intertwined with personal disputes and local politics. The party ties seemingly broken in 1848 had been only fractured, but the fractures remained far from healed.

THE RUSH TO CALIFORNIA

Nine days apart, two events, unrelated but inseparable, shaped the political and ideological battle in 1849 and 1850—and, indeed, long beyond. On January 24, 1848, James Marshall found gold at John Sutter's mill in northern California. Word spread of a mother lode. It became the benchmark for other mining rushes, from the Comstock Lode just across the Sierra Nevada to Colorado and Montana. It prompted a migration by land and sea that altered the dynamics of the American population during a time of considerable growth. It created wealth that changed the

American economy and damaged the long-standing Whig argument that prosperity depended on the economic regulation that only a national bank could provide. It helped finance such future developments as the transcontinental railroad, whose builders and their fellow businessmen dominated western politics and finance and influenced national affairs into the twentieth century.

All of the above might have happened without the second event, which by then seemed inevitable: the end of the Mexican-American War, which the United States won. On February 2, 1848, American envoy Nicholas Trist signed a treaty with highly favorable terms for his country. James K. Polk's war yielded California, all or part of six other states—Nevada, Utah, Arizona, New Mexico, Colorado, and Wyoming—and an expanded Texas boundary. Because Polk had fired Trist for disobeying his instructions, and Trist flouted Polk's announcement of his firing, those terms need not have ended the war. But with an election year in full swing and his policies still controversial, Polk concluded that because he had wanted California all along, he should let the Senate decide whether to approve the treaty. It did, but the Pandora's Box of slavery that David Wilmot's Proviso opened stayed open. In the end, acquiring about 500,000 square miles of land had cost the United States more than 13,000 casualties, $15 million in indemnification to Mexico, and growing agitation over slavery and its potential expansion into western territories.

The issue might have remained dormant or died if not for the discovery of gold in California. It took time for the news to make its way to the East Coast. The *New York Herald* published a letter from San Francisco on August 19—more than six months after the great find at Sutter's Mill—and Polk promoted the discovery in his December annual message to Congress. As the news spread, the mother lode prompted the mother of all rushes. California's population of white settlers, known as *forty-niners* for the year they arrived, quadrupled in one year—almost all of them between San Francisco Bay and the Sierra Nevada foothills, north of the Missouri Compromise line. Reverend Walter Colton, a Navy chaplain running California's government at Monterey, wrote, "What crowds are rushing out here for gold! What multitudes are leaving their distant homes for this glittering treasure!" They believed the exaggerations that inspired one writer to observe, "A grain of gold taken from the mine became a pennyweight at Panama, an ounce in New York and Boston, and a pound nugget in London." As the news traversed the world, fortune-seeking immigrants created a polyglot society in California. A significant percentage of the working miners had recently escaped their native Ireland's potato blight and found East Coast cities daunting for their size, the difficulty of making a living, and the anti-Catholic sentiment of some residents.[3]

What these forty-niners thought about major issues like slavery is unclear, but so is whether many of them thought about such matters at all. "The discovery of these vast deposits of gold has entirely changed the character of Upper California," wrote William Tecumseh Sherman, a young army lieutenant stationed in the area. "Its people, before engaged in cultivating their small patches of ground and guarding their herds of cattle and horses, have all gone to the mines, or are on their way thither; laborers of every trade have left their work benches, and tradesmen their shops; sailors desert their ships as fast as they arrive on the coast." Many of those moving to California dedicated themselves to pursuing profit in the gold fields or saw opportunity in the adjacent towns, where they could make money by providing services to the miners. Most settlers came from northern states. Getting there required many of them to visit slave territory, either on wagon trains that headed west from Missouri or on boats that went by southern ports, heading down the eastern seaboard on a long trip that would take them through the Isthmus of Panama or around the tip of South America. If they were predisposed to oppose slavery in the first place, personal exposure to the peculiar institution strengthened their resolve. Despite claims that Californians opposed the presence of both slaves and free blacks, and Mexican laws that outlawed slavery, a group of Texans tried to bring 15 slaves to a claim north of Sutter's Fort. Local miners held a meeting at a local bar and agreed "that no slave or negro should own claims or even work in the mines." The Texans took this and other hints and left. When two Chileans arrived in Yuba City with peons, virtually the equivalent of slaves, local miners hanged one of the South Americans and cut off the other's ears.[4]

More important than slavery was the issue of government itself. Without some organization, mining claims would remain in dispute and vigilante justice of the sort the Chileans were subjected to might prevail. Thus, the drive for some kind of government in California came from inside and outside. Californians gathered in September 1849 in Monterey to write a state constitution. The convention brought together both new arrivals and emigrants captivated by California's charms long before the discovery of gold. The members included William Gwin, a Mississippi Democrat who fought for control of his party throughout the 1850s; Henry Halleck, later famous and infamous as a Civil War general; and Lansford Hastings, whose professed knowledge of western trails led the Donner Party astray, killing more than half of its 87 members. Despite a southern presence, the convention unanimously outlawed slavery and declared, "Every white male citizen of the United States, of the age of twenty-one years . . . shall be entitled to vote."[5]

Californians were not alone in determining their form of government. In 1846, Mormons—the Church of Jesus Christ of Latter-Day Saints—began arriving in the eastern Great Basin under church president Brigham Young's leadership. Mormons had a difficult past. Their founder, Joseph Smith, had been controversial from the beginning. A nearly illiterate farm boy in the burnt-over district of upstate New York, he reported that an angel had led him to some plates whose mysterious writings he and his wife translated into the Book of Mormon. In 1830, the church began in Palmyra, New York, with six members. Located at the heart of the Second Great Awakening, the new church grew to 100 by 1831, but Mormons' beliefs and cooperation—what critics called clannishness—prompted moves to Ohio and Missouri before they settled in

Nauvoo, Illinois, in 1839. There they enjoyed financial and spiritual success until 1844, when Smith announced his candidacy for president. Illinoisans resented his abolitionist platform, voiced in a state where abolitionist Elijah Lovejoy had been murdered seven years before. Nor did they take well to Smith's belief in plural marriage that encouraged men to marry more than one woman. After many confrontations with church members and non-Mormons, Smith went to jail for disturbing the peace. In the summer of 1844, a mob attacked the jail and killed Smith and his brother.

When Young succeeded Smith as church leader, he moved Mormons west, using John C. Frémont's best-selling report of his western explorations as a guide. Young reasoned that Mormons needed to remove themselves as far as possible from their American critics. But less than a year after arriving in the Great Basin, in Mexican territory, they wound up back in the United States, thanks to the Treaty of Guadalupe Hidalgo. Neither thrilled nor daunted, Young came up with a plan of government: the state of Deseret, a word from the Book of Mormon for the honeybee, whose industrious habits Mormons tried to emulate. Although more realistic and organized than his predecessor, Young proved that when he dreamed, he dreamed big. Deseret would include most of the Great Basin and southern California, providing Mormons with room for growth, protection, and a port on the Pacific Ocean. While Mormons enjoyed success in the Gold Rush and in selling supplies to travelers en route to it, their belief in polygamy made the church's chances of turning this dream of Deseret into reality slim. But the Mormons' presence and success attracted non-Mormon residents to the Great Salt Lake area, making some form of government necessary. The population and its need for government paled in comparison with California's problems. That was the federal government's obligation—and one of many problems confronting the administration that followed Polk into office in 1849.

THE WHIG PRESIDENT AND THE WHIG PRESIDENCY

On March 4, 1849, the presidency was to pass from Polk to Zachary Taylor. But it was a Sunday, and Taylor refused to violate the Sabbath to take the oath of office. The legend developed that for one day, the presidency went to the next in line constitutionally, Senate president pro tempore David Rice Atchison. Whether Atchison actually became president for 24 hours, and slept or drank all day, fascinates historical trivia experts—and trivializes his significance. Many states have elected senators from each party, but Missourians had chosen two Democratic senators who despised each other: Atchison, who supported expansion if it benefited the South, and Thomas Hart Benton, who fought for westward expansion almost as ardently as he opposed slavery expansion.

Their visions reflected the debate that roiled the two major parties and the country over the next year-and-a-half, beginning on March 5, when Taylor took the oath of office. Amid wind, rain, and snow, he read an inaugural address clear neither in delivery—he mumbled—nor in intent. He cited George Washington's example of being above politics, demonstrating naiveté and the beginnings of a master plan to change the party system. On commercial and agricultural matters, he said, "It is for the wisdom of Congress itself, in which all legislative powers are vested by the Constitution, to regulate these and other matters of domestic policy. I shall look with confidence to the enlightened patriotism of that body to adopt such measures of conciliation as may harmonize conflicting interests and tend to perpetuate that Union which should be the paramount object of our hopes and affections." Ideologically disposed toward a powerful Congress and a deferential executive, Whigs had reason to welcome Taylor's sentiments.[6]

Unfortunately for Taylor, the dreams in his inauguration proved to be just that, dreams. One of his problems was the South. Deep South or Border South, urban or rural, slave owning or not, southerners could agree that the Wilmot Proviso and Free-Soil campaign were inherently insulting. Although not all southerners worried about whether slavery would expand into the West—and some who did, mostly in the Deep South, doubted it could or would—they resented northerners who presumed to decide for them, but divided over how best to voice that resentment. Responding partly to northern proposals to ban the slave trade in the nation's capital, John Calhoun held a congressional caucus after the 1848 election and issued his Southern Address, which called for southerners to unite. Several state legislatures and conventions adopted measures in line with Calhoun's thinking, but his effort failed, at least for the moment. Northerners eased tensions by backing away from efforts to stop the interstate slave trade. Most southerners in Congress refused to sign the address; few southern Whigs saw a need to be rigid when one of their own had just won the White House. Nor did they trust Calhoun, who had switched from nationalist to sectionalist to protect his political base in South Carolina and weaved from party to party in pursuit of the presidency.

Then, the South's most extreme advocates of slavery and states' rights planned a convention to meet in Nashville, Tennessee, where they complained loudly about their fate but found themselves outnumbered by moderates in the upper and lower South. How Georgia leaders responded to Calhoun and the Nashville meeting proved telling: Whigs Alexander Stephens and Robert Toombs preferred to give their party and its president time to prove themselves, whereas Democrat Howell Cobb suggested giving his party a chance to return to power. Thus, Taylor might not have to worry about southerners uniting behind secession, but he had to cope with a disunited South and southern Whigs who might disunite over any misstep.

Taylor had another problem: himself. Although politics is part of military life, and he engaged in his share of maneuvering for the presidency, he lacked experience with national politics and policies as well as those who made and practiced them. On the traditional ride to his inaugural with the departing president, he told Polk that with California and New Mexico so far west, they might be better off independent from the U.S. government, prompting Polk to deem him "exceedingly ignorant of public affairs, and, I should judge, of very ordinary capacity." Because Polk often disliked other Democrats, his criticism might be expected, but Taylor's supporters, too, were capable of disdaining him. A Mexican-American War opponent who had been slow to warm to Taylor but campaigned for his election, Horace Greeley told a friend, "Old Zack is a good old soul but don't know himself from a side of sole leather in the way of statesmanship." Seward said, "He is a sensible and sagacious man, but *uninformed about men,* and will fail to obtain a Cabinet politically strong." Others saw Taylor as indecisive: Webster, who had no use for him, said, "General Taylor means well, but . . . feels that he must rely on somebody; that he must have counsel, even in the appointment of his counselors."[7]

These criticisms cut to the heart of a problem greater than Taylor: Whigs expected too much and too little of their president, and paid for the contradiction. Whigs originally coalesced around the idea that "King Andrew" Jackson abused and overextended his office's powers and argued that the president should defer to Congress; however, the president took office in March and the next congressional session began the following December, leaving no Congress for the president to defer to. Nor could he easily overcome Whig history: when William Henry Harrison, expected to be a properly deferential Whig president, died, his successor, John Tyler, isolated himself from his party. With opposing precedents, and Taylor avoiding politics throughout his life, Whigs worried about the direction he would take.

Taylor tried to balance the cabinet between regions and wings of the party, but if sectional conflict made it hard for him to surround himself with leading Whigs, the personalities involved made it impossible. Traditional Whig leaders had no interest in serving in the cabinet. Clay disdained him openly, Webster disdained him privately, and Taylor felt similarly about them. One of Taylor's campaign managers, Truman Smith, revealed his displeasure with them when he wrote, "In nominating General Taylor we set aside man-worship—the bane and curse of the Whig party. The same rule should be observed in organizing the cabinet. I want *no everlasting great man* in that body."[8]

Taylor presumably satisfied him. His secretary of state, longtime Senator John Clayton of Delaware, a border state, had no use for slavery expansionists. But he veered between wings of the party, was temperamental, and liked to drink—poor traits for the nation's chief diplomat and, as secretaries of state were considered, as Taylor's chief lieutenant. A superb lawyer, Attorney General Reverdy Johnson, a border state moderate from Maryland, suffered from "a marked vein of indolence," as historian Allan Nevins charitably described his laziness. Ohio's Thomas Ewing had political skill, but the new, politically marginal Interior Department gave him few chances to show it. The other appointees lacked political stature, and his effort to include a recognized party leader failed: John Crittenden, who helped engineer his nomination, had just been elected governor of Kentucky and felt obligated to return home rather than give up that job for the cabinet. Nevertheless, Clayton peppered Crittenden with letters seeking advice. Worse, Crittenden's departure opened his Senate seat for Clay. Taylor lost an ally and gained a fellow Whig with his own agenda and a political magnetism that Taylor could never hope to match.[9]

Taylor's approach to patronage also antagonized his party. Although he played a larger role than many Whigs thought, he seemed to leave decisions up to cabinet members. They often bungled the choices, giving too many posts to one state or not enough to another, promising a position to one Whig and then naming another, or making poor selections. Local antagonisms and ambitions shaped the Whigs' response and displeasure. Taylor ally Alexander Stephens recommended retaining Georgia's Democratic postmasters to win support from moderate southern Democrats—and perhaps head off more radically proslavery Whigs. In New York, new Senator Seward and his antislavery Whigs battled Vice President Millard Fillmore and his conservative friends. That Seward usually won may have seemed surprising, given Fillmore's position—or not, because Seward and Thurlow Weed, his political partner, were shrewder than Fillmore and his backers. Representative Abraham Lincoln returned to Illinois to find the administration ignored his suggestions, gave jobs to Whigs who sat out the previous campaign, and offered him a dead-end position in Democratic Oregon Territory. "It is fixing for the President the unjust and ruinous character of being a mere man of straw. This must be arrested, or it will damn us all inevitably. The appointments need be no better than they have been, but the public must be brought to understand, that they are the *President's* appointments," Lincoln warned Clayton. "He must occasionally say, or seem to say, 'by the Eternal,' 'I take the responsibility.' Those phrases were the 'Samson's locks' of Gen. Jackson, and we dare not disregard the lessons of experience." But that was the opposite of what Whigs claimed to want in a president, leaving Lincoln's friend Edward Baker to grouse that "the administration is gone to the devil."[10]

Taylor also showed more Jacksonian decisiveness than other Whigs realized—or wanted. He moved on two key issues: the party's future and what to do about the territory acquired from Mexico. Despite his political inexperience, his praise for Washington's desire to avoid partisanship, and the presence of Clay and Webster, Taylor believed as president, he was his party's leader. He sought to remake the Whigs in his image, or as he perceived his image: beyond party and ideology. The controversial patronage appointments favored his allies. Because it was "committed to ultra measures" economically and tied to Clay and Webster, he replaced the Whig organ in Washington, D.C., the *National Intelligencer*, with the *Republic,* reflecting the term he and his supporters preferred: Taylor Republicans. Believing that "we won our victory as *Taylor* men—not merely as Whigs," Clayton wanted "to sink the name of the whig party in that of the Taylor Republican Party after the election." Taylor and his backers hoped being moderate and invoking the old Jeffersonian Republicans would attract moderate Democrats. Promoting a nationalism developed from

Taylor's long career of moving around the country on military assignments and argu-ing that rabidly proslavery southerners were a threat to states' rights, they hoped to appeal to Free-Soilers, especially if Democrats stuck with squatter sovereignty or favored expanding slavery into the newly acquired territories.[11]

But political problems—Democratic successes and Whig failures—hampered Taylor's efforts. In the 1849 state and congressional elections, Democrats found a way to paper over divisions on slavery. Their candidates simply ran as antislavery in the North and proslavery in the South. This technique probably would have failed in a presidential election with a national platform, but it worked in local elections. New York's Barnburners and other Democrats abandoned the Free-Soil movement, which, as a third party, would have isolated and marginalized their efforts to promote antislavery policies in Congress, and returned to their old party, at least until the next presidential election. Taylor had hoped to entice them with his Republicanism and unite them with northern Whigs opposed to slavery. But he remained silent, at least publicly, and antislavery Whigs feared that returning to their old political home would cede power in the Free-Soil Party to radicals such as Salmon Chase and hurt the movement against extending slavery. When Democrats gained ground in Congress and state offices, their success made Taylor and his plans look like a failure, worsening Whig divisions.

In proposing a political revolution, Taylor made the mistake of appearing too rev-olutionary, at least on slavery. His inexperience in politics and in the presidency made him ripe for shrewder Whigs to pluck—an opportunity for Seward and Weed. Almost from the moment Taylor took office, Weed visited Washington from his offices at the *Albany Evening Journal,* offering advice and friendship. Within a month after Taylor took office, Seward, not his more conservative foe in New York Whig politics, Vice President Fillmore, became a regular at cabinet meetings. Seward ingra-tiated himself to Taylor and most of the cabinet with his brandy and cigars, sense of humor, and talent for showing friend and foe alike that he was neither the radically antislavery bogeyman southerners hated nor the crook or ideologue that his north-ern rivals labeled him. But to conservative Whigs in the North and all Whigs in the South, Seward's influence suggested Taylor's defection to supporters of the Wilmot Proviso and efforts to restrict slavery to where it existed. As a Kentucky Whig told Clayton, "The Wilmot Proviso must never come before Genl. Taylor for his approval or rejection, if we intend to maintain our party ascendancy." That was as true for Whigs hoping to survive and prosper as a party as it was for Taylor's goal of replac-ing them with a new party.[12]

Concerned about the Whig response to restricting slavery, Taylor tried to settle the issue in the Mexican Cession with a plan that Michael Holt, the party's leading historian, has called "breathtaking in scope and ingenious in conception." Not so coincidentally, Taylor hatched it without consulting Congress, although the idea bubbled up from two ex-congressmen (Crittenden and William Preston, by then

Taylor's secretary of the navy) and a newly elected one (Baker). In tandem with Clayton, Taylor saw a way to avoid a fight about slavery in western territories: avoid creating western territories. Taylor's choice as Indian agent for the Santa Fe area, James Calhoun, would urge New Mexicans to write a constitution and seek statehood. Thomas Butler King, a moderate from Georgia, went to California to inspect mail routes and a possible location for a railroad across the Isthmus of Panama to ease travel from east to west, but with instructions similar to Calhoun's: encourage Californians to create a government and write a state constitution, but say nothing in it about slavery. Taylor sent moderate Missouri Whig John Wilson to the Salt Lake area as Indian agent with a message for Mormons: attach themselves to California and accept its state government. Then, he and representatives from the Mormon settlement would head for California's constitutional convention. For his part, King would stall the convention and lobby Californians to accept Mormons as part of their state. Clayton told Crittenden, "As to California and New Mexico, I have been *wide awake.* The plan I proposed to you last winter will be carried out. The States will be admitted—free and Whig." Because Mexican law forbade slavery, the institution never established a foothold in those regions, making it unlikely to grow. Whigs in Congress could vote on statehood without discussing slavery or the Wilmot Proviso, which applied only to territories.[13]

The problem was not Wilmot's Proviso but Murphy's Law: what could go wrong, did go wrong. Wilson easily persuaded Mormons to join California; with polygamy keeping statehood beyond their grasp, they could be assured of federal protection, and their isolation would guarantee their freedom to practice their religion. But before King arrived, Californians called a constitutional convention. Had he been able to stop it, subsequent relations—or the lack of them—between Mormons and miners in California and Nevada suggested any agreement might have been impossible to sustain. Instead, Californians chose an eastern boundary hundreds of miles west of the nearest Mormon settlement and proceeded with a constitution that banned slavery on grounds that Gwin, a slave owner back in Mississippi, explained: "In California, labor is respectable. In our mines are to be found men of the highest intelligence and respectability performing daily labor, and they do not wish to see the slaves of some wealthy planter brought there and put in competition with their labor, side by side." Meanwhile, New Mexicans contrarily held a convention and asked Congress to set up what Taylor wanted to avoid: a territorial government rather than a state. New Mexico's small population probably would preclude statehood in the immediate future, and the Wilmot Proviso would almost certainly come up for a vote.[14]

As King, Calhoun, and Wilson pursued their goals, Taylor toured Pennsylvania and New York. At Mercer, Pennsylvania, he announced, "The people of the North need have no apprehension of the further extension of slavery," and "the necessity of a third party . . . would soon be obviated." His hopes were not to be realized, but his words did nothing to allay southern fears that he had gone over to the other side. To

Calhoun, "The alienation between the two sections has . . . already gone too far to save the union." Slavery and whether it would exist in the West seemed to have brought the United States to the brink of disunion.[15]

THE THIRTY-FIRST CONGRESS:
COBBLING TOGETHER SUPPORT

With no settlement in sight for sectional issues in general and the new territory from Mexico in particular, Congress met in Washington, D.C., in December 1849. What happened in the next month was more ominous than the past year's failed maneuvering. Not only would Taylor's hopes of settling slavery expansion into the West prove to be a pipe dream, but members of Congress would demonstrate the depth and breadth of their disagreement on that subject. Indeed, they showed that slavery issues transcended party loyalty and foreshadowed further disputes.

The first and biggest problem was electing a speaker of the House. A dozen Free-Soil party members nominated David Wilmot, making clear their opposition to a speaker who supported or waffled on slavery. The remaining lawmakers split so closely between Democrats and Whigs that no one could win a majority—but the partisan division mattered less than the ideological one. The Democratic front-runner was Howell Cobb, a Georgian more moderate on slavery than most other southern Democrats—he refused to sign Calhoun's "Southern Address." This made him unacceptable to some southern Democrats, but his proslavery views made him anathema to many northern Democrats. Whig candidate Robert Winthrop of Massachusetts, the incumbent House speaker, was less radical on slavery than most of his fellow New Englanders, who resented his votes against the Wilmot Proviso, but even that was too antislavery for southern Whigs, who remembered his earlier support for the Proviso. Eight southern Whigs, including the usually moderate Alexander Stephens, walked out of the party caucus rather than vote for Winthrop.

The balloting went on for days, with congressmen even fighting over who would preside until they chose a permanent speaker, and southern Democrats refusing to support a northerner for the clerk's position. Tempers frayed: when New York Whig William Duer accused Virginia Democrat Richard Meade of advocating disunion, Meade denied it; Duer called him a liar, and other lawmakers cried, "Shoot him! Shoot him!" Robert Toombs, a heretofore moderate Georgia Whig, issued a warning that freed him of accusations of moderation: "I do not hesitate to avow before this House and the Country, and in the presence of the living God, that if, by your legislation, you seek to drive us from the territories of California and New Mexico, purchased by the common blood and treasure of the whole people, and to abolish slavery in this District, thereby attempting to fix a national degradation upon half the states of this Confederacy, *I am for disunion.*" Finally, the House agreed to accept a speaker with a plurality rather than a majority. Cobb squeaked past Winthrop, then chose moderate committee chairs, suggesting a chance of restoring order. But he gave several posts to Free-Soilers, which struck doctrinaire southerners as traitorous.[16]

With Congress ready, Taylor sent over his first annual message. Although critics considered it strangely written—due to its combination of contributors, it read nothing like Taylor wrote or spoke, and because a few sentences made no sense—the president made clear what he expected and wanted. As a good Whig, he called for a revised tariff and improvements in rivers and harbors, leaving details to Congress and assuring it that he considered the veto power "an extreme measure, to be resorted to only in extraordinary cases, as where it may become necessary to defend the executive against the encroachments of the legislative power or to prevent hasty and inconsiderate or unconstitutional legislation." But he took a Jacksonian stand on the Union: "Whatever dangers may threaten it, I shall stand by it and maintain it in its integrity to the full extent of the obligations imposed and the powers conferred upon me by the Constitution." Trying to avoid partisanship, subtly promote Taylor Republicanism, and defuse the battles over slavery, he also repeated Washington's warning against "characterizing parties by geographical discriminations."[17]

When Taylor addressed the geographical issue dividing the parties and the Union, he combined Jacksonian Unionism, state's rights, and southern Whiggery. Californians soon would seek statehood, and he expected New Mexicans to do the same. Hoping that Congress would approve both, he warned against sectional objections: "By awaiting their action all causes of uneasiness may be avoided and confidence and kind feeling preserved. With a view of maintaining the harmony and tranquility so dear to all, we should abstain from the introduction of those exciting topics of a sectional character which have hitherto produced painful apprehensions in the public mind." Indeed, leaving the issue up to those seeking statehood and simply voting for or against their constitutions might marginalize radicals on either side of the slavery debate.[18]

By the time Taylor submitted his annual message, it was too late, and not because the House delayed by fighting over the speakership, although that symbolized the problem. Rather, Toombs summarized the position that increasing numbers of southerners considered necessary. Parts of California and New Mexico were south of the Missouri Compromise line, but those states seemed destined for freedom. So did Oregon, which the proslavery Polk had acquired, and most of the existing territory in the United States. The northern population was growing more rapidly than the southern population. Senator John Bell of Tennessee suggested splitting Texas into several slave states—a practical response to what southerners deemed a practical issue, but it was also an emotional issue and thus harder to resolve. The Constitution's Three-Fifths Clause had enabled southerners to gain members in the House of Representatives and the Electoral College that they would have lacked otherwise, but not even those numbers could counter what migration, immigration, new states, and natural growth would do: give the North a majority large enough to legislate or someday pass a constitutional amendment against the South's peculiar institution. Southerners, especially in the Lower South, where slavery was more vital to the economy and society than in the Upper South, felt cornered.

The two-party system, as it then existed, offered no solution—and, again, the fight over the speakership was symbolic. Free-Soilers might join Democrats or Whigs on a variety of issues, but not on slavery. In this case, region defined the two parties more than party ideology. Democrats were rudderless. Among older Democrats, Polk withdrew from power and soon died, Cass relegated himself to the periphery by losing the presidential election, Buchanan was out of office and more follower than leader, and Van Buren had offended both sections. Younger Democrats like senators Stephen Douglas of Illinois and Jefferson Davis of Mississippi lacked the national reputation to represent their party to the country. The old Whig leaders, Clay and Webster, were in the Senate and had become legendary for compromising or—as critics would say—shifting their ground. In the White House sat Taylor, a southern slave owner willing to defer to Congress on the Wilmot Proviso and let new states decide on slavery for themselves. But while they rode his coattails to victory, few Whigs saw Taylor as wise or experienced enough to lead them to the fruits of that victory. Worse still, he adopted as his closest adviser Seward, whose best-known statement on slavery, delivered before a sympathetic Ohio audience, had been that it "can and must be abolished, and you and I can and must do it."[19]

Instead, Congress began 1850 by wrangling over slave owning interests and demonstrating the extent of sectional divisions. On January 4, Senator James Mason of Virginia, a Jacksonian Democrat educated in Pennsylvania and devoted to states' rights, proposed to expand federal power with a stringent new law governing the treatment of fugitive slaves and a $1,000 fine for anyone who tried to interfere with a slave's return. Seward responded with an amendment providing accused fugitives with a jury trial and the right to habeas corpus, causing a fierce debate. And this was not the only debate before the nation's leaders. Texas still had debts from when it had been the independent Lone Star Republic. Although the Mexican-American War had determined its southern boundary, it had yet to settle a dispute over how far north and west it extended—an issue important to southerners because Texas was a slave state and they wanted room for slavery to grow. No stranger to controversy, Benton introduced a bill to help Texas retire its debt in return for surrendering what would have been slave territory back to the United States. Henry Foote, a Whig senator from Mississippi, introduced a bill to create three new territories out of the Mexican Cession. That measure went to the Committee on Territories, chaired by Douglas, who believed in letting the residents of the territories decide the question of slavery. Northerners had backed away from efforts to end slavery and the domestic slave trade in the nation's capital, but that issue might resurface at any time. Within a few weeks in early 1850, all of the issues both parties had sought to avoid had come back with a vengeance, dividing Democrats and Whigs, northerners and southerners.

Whether slavery would expand westward seemed to have endangered the Union. Recent debates over slavery and the West, from the 1844 election and Texas annexation through the Wilmot Proviso and the Mexican Cession, had frayed nerves to the snapping point. Antislavery resolutions from Vermont, calling the institution "a crime against humanity," prompted representatives and senators alike to accuse each section of violating and threatening the other. Alabaman Jeremiah Clemens accused northerners of turning churches, often centers of abolitionism, into "sanctuaries of slander." Senator William R. King of Alabama, a usually conservative Deep South unionist, wrote to his friend Buchanan about northerners, "They must stop and at once their course of aggression, or nothing but divine interposition can prevent a dissolution of the Union. I am no alarmist, but I cannot be mistaken in this matter."[20]

THE COMPROMISE OF 1850

In the midst of a rainy Washington January, suffering from a cold and cough, 72-year-old Henry Clay bundled up and left his rooms at the National Hotel one night for a cottage several blocks away. There he sat down with 68-year-old Daniel Webster. For four decades they had been at the center of American politics and expansion, both economic and geographic. Now they were old, at least for their time, and feeling the effects of decades of overindulging in liquor and other forms of entertainment. Their careers had alternately united and divided them. They began as ideological foes: Clay supported war with Great Britain in 1812 to promote national pride, perhaps the acquisition of Canada, and a new brand of Jeffersonian Republicanism, whereas Webster feared the war's economic impact on his New England and retained old Federalist leanings toward England. Then they had united against Andrew Jackson in a failed effort to save the Bank of the United States and defeat him for reelection. Founders of the Whig Party, legendary for their oratory, they had fought for the presidency and power, clashing with each other and other would-be Whig leaders, and barely spoke through most of the 1840s. They had faced questions about their ethics, Clay for helping John Quincy Adams win the presidency in 1825 as part of a "corrupt bargain" that made him secretary of state and for shifting ground in his unending quest for the White House, Webster for receiving a retainer from the bank while defending it in the Senate.

Age left their ambition and Whiggery undiminished. Clay had lost bids for the presidency in 1824, 1832, and 1844, and felt betrayed when his party rejected him in 1840 and 1848, when he correctly believed that a Whig could be elected. On the ballot in 1836 and in the hunt for the nomination several other times, Webster had hopes for 1852. Both believed in the Whig concept of a president deferring to Congress, at least while they remained in Congress. Both disdained and envied Taylor, whom they considered ill-equipped for a job they felt they deserved more, especially in a crisis. Clay sought support for his plan to deal with that crisis, and Webster, who shared his Unionism, proved encouraging.

By January 29, Congress seemed calmer. After Foote accused Seward of trying "to spoliate upon the known and undeniable rights and interests of all the southern States of the Confederacy with pointed disapprobation, with hot contempt, with unmitigated loathing, and abhorrence unutterable," Seward's senior colleague from New York, Democrat Daniel Dickinson, spoke of the need for "kindness, and courtesy, and conciliation." Rejecting instructions from the Michigan legislature, Cass took that advice. Having run for president in 1848 on letting a territory's citizens decide whether to allow slavery, he vowed to oppose the Wilmot Proviso if it came up again for a vote. With his colleagues cooling their passion and rhetoric, Clay rose from his desk to "propose an amicable arrangement of all questions in controversy between the free and the slave States, growing out of the subject of Slavery." He sought to admit California as a free state, create two territories for the rest of the Mexican Cession without mentioning slavery, reduce the size and debt of Texas, abolish the slave trade in the District of Columbia, strengthen the fugitive slave law, and disclaim the power to interfere with the slave trade between the southern states. He asked the Senate to consider "viewing them as a system—viewing them together."[21]

Clay's proposal combined shrewdness, diplomacy, and a commitment to the Union. Taylor had a policy—no compromise and no partisanship—but it seemed doomed, if not already a failure. That gave Clay the chance to reassert his supremacy in the Whig party and in Congress, and he hoped to make the most of it. Twice he had been at the crux of a compromise that preserved a tenuous unity: the Compromise of 1820, which limited the spread of slavery, and the Compromise Tariff of 1833, which mollified South Carolinians claiming the right to nullify a federal law, southerners opposing a higher tariff, and northerners convinced that they needed one. Again, Clay proposed to ease sectional antagonisms and preserve the Union. And a week after introducing this newest round of compromise legislation, Clay delivered a two-day speech that made the Senate Washington's greatest attraction, with Clay where he liked to be: at the center of attention.

Clay outlined his case for compromise—and the middle ground in a political system divided among parties and regions. Urging southerners to cede California to the Free-Soil side, Clay said, "If . . . a decision of California has taken place adverse to the wishes of the southern States, it is a decision respecting which they cannot complain," because Californians "incontestably" had the right to decide—to which radically proslavery southerners could respond that Californians had no such right, because the Constitution protected property. For their part, northerners should forget about the Wilmot Proviso because it endangered the Union. Nor was it even needed. Because Mexican law banned slavery, it probably would never take root in California or New Mexico. "What do you want?—what do you want?—you who reside in the free States. Do you want that there shall be no slavery introduced into the territories acquired by the war with Mexico? Have you not your desire in California?" Clay said. "And in all human probability you will have it in New Mexico also. What more do you want? You have got what is worth more than a thousand Wilmot provisos. You have nature on your side—facts upon your side—and this truth staring you in the face." But antislavery northerners could respond that although nature had made slavery unprofitable, southerners still wanted to expand its boundaries. Clay denied southern claims that the Missouri Compromise line extended to the Pacific, which hardly made the claims go away, but suggested that southerners might benefit: slavery was almost certain not to expand northward, but without that 36° 30' line, it could do so.[22]

The rest of Clay's argument also lay open to contention. The Texas boundary "was unfixed," but it was a state and New Mexico was not yet a territory, a situation that raised constitutional questions about congressional authority on the subject. Clay claimed that Congress could end slavery in Washington, D.C., but with slavery in Virginia and Maryland that would be unwise—which southerners could read as a warning that someday it might be wise or even possible. He presumed northerners and southerners agreed the slave trade near Capitol Hill was "repugnant," but even if he was right, one section still might use the question of whether to get rid of it as a bargaining chip against the other. The biggest chip he offered southerners against the North was a more stringent fugitive slave law, much like Mason's. For those doubting his proposals, he had a stern reminder: disagreement might spawn secession, and "we may search the pages of history, and [find] none so furious, so bloody, so implacable, so exterminating" as "that war which shall follow that disastrous event—if that event ever happens—of dissolution."

The immediate response to Clay's bill and speech revealed the deep split among sections and parties. Democrats and Whigs divided not by party, but by region, and within their regions. Clay won praise from Unionists, including old political foes Van Buren and Francis P. Blair, while Sam Houston disputed his proposal for Texas as he pled for the Union. But conservative Massachusetts Whig Edward Everett told Winthrop, "Unless some Southern man of influence has courage enough to take ground against the extension of slavery, and in favor of its abolition in the jurisdictions of the United States, we shall infallibly separate; not perhaps immediately, but before long. This is the only compromise that will satisfy the North; that is, non-interference in the States, exclusion and abolition everywhere else. I am not saying what I think ought to satisfy the North; but I am saying what in my opinion will." Winthrop's successor as speaker, Cobb, a moderate by proslavery standards, surmised that Clay's actions would have a "bad effect" on northerners by convincing them that he "expresses southern sentiment, which is very far from being the fact." Indeed, the most ardent advocates of states' rights and slavery branded Clay a "humbug" and "charlatan." Complaining that he asked the South to give up too much, Jefferson Davis declared slavery could take root in California if given the chance. Free-Soilers proved no kinder, with Senator Salmon Chase of Ohio finding in Clay's ideas "sentiment for the north" and "substance for the south—just like the Missouri Compromise."[23]

As these responses suggested, northerners and southerners took a variety of stands on the compromise. Groups of senators and representatives caucused and hatched plans to pass Clay's proposals or something like them. The most rigid deep southerners threatened secession if Congress approved and Taylor signed any such measures. The cabinet was reportedly as divided as Congress. Conflicting reports emerged about Taylor's response, ranging from a plan to blockade the South to threatening to lead the army personally if it seceded. He announced during a visit to Fredericksburg, later the site of a battle the Compromise of 1850 was supposed to avert, "As to the Constitution and the Union, I have taken an oath to support the one, and I cannot do so without preserving the other."[24]

That distinguished Taylor from another southerner who felt strongly about Clay's ideas. On March 4, John Calhoun entered the Senate chamber on the arms of fellow South Carolinian Andrew Butler and Virginia's Mason, who read the last major speech Calhoun would write. Once described as "the cast-iron man, who looks as if he had never been born, and never could be extinguished," Calhoun was "so emaciated, pale, and cadaverous" from tuberculosis that he looked "like a fugitive from the grave." But Calhoun delivered a eulogy not for himself but for the Union—if the South went unheeded. "I have, Senators, believed from the first that the agitation of the subject of slavery would, if not prevented by some timely and effective measure, end in disunion," he began. He blamed "the long-continued agitation of the slave question on the part of the North, and the many aggressions which they have made on the rights of the South." Since the Constitution's ratification, he noted, the growth of the United States favored the North. That growth, producing more northern members in Congress, "will effectually and irretrievably destroy the equilibrium which existed when the Government commenced. Had this destruction been the operation of time, without the interference of Government, the South would have had no reason to complain; but such was not the fact." He cited legislation and tariffs as promoting northern growth at the South's expense. While recognized for the facts and logic with which he buttressed his positions, Calhoun showed a talent for the counterfactual that revealed the depths of southern anger. He claimed that if the federal government had not "extracted" southern capital and legislation such as the Northwest Ordinance of 1787, and the Missouri Compromise had not "excluded" the South from new lands, the South would have maintained equality. Thus, "the loss then of the equilibrium is to be attributed to the action of this Government."

Ironies—or "syllogisms," as one historian put it—dripped from Calhoun's speech. In the decades to come his depiction of the South as a conquered province would resonate with westerners claiming to have been a colony of eastern power. In addition, where westerners would stand in the Union and on slavery had much to do with the compromise Clay proposed and Calhoun scorned. While deeming it "a great mistake to suppose that disunion can be effected by a single blow. The cords which bind these States together in one common Union are far too numerous and powerful for that," Calhoun threatened disunion if the North refused to accommodate southerners by letting them bring their slaves into new western states and territories, helping them recapture fugitive slaves, and supporting a constitutional amendment to restore the earlier equilibrium. According to Calhoun, these measures would "satisfy the States belonging to the southern section that they can remain in the Union consistently with their honor and their safety." The North would agree "if she has half the love of the Union which she professes to have, or without justly exposing herself to the charge that her love of power and aggrandizement is far greater than her love of the Union"—a demand on the North that he seemed not to make of the South.[25]

With proper deference to Calhoun's stature and precarious health, northerners and southerners criticized his speech. That northerners objected was unsurprising, with the first lengthy response coming from Maine's Free-Soil Democratic senator, Hannibal Hamlin, later Lincoln's vice-president. Hamlin saw "the simple question" as whether California had created a republican form of government; if so, "it is a State, and *it will be* a State of this Union, when we shall have admitted it within our limits, and when we shall have passed the necessary laws to make it so, *as we will*." John Tyler, the accidental president from Virginia who had named Calhoun secretary of state, deemed his remarks "too ultra." King, an Alabama moderate, voiced sentiments similar to Tyler's. Foote, a Mississippian with a talent for disagreeing with his colleagues about almost everything, proposed a Committee of Thirteen in place of Calhoun's constitutional amendment. He suggested that many Whigs and northern Democrats, "who, though they are not the zealous advocates of slavery, and are unable to appreciate the manifold advantages which we hold to belong to our system of domestic labor, are, notwithstanding, not *hostile* to it. . . ." Calhoun replied that "as things now stand, the southern States cannot with safety remain in the Union," and added, "Every portion of the North entertains feeling more or less hostile to the South." Southerners were divided over the issues, and over whether northerners actually hated them.[26]

But some northerners associated with the antislavery movement, especially in southern minds, felt differently than Calhoun thought. "Mr. President, I wish to speak to-day, not as a Massachusetts man, nor as a northern man, but as an American. . . . I speak to-day for the preservation of the Union. 'Hear me for my cause,'" Webster began on March 7. Although an observer once had said "no man can be as great as he looked," the "Godlike Daniel" was, like Clay, in decline. Yet he still could hold an audience rapt. Reminding the North it once had slavery and the South it once saw the institution as evil, he said that "as to California and New Mexico, I hold slavery to be excluded from those territories by a law even superior to that which admits and sanctions it in Texas—I mean the law of nature—of physical geography—the law of the formation of the earth. That law settles forever, with a strength beyond all terms of human enactment, that slavery cannot exist" there. He derided the Wilmot Proviso and decried abolitionists: "I do not think them useful. I think their operations for the last twenty years have produced nothing good or valuable." He supported a harsher fugitive slave law, admitting, "I say that the South has been injured in this respect, and has a right to complain; and the North has been too careless of what I think the Constitution peremptorily and emphatically enjoins upon it as duty."[27]

However beautifully Webster stated his case, his speech proved more important to his political fortunes than to the debate. His plea in itself probably prompted no one to switch sides, although adding his New England voice to a Kentuckian's may have had an impact. His stand did no harm to his relationship with Taylor—they had no relationship—but bore fruit with backers of the compromise, whom he hoped to count among his friends for his next presidential run. Antislavery Whigs and abolitionists who at least considered him sympathetic, voiced horror and disappointment, exemplified by poet John Greenleaf Whittier's "Ichabod":

> So fallen! So lost! The light withdrawn
> Which once he wore!
> The glory from his gray hairs gone
> Forevermore! . . .
>
> Let not the land once proud of him
> Insult him now,
> Nor brand with deeper shame his dim,
> Dishonored brow. . . .
>
> All else is gone; from those great eyes
> The soul has fled:
> When faith is lost, when honor dies,
> The man is dead!

Yet for all of the criticism—by one editor's count, all but 6 of 76 Whig publications in New England attacked him—Webster had opposed nullification and southern nationalism because it detracted from American nationalism, not because he was antislavery. Like Clay, he harbored ambitions to save his country, but Webster wanted to be president and saw southern support as vital to that goal.[28]

Four days later, another ambitious, often misunderstood senator took his turn. Seward's words seemed especially important because he was Taylor's closest adviser on Capitol Hill. But he shared Clay's and Webster's Whiggish belief in a strong government and an integrated economy; their dislike for slavery, albeit a more ardent one than theirs; their ability to wine and dine even their foes; and their love for the political game. He played no game on March 11, 1850, with a monotonic but more controversial speech than Webster's. Like Taylor, Seward opposed the compromise. He had no doubt that Congress could legislate against slavery in the territories and that slavery eventually would disappear. Understanding southern anger but seeing no crisis, "I shall vote for the admission of California directly, without conditions, without qualifications, and without compromise."[29]

Then came a sentence that reverberated well beyond the compromise debate. Seward declared, "There is a higher law than the Constitution." Although he went only slightly beyond Webster's point about forces of nature settling slavery, doing so in a simple, declarative sentence caused an uproar. Southerners were livid and his ally Weed was distraught. A New Hampshire Democratic editor concluded, "If Mr. Seward's doctrines were to be endorsed by the people at large, there would be an end not only of the Union but of every rational form of government." Taylor distanced himself from the New Yorker, at least publicly. Granting that Seward had been trying to help his antislavery allies in New York in legislative and patronage battles against Fillmore's conservatives, the "higher law" speech did him no political good. This seeming radicalism trailed Seward for the rest of the decade and helped cost him the 1860 Republican presidential nomination.[30]

Just as the troika of Clay, Webster, and Calhoun adopted different views, so did their younger Senate colleagues. Davis, who had served heroically under Taylor in the Mexican-American War and been Taylor's son-in-law until his wife's death, lambasted compromise, defended slavery, and suggested extending the Missouri Compromise line to the Pacific. The new Free-Soil Democratic senator from Ohio, Chase, so ardent in his views and so willing to defend them that he became known as the attorney general for runaway slaves, opposed compromise and doubted southern claims of insult and injury. Douglas, an Illinois Democrat who managed a slave plantation his wife inherited, disdained all extremists. "The excitement is subsiding and reason is resuming its supremacy," with the public demanding an end to sectional antagonism, Douglas said. "The Union will not be put in peril; California will be admitted; governments for the territories must be established; and thus the controversy will end, and I trust forever."[31]

Douglas proved unduly optimistic. For the rest of the spring and summer of 1850, members of Congress wrangled over the details of the compromise in a series of votes on bills and amendments to bills. They stopped long enough to mourn Calhoun's death on March 31—except Benton, who told Webster, "He is not dead, sir—he is not dead. There may be no vitality in his body, but there is in his doctrines. . . . Calhoun died with treason in his heart and on his lips." Nevertheless, the senator from Missouri later promised not to attack Calhoun further: "When God Almighty lays his hand upon a man, sir, I take mine off." Most members of Congress welcomed reports that the Nashville Convention, where Calhoun had hoped southerners would take a stand, delayed action. After all of the oratory and wrangling, what made the Compromise of 1850 possible were summer heat, three failed southern politicians, and one shrewd northerner who had either no principles or just enough of them to pass the legislation.[32]

THE ROAD TO COMPROMISE

The heat was especially bad on the Fourth of July in 1850. As in most places, people in Washington, D.C., gathered for patriotic speeches. Those attending included Taylor, who at 66 was aged by the standards of the time and susceptible to digestive disorders. He had had a difficult week: fellow Whigs had introduced a resolution censuring his administration over a payment on a land claim his cabinet had approved that benefited his secretary of war, prompting demands for resignations and even impeachment. Making matters worse, Texas appeared ready to fight for its claim to New Mexico, specifically the area around Santa Fe. When Taylor pondered sending soldiers to Santa Fe to defend against Texas, Stephens, Toombs, and other southern Whigs threatened impeachment, with Stephens declaring that "freemen from the Delaware to the Rio Grande" would "rally to the rescue" of Texas. Secretary of the Treasury George Crawford of Georgia told Taylor that he would refuse to support him. Taylor replied that he would take action himself—a Jacksonian moment, but a sign of Whig splintering.[33]

With these problems looming, Taylor went to the celebration in Washington, D.C. After listening to speeches in the broiling sun, he drank cold water or milk, and ate raw fruit or vegetables—the kind of diet even his administration organ, the *Republic,* advised against. The next day he awoke with a stomach ache, a common affliction for him, but it turned into acute gastroenteritis. He quickly declined and died on July 9, his death proving so convenient to pro-compromise forces that rumors long persisted of foul play. Fillmore, his successor, added to the ticket in 1848 almost as an afterthought to appease conservative northern Whigs, had told Taylor that if forced to cast a tie-breaking vote in the Senate, he would support a compromise. That doing so would fly in the face of the president and Seward, his opponent for party control in New York, seemed not to bother him.

The failed politicians were three southern senators: border state men Clay and James Pearce of Maryland, and Foote of Mississippi, whose bombast exceeded his proslavery views. Advocating a 13-member committee to shepherd the measure, Foote convinced Clay that bundling most of his proposals into one bill, known as the Omnibus, would ease the compromise's passage. Unfortunately, Clay forgot history—his own history. He had shepherded the Missouri Compromise through Congress by breaking up the measures involved so that members could vote for what they liked and against what they opposed—the kind of approach that, his contemporaries in 1850 and historians later would suggest, made what happened in 1850 anything but a compromise. The Omnibus plan's success proved debatable—and moot. Pearce, managing the bill on the floor, entangled himself in parliamentary maneuvers by withdrawing Clay's bill for amending. At that point, other senators piled on, removing other portions until the only part that remained was the plan to create Utah territory. "The omnibus is overturned, and all the passengers spilled out but one," Benton declared. After blaming Pearce's handling of the bill as "the immediate cause" of its defeat, Clay left for New England to escape the Potomac heat, nurse his fragile health, and lick his wounds. Assessing the measure's defeat, Douglas wrote, "I regret it very much, although I must say that I never had very strong hopes of its passage. By combining the measures into one Bill the Committee united the opponents of each measure instead of securing the friends of each. I have thought from the beginning that they made a mistake."[34]

Events proved Douglas right. Clay said, "I was willing to take the measures united. I am willing now to see them pass separate and distinct, and I hope they may be passed so without that odious proviso which has created such a sensation in every corner of the Union." Douglas teamed with several colleagues to achieve Clay's goal. Knowing how to count votes, Douglas saw other northern Democrats backed the Omnibus, but northern Whigs and southerners of both parties varied in their attitudes toward it. As he wrote, "The Compromise Bill was defeated by a union between the Free Soilers & Disunionists & the administration of Gen'l. Taylor." So, he took the bill apart, brought up the sections individually, and cobbled together a majority for each. Not only did he deserve the credit for passing the compromise, but he enabled colleagues to stay true to their views and constituents by voting for or against the measures—or not voting and avoiding a disagreeable stand. At the end, Davis, his opponent, said, "If any man has a right to be proud of the success of these measures, it is the Senator from Illinois."[35]

Not that Davis and his fellow anti-compromise southerners liked it, and they did nothing to hide it. Their rhetoric suggested the depths of their displeasure and foreshadowed graver developments. Objecting to the ban on slavery in California, Democrat Pierre Soulé of Louisiana asked his colleagues whether "they think that the people of the South will long brook and endure such enormities?" Twisting the ideas of those who feared southern secession, Davis said, "Those who endeavor to sap and undermine the Constitution on which that Union rests are disunionists in the most opprobrious understanding of that term; such being the crime of disunion, I ask by whom, and how is this spirit of disunion promoted?" Calfornia's addition exhibited, he said, "that spirit of a dominant party which regards neither the Constitution nor justice, nor the feelings of fraternity which bind them to us."[36]

While Soulé and Davis were not alone, their allies were too few to stop Douglas. Besides approving California's admission as a free state, senators created Utah and New Mexico territories and left slavery up to their residents—repealing the Compromise of 1820's ban on slavery north of Missouri's southern border, but so implicitly and quietly that it went unnoticed. Lawmakers agreed to pay the debt Texas racked up as an independent republic. They settled the boundary between Texas and New Mexico, not to the liking of the Texans, but taking enough of New Mexico's claim to pacify them. They approved the new fugitive slave law the South wanted. They prohibited the slave trade in the District of Columbia. Together, these measures comprised the Compromise of 1850.

They also had to win the approval of another house of Congress. The House's discussion of the compromise has received far less attention than the Senate's. No leaders or orators of the fame of Clay and Webster shepherded the bills through the House, and none of those involved became lightning rods during the 1850s, as Douglas did, or cabinet officials of historical significance, as Seward and Chase did. But the measures passed through techniques similar to those in the Senate. Cobb justified the fears of those who considered him too moderate by ruling for the compromise forces on procedural questions. Kentucky's Linn Boyd, his appointee to chair the Committee on Territories, shared his moderate Democratic leanings and helped guide the legislation. Again, northern Democrats dominated the pro-compromise voting, joined by moderates of both sections and parties. If the House debate proved less dramatic, that can be blamed partly on having to follow the Senate and partly on comments like Boyd's: "I am astonished at the patience with which our constituents have borne our procrastination. I think we have talked enough—in God's name let us act." The House passed the legislation.[37]

But what would the president do? Contrary to the Whig idea that the president should leave Congress to do its business, Fillmore worked behind the scenes with his new secretary of state, Webster. He kept the Texas boundary dispute from driving a wedge between the compromise's supporters. He made clear to both sides that he would tolerate no fighting between the factions and squelched New Mexico's attempt to win immediate statehood while the dispute continued—an issue over which Texans and New Mexicans appeared ready to fight. Thus, as David Potter said, he "settled a very inflamed crisis—in some ways more explosive than the one on which Clay had been working—and settled it with such adroitness and seeming ease that history has scarcely recognized the magnitude of his achievement." More than that, Fillmore signed the compromise measures, averted disunion, and helped avoid the possibility of a much larger battle between the North and the South. Seward and his allies saw him as a doughface—a northern man with southern principles—but he eased sectional tensions.[38]

THE SIGNIFICANCE OF THE COMPROMISE

How and why the Compromise of 1850 mattered often seems lost in the drama of its passage. It marked a changing of the guard from an older generation, whose time already might have passed, to a new generation whose time had yet to come.

Clay, Webster, and Calhoun—and Taylor, generationally and militarily but not politically—had fought these battles for decades. All had baggage. Douglas blamed the Omnibus's failure partly on its identification with Clay, who caused apprehension (Democrats feared his presidential aspirations) and anger (Taylor's forces resented his assumption of leadership). Webster and Calhoun shifted ground so often during their careers that even their allies doubted their influence. For his part, Taylor demonstrated the nonpartisan nationalism Whigs had hoped for in nominating him, as well as a general's belief that the orders he gave were to be followed.

But the transition to the next generation came before that group was ready to lead, at least to the degree of Clay, Webster, and Calhoun, or even Benton and Sam Houston. Douglas demonstrated considerable acumen, but in modestly deflecting credit for his accomplishment, he bowed toward Clay for putting together the legislation in the first place. In his home state of Illinois, for all his talk of popular sovereignty, he had to navigate between groups divided on the compromise and slavery. Seward remained true to his antislavery ideology, but at the price of jeopardizing both his reputation as a Taylor administration spokesman and his own political power, proving almost as attentive to how his views would affect his divided state Whig Party as to what they would mean to the country's future, and revealing a surprising naiveté about the force of his words. Chase believed as strongly in free soil as Davis did in slavery, and both proved it, demonstrating the depth of their principles but costing themselves support outside their immediate circles. Fillmore's actions won him no support from anti-compromise forces on either side of the Mason-Dixon Line or the political aisle: as a Whig, he had no reason to expect pro-compromise Democrats to embrace him, and supporting a compromise that kept everybody slightly unhappy was no way to prepare for a presidential campaign in 1852, especially when Webster had similar hopes. To varying degrees, all of them saw their future political careers blocked by the existing political system. When a new system emerged, largely in response to the issues that led to the compromise or that the compromise ignored, the new generation of lawmakers would move to the forefront.

The compromise was significant not just for who was involved, but for what it involved. The major issues concerned slavery and the West: California's admission as a free state, the status of slavery in the rest of the Mexican Cession, and the Texas boundary dispute and debt. The other controversies—the fugitive slave law and slave trade—not only involved slavery, but also became hostages to the fortunes of the other measures, making them inseparable. Emerging from this debate with victories and defeats, pro- and antislavery forces showed how deeply western lands and the possible existence of slavery there mattered to them.

An important question is whether anyone won the compromise. The immediate victor was the South. Southerners objected strongly to adding a free state and thereby upsetting the Senate's balance of power, but Californians elected Free-Soiler John Frémont and southerner William Gwin, maintaining the balance. Furthermore, they later replaced Frémont with John Weller, an Ohioan with southern sympathies, giving proslavery forces an advantage. Leaving the decision on slavery up to the territories could have helped the South because Utah and New Mexico permitted the institution. Texans received more land and Texas bondholders more money than they expected—results neutral or helpful to the South. Sales of slaves went on in Washington, but less formally. The Fugitive Slave Law of 1850 enabled the South to regain some of its runaways and demonstrated southern power in the federal government, which also came at the price of deepening sectional animosity.

The Compromise of 1850 had the long-term effect of helping the North win the Civil War. A decade later, the northern growth that worried southerners had continued unabated. Industrial development enhanced the North's advantages. The northern leadership that emerged during the Civil War gained experience in the decade to come: Lincoln returned to the political fray and Seward, and to a lesser extent Chase, developed more finesse, to the Union's benefit. By contrast, during the 1850s Davis and Stephens changed little, to the South's detriment.

For the short term, the compromise averted a greater disaster. Chase was right when he said, "The question of slavery in the territories has been avoided. It has not been settled." But Douglas had a point when he said, "My object was to settle the controversy, and to restore peace and quiet to the country. . . . The measures are right in themselves, and collectively constitute one grand scheme of conciliation and adjustment. They were all necessary to the attainment of this end. The success of a portion of them only would not have accomplished the object; but all together constitute a fair and honorable adjustment." Within the adjustment, though, were the seeds of further tension for both parties and the Union over the issues the compromise was supposed to settle.[39]

THREE

"A HELL OF A STORM": THE AFTERMATH OF COMPROMISE

"The party is dead—dead—dead!" One Ohio Whig's post-mortem on the 1852 election summarized his party's plight. Democrat Franklin Pierce buried Whig presidential candidate Winfield Scott. Pierce won 27 of 31 states and Democrats gained in Congress and in local elections. A Pennsylvanian described Whig efforts to stem the tide as "like pissing against the wind." Young Whigs like Indiana's Schuyler Colfax, the future House speaker, considered the party "almost annihilated," while veterans like Thurlow Weed of New York said, "There may be no political future for us." Granted, devastating losses often breed doomsaying, but time and events proved these Whigs right. Despite campaigning and winning in several state elections in 1853, their share of the vote declined sharply. Their party never recovered from the smashing defeat, and the Kansas-Nebraska Act of 1854 and its aftermath all but completed the dissolution of the Whig party.[1]

Part of the party's problem was its cult of personality. Two Whigs towered above all others. In 1852, both died: Henry Clay on June 29 and Daniel Webster on October 24. Lightning rods throughout their careers, attacked by antislavery Whigs for their role in the Compromise of 1850, they also carried weight as founders and leaders whose reputations predated the party. Their presidential ambitions may have hurt the Whig party as much as they helped it, but they also attracted at least as many followers as they repelled. More crucially, their belief in the Union above all and an expansive federal government underpinned Whig ideology. With their deaths, and a combination of new issues or different versions of old issues, keeping the Whig party together became harder, perhaps impossible.

Although its intent was far different, the Compromise of 1850 sowed the seeds of these events. Northern Democrats basked in the glow of Senator Stephen Douglas's success in passing it, southern Democrats recalled their Jacksonian roots and celebrated the Union's preservation, and secessionist Democrats gnashed their teeth or sought a new political home, although their behavior was not enough to ruin their party. Whereas conservative and Upper South Whigs found Clay's plan acceptable, even ideal, Deep South and antislavery Whigs were another matter. Despite divisions over slavery that permitted the Free-Soil party's growth in 1848, Democrats felt more party loyalty than Whigs. Not only had success bred unity, but Democrats also shared a unifying ideology of states' rights. Whigs believed in economic development and limited executive power—goals that mattered less to southern Whigs than protecting slavery and less to northern Whigs than limiting it.

While the Compromise's passage and the reaction to it suggested a desire to avoid further controversy, the sectional consensus, even if only an agreement to disagree, proved short-lived. After receiving little attention in debates over the Compromise, the Fugitive Slave Act became a major issue. Continued attempts at westward and southern expansion divided regions and parties. Both parties struggled to find new leadership—or seemed to find it and regretted it. As the Kansas-Nebraska Act proved, the regions and parties remained split over slavery and its expansion into the West. Although Democrats proved better at papering over their disagreements in the wake of the Compromise than were the Whigs, they were hopelessly divided, too. After his defeat as vice-presidential candidate on the 1852 Free-Soil ticket, George Julian proved prescient: "One of these strongholds of slavery has perished, the other has thus been deprived of its antagonist, and must follow in its footsteps; for although intensely hostile, they have been in support of each other."[2]

THE COMPROMISE OF 1850: VOTERS' POST-MORTEM

Before the Pierce landslide or the political earthquake caused by the Kansas-Nebraska Act, voters expressed their opinion of the Compromise of 1850 in elections later that year and in 1851. Whether the voting came amid rumors that new president Millard Fillmore would approve the Compromise or after he did so, Whigs lost ground—even when they triumphed. The key issue for both parties was the Compromise and what it meant for slavery and its westward expansion. Whigs hoped to win back defectors to the Free-Soilers in 1848 but found their association with the Compromise, due mainly to Fillmore and Clay, an obstacle. They also ran into difficulty with the remnants or resurrection of Zachary Taylor's efforts to redefine the Whigs as a non-partisan group of Centrists and Unionists. Thus, in the North's strongest antislavery areas, Whigs fared badly in the 1850 midterms by running on a pro-Compromise platform and through guilt by association with Fillmore. Fusing with Free-Soilers helped them; in Ohio, for example, a Whig/Free-Soil coalition elected Benjamin Wade to the Senate to serve with Democratic Free-Soiler Salmon Chase.[3]

Massachusetts presented a conundrum for Whigs and Democrats. Antislavery Democrats and Free-Soilers grew closer, with Conscience Whigs excoriating Webster for his Seventh of March speech and becoming Fillmore's secretary of state. Returning the favor, he said, "I much prefer to see a responsible Democrat elected to Congress than a professed Whig, tainted with any degree of Free Soil doctrines or abolitionism." Webster moved allies into his old Senate seat and a vacant House seat and proved more willing to compromise with the South than with antislavery Whigs. These attitudes cost Whigs in the 1850 election, enabling Free-Soil Democrat George Boutwell to become governor. Early in 1851, after a long battle, the legislature elected Conscience Whig Charles Sumner to the Senate, which he called "a mighty pulpit from which the truth can be preached," and where he became a vocal critic of slavery and the South.[4]

If Massachusetts symbolized the divisions within the two parties, New York's Whigs showed how rickety their party had become. Although Fillmore was his vice-president, Taylor gave most of New York's patronage to Seward and Weed. When Taylor died, Fillmore removed some appointees but, hoping for some unity, avoided a political slaughter. But slavery expansion had long divided New York Whigs, and the 1850 elections proved no different. Fillmore opposed any anti-Compromise platform that would "sacrifice the Whig party of the Union for the sake of a temporary triumph in the State of New York." When Whigs met in September, Weed had no objection to Fillmore ally Francis Granger presiding. But when the convention divided over praising Seward's record, Fillmore's group bolted, Granger's mane giving them their name, the Silver Grays. Then, for governor, Sewardites backed Washington Hunt, who had kept one foot in each camp, convincing both sides that they controlled him. Whereas New York City Whig merchants abandoned him as too radical, Silver Grays swallowed their displeasure. Hunt barely defeated Democrat Horatio Seymour while Whigs gained enough legislative seats to elect Hamilton Fish, a conservative Seward ally, to the Senate. Those results and an agreement to seek an internal improvements bill convinced Fillmore of "the *union* of the Whig party in N. York."[5]

Fillmore was too optimistic. When rumors spread that conservative New York Democrats—always battling their antislavery intraparty rivals—and Whigs would "clear our skirts of Sewardism" by forming a new party, Seward's friends inclined to let them go. The Silver Gray editor of the *New York Express* tried to insult Weed by likening him to Frederick Douglass as an abolitionist, and Weed replied that "we think better of him as an Editor and a Man, than we do of the *Express* and its Editors." But when

Whigs lost most state races in 1851, recriminations inevitably followed. Antislavery Whigs accused Fillmore of sacrificing his party's success to keep them out of power. Other Whigs charged them with putting opposition to slavery expansion above all else. Either way, Whigs were in sad shape when the party in the president's home state was in such a shambles and the more powerful faction was the one opposed to him. If Fillmore hoped to win a term in his own right, New York was a bad omen.[6]

In slave states, too, traditional rivalries helped explain the 1850 results, but so did the distinction between protecting southern rights and backing disunion—a dispute similar enough to that in the North to keep the Compromise at the center of political debate. In Democratic Missouri, Senator Thomas Hart Benton had fought slavery expansion through five terms. In 1850, his attitude finally cost him his seat in an electoral preview of future party divisions. With divided Missouri Democrats refusing to compromise, and Benton still flaying the Slave Power—which included Missouri—anti-Benton Democrats helped Whigs slip in their candidate. A similar situation hurt Delaware Whigs. Taylor's secretary of state, John Clayton, often leaned toward free-soil in that slave state, and those leanings, combined with other issues and the remnants of Whig displeasure with Taylor, helped Democrats gain Clayton's old Senate seat in addition to a long-standing Whig House seat.[7]

Southern Whigs mirrored their northern counterparts. Divided over the Compromise, they had to bridge the chasm between conservative and radical responses to issues tied to slavery and found it hard to do. They also faced the question some northern Whigs asked: Should they stay in the party? Northern Democrats reunited after 1848 by tamping down differences over slavery, emphasizing unionism, stressing local issues, and not running nationally oriented campaigns. But for northern Whigs committed to federal activism and southern Whigs who believed less strongly in it for economic purposes and not at all when slavery was at issue, the twain was unlikely to meet. Worse, even if they were broader-minded than Deep South Whigs, border state Whigs still had to overcome the sense spreading in the South that the North had no respect for southern rights.

Southern Democrats felt even more strongly about these issues. Just after California's admission on September 9, 1850, Democratic governors in Georgia and Mississippi called for secession, and their South Carolina and Alabama colleagues hoped for the same; the next May, about 450 South Carolinians met in a convention and endorsed secession. Those sentiments should have played into Whig hands: southern Whigs opposed secession and could have bolstered Fillmore's efforts to unite Whigs behind the Compromise. But when Webster proposed a fiery Unionist response, Fillmore said no. Why he did so may have resulted from southern Whigs advising against it, or he saw that Webster's desire to win the 1852 nomination gave him selfish reasons to appease northern Whigs who would welcome such a statement. But with Democrats getting their way in the Compromise, most secessionist sentiment seemed to go into hibernation.

Hoping to gain support and stave off fire-eaters, as secessionists were called, unionist southern Whigs sought to fuse with like-minded Democrats. But with Democrats more popular in the South, Whigs would be secondary, a risky sacrifice. Beyond Unionism, ambition enhanced their desire for fusion. In Mississippi, Senator Henry Foote angered other Democrats by backing the Compromise. Joining a Unionist party saved Foote's career: he defeated states' rights Democrat Jefferson Davis for governor. In Alabama, the Unionist coalition enabled a few Whigs to win normally elusive offices, but not as Whigs, doing nothing for party loyalty. Whigs were strong only in one southern state, Georgia, where they imploded. Pro-Compromise Whigs, led by Alexander Stephens and Robert Toombs, hoped to take over their party, unite with unionist Democrats, and marginalize secessionists. Benefiting from an upturn—prosperity discouraged secessionism—they aligned with Democrat Howell Cobb in a Union party that elected Cobb governor and Toombs senator. But their platform declared "that upon a faithful execution of the *Fugitive Slave Law* . . . depends the preservation of our much beloved Union"—a condition disagreeable to many northern Whigs and a significant number of southern Whigs. Thus, Stephens and Toombs helped shelve the Democratic party temporarily, but divided the Whig party permanently.[8]

Indeed, playwright George Bernard Shaw's description of the United States and England as two countries separated by a common language applied to the North and South in the 1850s. William Freehling has written, "This image of *a* South, united in abnormal conspiratorial control of democracy, missed everything important about the divided South." The same could be said of the North. Differences existed between states—Massachusetts was more antislavery than Indiana, Virginia more ambivalent about slavery than Alabama—and within states. Differences existed between the parties, but in several states, antislavery or doughface members of the two parties discussed creating new coalitions based primarily on issues related to slavery and its expansion. Increasingly, both sections saw the other as monolithic. That was a recipe for trouble.[9]

"TRAMPLE THIS INFAMOUS LAW UNDERFOOT"

Antislavery forces seemed to have no cause for complaint about the Fugitive Slave Act of 1850 beyond moral opposition to anything that perpetuated or protected slavery. The law was constitutional: Article IV, Section 2 of the Constitution guaranteed slave owners the right to regain escaped human property, and Congress passed legislation to that effect in 1793. In the 1830s, responding to the reinvigorated abolitionist movement and southern efforts to restrict speech and discussion related to slavery—several northern states passed personal liberty laws giving African Americans the rights of habeas corpus, jury testimony, and trials, and imposing penalties on kidnappers. In 1842, in *Prigg v. Pennsylvania,* the U.S. Supreme Court overturned state laws that conflicted with the fugitive slave law, but held the federal government, not the states, responsible for enforcing it—which the 1850 measure proposed to do.

But several aspects of the Fugitive Slave Act foreshadowed problems. "Here was a firebrand vastly more inflammatory than the Wilmot Proviso," David Potter wrote. "The Proviso had dealt with a hypothetical slave who might never materialize; the Fugitive Slave Act, on the contrary, dealt with hundreds of flesh-and-blood people who had risked their lives to gain their liberty, and who might now be tracked down by slave-catchers." Existing personal liberty laws suggested northerners' readiness to ignore or fight what they found disagreeable, and bringing the issue to their doorsteps promised more resistance. Most important, the act's provisions strongly favored the South. Federal officials would appoint commissioners to issue warrants for the arrest and return of fugitives. Besides ordering citizens to help enforce the law or face fines or jail, they would hear pleas and be paid per case—$10 if they found in favor of the slave owner, $5 if they found for the accused fugitive. Slave owners needed only an affidavit claiming ownership as "proof." The accused fugitives would have no right to testify.[10]

If the act outraged northerners, its undertones made matters worse. Amid the controversy over the rest of the Compromise, the Senate devoted little time to fugitive slaves and the House even less. What time they spent on it proved that southerners remained dug in on their demands for the return of fugitives, although the issue mattered more to border slave states than to the Deep South, where fewer slaves escaped. Most northerners showed little inclination or moral compass to fight over the specifics, especially with so much anger swirling around—or, as Transcendentalist minister Theodore Parker put it, "Southern Slavery is an institution which is in earnest. Northern Freedom is an institution that is not in earnest." But angry antislavery northerners noted the contradictions: southerners had sought expanded federal activism, which they considered evil if it threatened slavery or their prosperity. Furthermore, while southerners and doughfaces dismissed the Wilmot Proviso as impractical, antislavery forces had to accede to a fugitive slave law the Deep South wanted although it affected mainly the Upper South. For their part, southerners saw it a test of northern resolve: if northerners refused to do their part, they were disobedient, and disunionist, and contributed to the agitation over slavery that the Compromise was supposed to end.[11]

Instead, once they understood what it did, northerners saw the Fugitive Slave Act as too bitter a pill to swallow. By literally bringing the issue into their homes, the law turned slavery from an intellectual exercise into a stark reality. They might have to join posses to hunt fugitives, turn neighbors in to the authorities, and testify against people they had known for decades. As William Cullen Bryant wrote in the *New York Evening Post,* "The people feel it to be an impeachment of their manhood, to be asked to assist in manacling, for the purpose of reducing to slavery, one who has lived among them the life of an industrious and honest citizen; whom for years they have been accustomed to meet in their daily walks, and with whom, perhaps, they have broken bread." Abolitionists and their allies took advantage of these feelings with heartfelt stories of former slaves ripped from their families and equally heartfelt vilifications of the law and its supporters. Calling it a "filthy" law, Ralph Waldo Emerson said, "As long as men have bowels, they will disobey." Representative Joshua Giddings, an Ohio abolitionist, said, "Let the President . . . drench our land of freedom in blood; but he will never make us obey that law."[12]

Indeed, northerners soon engaged in civil disobedience, though not so far as Frederick Douglass suggested: "The only way to make the Fugitive Slave Law a dead letter is to make a half-a-dozen or more dead kidnappers." Instead, Parker and other antislavery Bostonians set up a vigilance committee. The first battle over fugitives involved William and Ellen Craft, who escaped north (Ellen cut her hair short and posed as a sickly planter accompanied by "his" servant), joined Parker's church, and faced return to Macon, Georgia. The committee hounded the two "man stealers" sent to retrieve them until they left after five days. When Fillmore ordered the warrant for the Crafts' arrest enforced and threatened to send federal troops, the committee spirited the Crafts to a new home in England. Parker spoke for many foes of slavery when he wrote to Fillmore, "I would rather lie all my life in jail, and starve there, than refuse to protect one of these parishioners of mine. . . . You cannot think that I am to stand by and see my own church carried off to slavery and do nothing to hinder such a wrong."[13]

Bostonians had more wrongs to hinder. Early in 1851, a fugitive known as Shadrach sat imprisoned, arrested at his job as a waiter at Taft's Cornhill Coffee House. As attorney Richard Henry Dana described it, "we heard a shout from the courthouse, continued into a yell of triumph, and in an instant after down the steps came two negroes bearing the prisoner between them with his clothes half torn off, and so stupefied by his sudden rescue and the violence of his dragging off that he sat almost dumb, and I thought had fainted; . . . and they went off toward Cambridge, like a black squall, the crowd driving along with them and cheering as they went." With Shadrach transported to Canada, Fillmore responded by ordering eight of his liberators prosecuted, but no jury would convict them. Nor did Boston easily let down its guard. The federal government's most notable early success in returning a fugitive to the South from Boston required 300 soldiers to remove Thomas Sims in the middle of the night. Webster wrote to Fillmore that the "abolitionists & free soilers . . . are insane, but it is an angry & vindictive insanity," and Fillmore replied that Sims's return "wiped out the stain of the former rescue." This disdain for abolitionists crossed partisan lines: Stephen Douglas told the Senate, "I hold white men now within the range of my sight responsible for the violation of the law at Boston. It was done under their advice, under their teaching, under their sanction, under the influence of their speeches."[14]

The northern rebellion against the Fugitive Slave Act extended beyond New England, which was known as "the cradle of abolitionism." In September 1851, a posse arrived in Christiana, Pennsylvania, to bring two escapees back to Maryland. The Quaker town near the Maryland border had a record of aiding fugitives. More than 20 blacks blocked their way, shots rang out, and the slaveholder was killed. Federal marshals arrested 40 men, whom the Fillmore administration indicted for treason—a capital offense. With Whig congressman Thaddeus Stevens, owner of a nearby iron-works, defending them, the jury found them not guilty.[15]

Soon after the confrontation in Christiana, an attempted capture in Syracuse, New York, caused a similar uproar. William Henry, called "Jerry," was a cooper who had escaped a couple of years earlier from Missouri. He came before a federal commissioner, an abolitionist who felt bound to uphold the law. The commissioner told his wife what happened, and she spread the word—and it spread quickly; Syracuse lay at the heart of the burnt-over district, where the Second Great Awakening had begun and antislavery sentiment was strong. Unitarian minister Samuel May reflected the attitude of the Act's foes when he told his congregants, "We must trample this infamous law underfoot, be the consequences what they may. It is not for you to choose whether you will or not obey such a law as this. You are as much under obligation not to obey it, as you are not to lie, steal, or commit murder." After Jerry's first escape attempt failed, a crowd knocked down the door to the jail where he was held, and his rescuers—including a proslavery Democrat who pivoted to abolitionism after seeing Jerry dragged in chains through the Syracuse streets—removed him to Canada. The indictment of 26 participants led to one conviction—and that man died awaiting an appeal.[16]

The Fugitive Slave Act ultimately brought few benefits to the South and its slave owners. During the 1850s, federal officials sent 332 African Americans into southern slavery and declared only 11 free. Those percentages favored the South, but demonstrated the Act's futility: those returned to slavery fell far short of the number of slaves who escaped. In many cases, the slave owner paid more to travel north and cover court costs than he could hope to recoup from the slave's monetary value. News of a slave owner's impending arrival prompted fugitives and free blacks to put themselves out of reach. An estimated 3,000 free blacks—fugitives or not—fled into Canada by the end of 1850, and the black population in the Canadian province of Ontario doubled during that decade.

Their failures, from Boston to Syracuse, heightened southern distrust for the North. For southern Unionists, the issue was the law, or the North's disobedience of it. When northerners defied the Fugitive Slave Act, they broke the law and deprived southerners of their most important gain from the Compromise of 1850. Although critical of the South's claims of the number of slaves who had run away to the North, Henry Clay could think of "no instance in which there was so violent and forcible obstruction to the laws of the United States" besides the Whiskey Rebellion of 1794, which George Washington put down with troops. Clay continued, "I condemn all violent interference with the due and regular execution of the laws." Fillmore felt similarly and hoped to unite Whigs around that ideal. In his annual message to Congress in December 1850, he called the Compromise "a settlement in principle and substance—a final settlement of the dangerous and exciting subjects which they embraced." He added, "It may be presumed from the opposition which they all encountered that none of those measures were free from imperfections, but in their mutual dependence and connection they formed a system of compromise, the most conciliary [sic], and best for the entire country, that could be obtained from conflicting sectional interests and opinions."[17]

But the controversy over fugitive slaves revealed the North's mixed emotions. What Fillmore said publicly upheld the Compromise of 1850 in all of its good and bad elements. Privately, he said, "God knows that I detest slavery, but it is an existing evil for which we are not responsible, and we must endure it and give it such protection as is guaranteed by the Constitution, till we can get rid of it without destroying the last hope of free government in the world." By late 1851, resistance to the Fugitive Slave Act had waned, and Charles Sumner lamented that "this is the darkest day of our cause." But easing anger was one thing—eliminating it proved to be a totally different matter.[18]

THE POLITICS OF LITERATURE, THE LITERATURE OF POLITICS

In the summer of 1851, newspaper readers encountered two distinct approaches to major issues from two people who shaped coming events in unexpected ways. In June, *Uncle Tom's Cabin; Or, Life Among the Lowly* began appearing in serial form, to be published as a book the next spring. In September, a new morning newspaper, *The New York Times,* debuted. Legend has it that Abraham Lincoln called the book's author "the little lady who made this big war," and the journalist oversaw the president's reelection campaign in the midst of that war. But both Harriet Beecher Stowe and Henry Jarvis Raymond contributed to the impending crisis in their own ways.

A writer for the Whig press in his teens, Raymond was only 31 when he and partner George Jones began publishing *The Times.* Raymond had worked for both Horace Greeley, the eccentric radical who edited the *New York Tribune,* and James Watson Webb, the eccentric conservative who edited the *New York Courier & Enquirer.* Greeley and Webb shared Whiggery and strong opinions, but Greeley was noisily antislavery whereas Webb was less vocal, reflecting the New York party split. While he imbibed Greeley's open-mindedness, Webb's practicality, and both men's political ambition, Raymond also saw that readers wanted news. The "penny press," as New York's one-cent dailies were called, varied from the sensationalism of James Gordon Bennett's *Herald* to the reformist intentions of Greeley's *Tribune.* In the first issue of *The New-York Daily Times,* as it was known, Raymond wrote, "Upon all topics,—Political, Social, Moral and Religious,—we intend that the paper shall speak for itself;—and we only ask that it may be judged accordingly. We shall be *Conservative,* in all cases where we think Conservatism essential to the public good;—and we shall be *Radical* in everything which may seem to us to require radical treatment, and radical reform. . . . We do not mean to write as if we were in a passion,—unless that shall really be the case; and we shall make it a point to get into a passion as rarely as possible."[19]

But Raymond proved passionate about politics, with long-term national effects. His declaration of principles targeted Greeley, the Seward-Weed machine's main voice in New York City. Ideologically, Greeley was closer to Seward and Weed on slavery. But his support for other causes, from dietary reform to utopian communities, put them in difficult positions and disinclined them to give him a political position. Both editors hungered for office, but Raymond was more reliable and likelier to follow the leaders than Greeley. By founding *The Times,* Raymond made a major contribution to serious journalism and had a political impact that reshaped the electoral landscape—and the rest of the American landscape. In 1854, when they backed Raymond for lieutenant governor instead of the *Tribune* editor, Greeley broke with Seward and Weed and exacted revenge by helping to deny Seward the presidency in favor of Lincoln in 1860. Meanwhile, Raymond became more important behind the scenes in party councils; he was responsible for the first Republican platform in 1856 and chaired Lincoln's campaign in 1864.

But all of that was in the future when *The Times* was born, and how those events unfolded had a great deal to do with what Raymond claimed to avoid: passion for a cause. In the early 1850s, no one expressed that passion more successfully than Stowe, a veteran writer whose brother Henry Beecher followed their father into the ministry, earning fame for his sermons and abolitionism. Stowe's sister-in-law told her that "if I could use a pen as you can, I would write something that will make this whole nation feel what an accursed thing slavery is," and Stowe did. She began a series of stories about slavery in the abolitionist *National Era.* In March 1852, they appeared in book form as *Uncle Tom's Cabin,* and sold about three million copies in the United States. It sold even better overseas, where the British leader Lord Palmerston praised the book not for "its story but for the statesmanship of it"—a reminder that other nations had ended slavery and might look askance at Americans who claimed to love liberty but allowed slavery to exist and even flourish.[20]

While Stowe never claimed it was a literary classic, *Uncle Tom's Cabin* may have been the most politically significant piece of fiction ever published. Its style could be plodding and Victorian, its characters simplistic, its plot moralistic and clunky, and its conclusion—the idea of slaves returning to Africa and thereby solving the racial problems afflicting the United States—unlikely. Few cared. Readers, and audiences at the many plays based on the series and the book, lived and died with Uncle Tom.

Uncle Tom was a slave who refused to acknowledge his overseer as a greater power than God, but he became known to generations as a symbol of blacks bowing down before whites. Audiences hissed at Simon Legree, who brutalized Tom, and mourned Little Eva, whom Tom had saved but whose death ultimately led to his sale and demise. Indeed, caught up in *Uncle Tom's Cabin,* they missed Stowe's larger point in making the Vermont-born Legree the villain and several southerners sympathetic: slavery was a national blot for which the North could not evade responsibility, and the slaves themselves offered the means of redemption for northerners and southerners alike.

More important, northerners and southerners bought Stowe's book in large numbers and reacted forcefully to it. For northerners, *Uncle Tom's Cabin* opened the eyes of many who had thought little about slavery and seemed to confirm the worst suspicions of those who considered it cruel and backward. Abolitionists objected to its support for colonization and its oversimplifications, but welcomed the widespread support it engendered for their cause. To southerners, it reflected the typical northern outlook—anti-southern and antislavery—and hypocrisy, because a northern author dared to criticize their peculiar institution. It prompted novels depicting slaves as better off than northern wage laborers, including *Uncle Robin in His Cabin in Virginia and Tom Without One in Boston.* Southerners referred to Stowe as "detestable," "monstrous," and "the vile wretch in petticoats." In his *Knoxville Whig,* William "Parson" Brownlow, a unionist during the Civil War, called Stowe "a deliberate liar" and "as ugly as Original sin—an abomination in the eyes of civilized people. A tall, course [sic], vulgar-looking woman—stoop-shouldered with a long yellow neck and a long peaked nose—through which she speaks"—although the chances he had ever seen her were slim to none.[21]

But other authors contributed to the debate over slavery and its political connections in the early 1850s. Nathaniel Hawthorne dedicated himself to the doughface cause as a Democrat and author of a campaign biography of his college classmate and friend, Franklin Pierce. The Whiggish and scholarly Edward Everett wondered, "Why in this fearful struggle which we are obliged to sustain is he on the side of barbarism & vandalism against order, law & constitutional liberty?" Sharing Hawthorne's sense that Whigs like Everett felt superior, James Fenimore Cooper celebrated the democratic frontiersman in such works as *The Deerslayer* and in political tracts, and his final works lamented the Union's future and that "we do not believe any more in the superior innocence and virtue of a rural population." One of the country's most distinguished poets, William Cullen Bryant, edited the antislavery and Democratic *New York Evening Post.* Although *Leaves of Grass* would not appear in print until 1855, after which he was known primarily as a poet, Walt Whitman wrote for several newspapers in the late 1840s and early 1850s, expressing Democratic and antislavery views. Another Democrat, Herman Melville, tried political fiction, but turned to *Moby-Dick; or The Whale,* which some readers saw as an antislavery allegory, whether or not that was so.[22]

Slavery inspired other fiction. In 1853, fugitive slave William Wells Brown, living in London to avoid capture back home, published *Clotel; or, The President's Daughter: A Narrative of Slave Life in the United States,* the first novel by an African American. Brown had written an account of his life as a slave and fugitive. His next literary effort noted, "On every foot of soil, over which *Stars* and *Stripes* wave, the negro is considered common property, on which any white man may lay his hand with perfect impunity." Clotel escaped by posing as a man, but was crossing a narrow bridge across the Potomac River from Washington, D.C., into Virginia, trying to evade her would-be captors, when "with a single bound, she vaulted over the railings of the bridge, and sunk for ever beneath the waves of the river! Thus died Clotel, the daughter of Thomas Jefferson. . . ." Brown was neither the first nor the last to suggest what history and science have proved: that Jefferson fathered black children with Sally Hemings. But for anyone, especially a fugitive slave, to suggest Jefferson's involvement with an African American was shocking at the time. To do so reflected the anger that Americans felt about the issue of slavery.

PIERCING THE WHIGS

"We 'Polked' 'em in '44," Democrats crowed about the Whigs, and "we'll 'pierce' 'em in '52." Despite the lameness of their slogan, Democrats achieved that goal—or Whigs did it for them; either argument is plausible. Clearly, though, neither party entered the 1852 presidential campaign with an obvious front-runner. Nor did the issues that united and divided them seem likely to produce one, as the process of choosing a nominee showed.

The Democratic possibilities seemed too old or too young. At age 61, James Buchanan had legislative experience in the House and Senate, cabinet experience as Polk's secretary of state, and diplomatic experience in that job and as minister to Russia. Embodying the doughface, Buchanan favored the Compromise of 1850 and states' rights, excoriated opponents of slavery, and felt more comfortable politically with southerners than with northerners. He even saw his chances as "in great part derived from the general impression that I am strong with all branches of the Southern Democracy." But he faced problems. In his native Pennsylvania, he fought Democrat Simon Cameron for primacy. Seeking backing in New York from William Marcy, an ally of party powers Martin Van Buren and his son John, Buchanan complained that "the Van Burens began to tickle Marcy with the idea of being President himself." Polk's war secretary and a former governor, the 65-year-old Marcy was one of New York's Hunkers, conservatives who cared less about slavery than holding office. But Marcy was a "soft" Hunker, willing to reconcile with the Barnburners and thus suspect. Like Buchanan, he seemed committed to no particular cause.[23]

The same could be said of Lewis Cass. Almost 70, he had been war secretary, minister to France, senator, and Democratic nominee in 1848. Coming from Michigan, he might attract western support, especially in the antislavery Old Northwest. But he had come up with the idea that Douglas turned into popular sovereignty, which showed more ambivalence toward the South than either region would tolerate, and his defeat four years before made him damaged goods. Nor was he popular enough to escape the attacks that had contributed to that loss, such as Greeley's description of him as "that pot-bellied, mutton-headed cucumber."[24]

The rest of the field had no more appeal, even to Democrats. Cass' running mate from 1848, Kentuckian William Butler, voiced interest, as did Sam Houston, a governor, senator, and symbol of Texas independence. But with support for their states' rights views strong in the South, Democrats needed a northerner who could bridge the gaps between regions and the divisions within those regions. Old Jacksonians Benton and Francis Preston Blair looked to Levi Woodbury, a New Hampshire warhorse of moderate views on slavery who had been a governor, Navy and Treasury secretary, senator, and, since 1845, a Supreme Court justice. But in the fall of 1851, Woodbury ruined the whole plan by dying.

Douglas hoped political savvy and support would outweigh experience. Not yet 40, he sought the presidency with support from his friends in "Young America," a nationalistic movement redolent of the belief in Manifest Destiny that was so crucial to Democratic politics in the 1840s. But Young Americans were even more interested in promoting nationalism in the sectionally minded party than in expansion, and critical of what they called "old fogies"—a term that fit most of the candidates. Douglas reflected their views in a speech on the "Great West": "The North and South may quarrel and wrangle about a question which should never enter the halls of Congress; but the Great West will say to the South, You must not leave us; and to the North, You must faithfully observe the constitution—with all its compromises." Douglas sought an end to the debate over slavery, a subject of little importance to him. He preferred to concentrate on westward growth, which, it turned out, proved impossible without reviving the slavery issue.[25]

As that conundrum suggested, Douglas managed to be his own best friend and worst enemy. A reporter said, "We Eastern men are all more or less mongrel. We have an English education and French manners. Our models and types are usually from the other side of the sea. . . . But the Western man is as original as the Indian." But if Douglas combined several American characteristics, so did his supporters, who came from all regions and points on the ideological spectrum, making them hard to control or to keep from contradicting one another. John Slidell of Louisiana called them "trading politicians and adventurers, with a very slight sprinkling of well-meaning men," while another Buchanan ally, Senator William King of Alabama, wrote, "Every vulture that would prey upon the public carcass, and every creature who expects the reward of office, are moving heaven on earth in his behalf." That comment could apply to any candidate's operatives, but the political establishment was shocked when Douglas took the then-unheard-of step of choosing a running-mate at the start—Senator R.M.T. Hunter, a Virginia Unionist slightly older than Douglas—and the almost unheard-of step of openly seeking the presidency when the tradition, at least publicly, was for "the office to seek the man." Seeking support, Douglas's backers bought the *Democratic Review* and declared in their first issue, "The statesmen of a previous generation, with their personal antipathies, and their personal claims, with personal greatness or personal inefficiency, must get out of the way" for "young blood, young ideas, and young hearts." The criticism soon became more personal and vitriolic. Whereas candidates had said worse about one another privately, they had avoided doing so in public. Looking too young in too many ways, Douglas's campaign survived, but barely.[26]

When Democrats met in Baltimore in July, no front-runner stood out, but a dark horse loomed. Woodbury's old backers teamed on behalf of Franklin Pierce, a former governor and senator from New Hampshire. Their reasons varied—a desire for patronage, a hatred for Whigs (especially possible nominee Winfield Scott), and the quest for a doughface. Pierce had the advantage of sympathy for the South melded with New England roots, youthfulness that might counter the Young Americans working for Douglas, and a reputation for following his leaders. His disadvantages were more personal than political. His wife opposed his political career, and he resigned a Senate seat and declined Polk's offer to become attorney general partly for those reasons. She also talked him into declining offers of support early in 1852 and believed that he planned to stay out of politics. Their first two children had died young, worsening Jane Pierce's physical and emotional fragility, and leaving her husband without the kind of support at home that he needed. Another reason for his departure from Washington was alcohol, which was crucial to doing business on Capitol Hill. Pierce handled it badly when he handled it at all. He had volunteered for the Mexican-American War and built a nondescript military record, mainly through bad luck: his horse pitched him one day and he injured his pelvis on the saddle horn, an injured knee kept him out of one battle, and diarrhea sidelined him another time.

Whether Pierce's luck improved at the convention depends on one's view of Pierce and luck. After 48 ballots of maneuvering between better-known candidates, his supporters convinced the delegates that he could unite the divided party. A stampede nominated him on the next ballot and named King of Alabama to run with him, pleasing party elders. The party platform backed the Compromise and opposed further discussion of slavery. Democrats were happy—or, more accurately, delusional: both David Wilmot and Jefferson Davis claimed Pierce shared their views. But a friend of Pierce's said in New Hampshire, "where everybody knows Frank Pierce, and where Frank Pierce knows everybody, he's a pretty considerable fellow. . . . But come to spread him all over this whole country, I'm afraid he'll be dreadful thin in some places." One of the few Democrats left unconvinced, antislavery New Yorker Preston King—no relation to Alabama's King—called the platform "mischievous in its present and future consequences upon the party and upon the country. There is however imperishable life in the principles of Democracy and the party will fight through in spite of all evil."[27]

While Democrats dreamed, Whigs dissolved. Northern Whigs sought areas of agreement but warred over the Compromise. What few triumphs Whigs achieved came by fusing with Free-Soilers and other antislavery men—a bad sign if the party hoped for a united sectional front. Slavery and its possible growth westward had divided Whigs within and across regions. Worse, Whigs could find no way to close the chasm. Their economic policies lost resonance with the prosperity produced by, among other factors, the Gold Rush. What might happen in the West divided them and what was happening in the West kept them from reuniting.

Nor did Whigs have a clear front-runner to coalesce around. As commanding general during the recent war, Scott offered the possibility of a third victory with a military hero. Connecticut's Truman Smith wrote, "We are a minority party and can not succeed unless we have a candidate who can command more votes than the party can give him"—in other words, Scott. As a Virginian, he could appeal to both regions and would abide by the Compromise. But Scott suffered from the perception that he was a tool of Seward and Weed, which would help him with northern antislavery Whigs but hurt him everywhere else. One southern Whig even said Scott was fine, the problem was everyone around him—although Weed preferred to cede the nomination to southern Whigs because he expected the Democrat to win and wanted to keep his side from taking the blame for it. Unlike William Henry Harrison and Zachary Taylor, who had been political and hid it, Scott was politically inept and constantly showed it. He often dabbled in politics during his military career and lacked the common touch of the other Whig generals who won the White House—not surprising for a commander called "Ol' Fuss and Feathers" and "Ol' Spit and Polish." Stuck with a candidate and a platform mostly silent on slavery as the only way to hold the party together, Greeley told a friend, "I suppose we must run Scott for President, and I hate it."[28]

Antislavery Whigs had few other options. Clay was dying and knew it. Webster was dying and did not know it, and after seeking the presidency for decades, he saw no reason to let age and ailments stop him in 1852. As secretary of state, he had a prominent platform from which to run. Despite his Unionism and Whig economic orthodoxy, his pro-Compromise stance cost him among antislavery Whigs. Rather than meeting them even partway, he preferred to try to force them to his side. That was hardly the best road to party unity, unless Webster hoped to replicate the southern Union parties in the North by uniting pro-Compromise Democrats and Whigs. But the southern parties proved short-lived or unable to translate their local success to the national race. The other issues dividing the two sides and many years of partisan battling were too great.

Webster also found high office kept him in the public eye but forced him into volatile situations. In 1851, Louis Kossuth toured the country, drawing hundreds of thousands along the East Coast to applaud his efforts in 1848 to overthrow Austria's Hapsburg Empire. But Kossuth wanted the United States to fund another Hungarian revolt. Whereas expansionist Democrats could advocate the spread of democracy in Europe as easily as they did in Mexico, Whigs were in a bind. Webster had diplomatic reasons to handle Kossuth gingerly, lest he offend European powers. His political reasons were more explosive: southerners and conservative northerners had no desire to hear about the downtrodden securing the blessings of liberty because that kind of talk could lead to trouble in slave states. Worse, from their standpoint, Seward—antislavery, committed to courting immigrant votes, and legitimately a believer in his cause—became Kossuth's American champion. That tied Kossuth to Scott, helped keep Webster from embracing him, and made him anathema to Fillmore.

Complicating Webster's plans, he was not even the only candidate to emerge from the administration. Unsure whether to run or back his secretary of state, Fillmore seemed indecisive and weak, as the Seward-Weed portion of the party claimed. Actually, Fillmore was in a bind. He had disavowed interest in a term of his own and admired Scott and Webster. But Scott had little hope of southern Whig support or winning the general election unless he swept the North, and no chance of winning enough Democratic votes to overcome southern or conservative northern Whig defections. Webster had hurt himself with antislavery Whigs, but backing the Compromise did nothing to erase southerners' memories of listening to him demand their support for Union and Whig doctrines beneficial to the North. Southern Whigs had no faith in the southern candidate, northern Whigs had no faith in the northern candidate, and antislavery Whigs had no faith in either of them. Just as Pierce's presence, though not necessarily Pierce himself, might unite Democrats, Fillmore—or what he did or did not stand for—might unite Whigs. Whether or not he wanted to run, for his party's sake, he had to run.

Perhaps the best summary of the Whigs' problem came from Christopher Williams, serving his fifth and final term as a representative from Tennessee. He joined Democrat Cobb and Whigs Clay, Stephens, Foote, and Willie Mangum of North Carolina in pledging to oppose any candidate who reopened the issue of slavery and the Compromise. He said, "I can never become a Democrat. I differ with them about the disposition of the public lands, tariff, and nearly all questions of expediency. I further believe, that the party with which I have been ever acting understands better the wants and interests, the character and genius of the American people than the opposition party." But he found it incomprehensible that Scott supported the Compromise, as his backers claimed, yet refused to say so publicly and could still be nominated over a sitting president or as distinguished a leader as Webster. Without mentioning the divisions among New York Whigs, he saw the only objection to Fillmore as "that he has been faithful to the obligations of his official oath" by signing the Compromise. Williams added, "I seek not to do General

Scott injustice. I have an object infinitely above the success of this or that man for the Presidency. I am struggling to maintain the nationality of the party to which I have ever belonged, and to conserve the interests of my country." But when he asked the House where Scott stood, Tennessee Democrat William Polk replied, "He is for it in the South, and against it in the North"—a reply that, as James Polk's brother, he doubtless made with great pleasure. Scott's position might work in local and state elections, but it would be disastrous at a national level.[29]

Accordingly, the Whig convention proved even more contentious than the Democratic gathering. Southerners threatened to bolt, which Seward and other Scott supporters would have found agreeable, but Fillmore and Webster, thinking of the party's future and their own hopes, helped quell the uprising. Raymond claimed northerners approved a wishy-washy platform in return for the South accepting Scott, and southerners demanded Raymond's expulsion from the convention—one even challenged him to a duel. Both loyal Whigs, both antislavery, Raymond could agree with Greeley, who wrote of the platform, "We defy it, execrate it, spit upon it." Whigs took even more ballots than Democrats to pick a candidate—53. Fillmore and Webster split the southern Whig vote, with neither man willing to make a deal to head off Scott or even speaking despite being hundreds of yards from each other in Washington. At one point, Fillmore and Webster simultaneously asked to withdraw their names, but their delegates also were stubborn and refused. Finally, Whigs chose Scott and, needing a southerner for balance even with Scott's Virginia roots, North Carolina's William Graham as vice-presidential candidate. Graham had been a governor, senator, and Fillmore's navy secretary, thus offering the prospect for unity. Or so they hoped.[30]

But both parties emerged from their conventions in sorry shape. Democrats united behind Pierce, an unknown quantity of marginal quality. The divided Whigs were stuck with a war hero without a lovable nickname and known for malapropisms and gaffes even when he stayed with a prepared text. Worse, other Whigs considered Scott putty in the hands of antislavery forces, especially Seward. The southern-oriented, states' rights, proslavery, or doughface Democrats chose a northerner with no record on slavery or much of anything else, except that he was a loyal partisan and could be counted on to follow rather than lead. The divided, northerly-inclined Whigs chose a southerner who was moderate on slavery and whom they hoped would say nothing about anything.

More crucially, the issues of the Compromise remained too important for either side to dismiss easily. Resenting their failure and despising Scott and Seward, Webster and his supporters planned to support Pierce but kept quiet about it. Whether Democratic or Whig, a significant number in the Deep South distrusted Scott and his party. Although presidential candidates were supposed to avoid campaigning, Scott's status as a general gave him reason to travel, enabling Whigs to put him on a tour to show that his views on slavery and immigrants were acceptable. Unfortunately, Scott spoke.

Responding to a crowd in Cleveland, he said, "I love to hear the Irish brogue. I have heard it before on many battlefields, and I wish to hear it many times more!" His clumsy remarks alienated both sides. Catholics felt patronized and remembered accusations of Scott's nativism. Whigs made the mistake of viewing their faith as monolithic when Catholics reflected the divisions that existed among most Americans of the time. Protestants who shared Scott's reported anti-immigrant views—and found the growing number of immigrants threatening—felt betrayed when he praised Catholics. One Whig expressed a common response when he described Scott as "a d——d old fool—a brainless bundle of wind & vanity."[31]

Meanwhile, Democrats could just watch the Whigs implode. Unable to accept Scott, some Whigs turned to the remnants of the Free-Soil party, which nominated Senator John P. Hale of New Hampshire—offering the added pleasure of pitting enemies from the same state—while conservatives stayed home, backed Pierce, or formed separate tickets. But Democrats were more united, and their candidate had done less to offend supporters or opponents. Whigs accused Pierce of abolitionist tendencies and attacked him as "the hero of many a well-fought bottle" and the "fainting general," which was partly true but only partly fair—and failed to attract enough temperance advocates to change the outcome. Democrats countered that and hammered Scott, with greater accuracy, as pompous and churlish. They set up "Granite Clubs" and "Hickory Poles to the Honor of the Young Hickory of the Granite Hills," tying Pierce far more than he deserved to Andrew Jackson.

When it was over, voter turnout had dipped since 1848, and Whig fortunes had fallen through the floor. Nationally, Pierce defeated Scott only by a margin of 1,601,474 to 1,386,580, but his lead covered almost the entire electoral map. Whig defeats extended beyond the White House into Congress and statehouses. In New York, where the number of Whigs in the House declined by two-thirds within four years, Hunt lost his reelection bid to Seymour, whom he had beaten two years before. Democrats gained governor's offices in Illinois, Michigan, and Louisiana, leaving Whigs with only 5 of the nation's 31 governors.

The post-mortems reflected shock and surprise on both sides. One Democrat wrote, "Who ever dreamed that Whiggery would squat & shrivel—& collapse and die of overfeeding on its own ailment—humbuggery?" Toombs dreamed it: "We can never have peace and security with Seward, Greeley & Co. in the ascendancy in our national councils, and we can better purchase them by the destruction of the Whig Party than of the Union." Several Whigs likened their losses to Napoleon's loss at Waterloo. Raymond could "see no resurrection of the Whig party *as such,*" and Greeley suggested disbanding the party and uniting with friendly Democrats.[32]

An exchange between two antislavery men proved illuminating. Sumner, who could be politically cunning while seeming to float above it all, told Seward, "Out of this chaos the party of freedom must arise." The New Yorker responded, "No new party will rise, nor will any old one fall." For the moment, Seward was right; in the long term, so was Sumner. But just as the Whigs spent most of their existence reacting to Jackson and his Democratic successors and allies, how the parties reconstituted themselves would depend mainly on the efforts of two Democrats, Pierce and Douglas, and what they did about the issue both sides had tried to bury: the expansion of slavery into the west.[33]

THE MAN IN THE MIDDLE

On January 6, 1853, Pierce, his wife Jane, and their 11-year-old son Bennie boarded a train at Boston, where they had been visiting. Two months before, Pierce had been elected president, and he had spent much of that time discussing and thinking about his cabinet. On this morning, politics became less important. An hour into their trip, the car in which they were riding uncoupled from the rest of the train and went down an embankment. Pierce and his wife were unharmed. The wreckage crushed their son to death before their eyes.

They were devastated. Seeking an explanation, they concluded that God's will had been to keep anything from distracting Pierce from his duties. Later, while talking with one of their friends on the trip to Washington, Jane found out that although her husband had told her he had no interest in the presidency, he had actually sought it. As Roy Nichols, Pierce's biographer, put it, "She'd lost her son; now she lost her faith in her husband. When she reached the White House, she went upstairs and locked the bedroom door. That, presumably, was more than Pierce's unstable nervous system could assimilate. Thereafter nothing went right."[34]

By that, Nichols meant "alcoholic exaggeration. It wasn't that he drank so much, but he couldn't drink anything without getting high." In July 1853, six months after the tragedy, Pierce went to New York for the first world's fair held in the United States with several cabinet members and John Forney, an editor of the administration's organ, the *Washington Union*. Pierce and his ministers made several speeches along the way, and the president took advantage of his visit to Pennsylvania to persuade James Buchanan to serve as his minister to Great Britain. But, Forney told Buchanan, all was not well: "He drinks deep. The place overshadows him," and "he seeks refuge."[35]

Pierce's problem was not so much alcohol as politics and his failure at it, starting with his cabinet. As presidents do, he tried to appeal to all regions and wings of his party—and failed. As secretary of state, Marcy had the diplomatic and management skills needed in his department, and shared Pierce's Young America-style expansionism. A logical choice for war secretary, Jefferson Davis ran the army well despite the stubborn streak that later marred his tenure as Confederate president. Attorney General Caleb Cushing of Massachusetts shared Pierce's views of slavery and the South, making the two of them so unusual in New England that they seemed fated to be together. Kentucky entrepreneur and politician James Guthrie was little known outside of his state before Pierce tapped him as Treasury secretary. Choosing Pennsylvanian James Campbell as postmaster general pleased Buchanan's wing of the party. North Carolina's James Dobbin aided Pierce at the convention, and Pierce hoped his presence in the Navy Department would satisfy southern Unionists, but Dobbin had opposed the Compromise of 1850 and dallied with secessionists. Governor Robert McClelland of Michigan had abandoned the Wilmot Proviso for the Compromise, and that combined with his friendship with Cass to win him the Interior seat.

Unfortunately, Pierce's cabinet provided little help in political and policy battles. Seeking friends and representatives of all regions and views, he wound up with a divided, unprepossessing group—or to make a comparison with another inexperienced president who chose a diverse cabinet, Abraham Lincoln selected party rivals or well-known figures he had the finesse to manage. Pierce's choices lacked the stature and savvy of Lincoln's and brought along ample baggage. Marcy's efforts to reconcile with New York's Free-Soilers hurt him politically with hard-line Democrats, worsening a party split there that rivaled the battles between the Seward-Weed forces and conservative Whigs. Cushing publicly denounced the Democratic–Free-Soil coalition in Massachusetts as "hostile in the highest degree to the determined policy of the Administration," which was to ferret out "the dangerous element of Abolitionism," a statement that hurt Pierce and the party throughout New England. Worse, the presence of Davis and Cushing in particular left pro-Compromise Democrats and southern Unionists feeling ignored or represented only in politically insignificant positions, and neither man ever gave the slightest sign of hearing any opinion but his own.[36]

In doling out patronage, always important in building political support, Pierce did no better. Douglas's rivals, led by proslavery senator Jesse Bright of Indiana, tried to limit his power outside of Illinois in hopes of stymieing his presidential hopes, and their success impaired relations with the Little Giant. Pierce named Marcy's rival, Daniel Dickinson, to the plum job of New York port collector, who was responsible for collecting tariff fees, which were then the major source of federal revenue. But Pierce tried to install as his assistant John Dix, who had fought both Dickinson and Marcy and barely won Senate confirmation—and then Dickinson refused the post. Pierce irked the more moderate Slidell by offering him a minor post, then gave Louisiana's top appointment to Pierre Soulé, a proslavery expansionist whose service as minister to Spain created diplomatic problems there. This opened a Senate seat filled by Slidell, who had no warmth for Pierce. A Douglas ally muttered about Pierce, "His efforts have entirely failed to unite the party. It is torn into shreds and tatters." In yet another tragic twist, Vice President King had gone to Cuba to ease his tuberculosis and died less than two months after the inauguration, making his the shortest vice-presidential term ever. King's death deprived Pierce of a wise old hand, well-known in the party and in Washington.[37]

Pierce's inaugural address offered more promise than his cabinet did. Bowing to the Young Americans, and suggesting that he considered the slavery debate settled, he claimed to have no "timid forebodings of evil from expansion"—indeed, it was "eminently important" for the sake of commerce and national security. On domestic issues, he sounded traditional party themes. "If the Federal Government will confine itself to the exercise of powers clearly granted by the Constitution, it can hardly happen that its action upon any question should endanger the institutions of the States or interfere with their right to manage matters strictly domestic according to the will of their own people," he said, striking Jacksonian, states' rights and proslavery notes. Addressing the South and endorsing the Compromise of 1850, Pierce said, "I believe that the constituted authorities of the Republic are bound to regard the rights of the South in this respect as they would any other legal and constitutional right, and that the laws to enforce them should be obeyed, not with a reluctance encouraged by abstract opinions as to their propriety in a different state of society, but cheerfully and according to the decisions of the tribunal to which their exposition belongs," and that "no sectional or fanatical excitement may again threaten the durability of our institutions"—if abolitionists or secessionists had any threatening ideas.[38]

Pierce and his cabinet had expansionist ideas and acted on them. Amazingly, they did not precipitate a new battle over slavery, but they did not gain much, either. Davis managed to install an ally, South Carolina railroad promoter James Gadsden, as minister to Mexico, and in 1853 he negotiated a treaty to buy 38,000 square miles for $15 million. Acquiring the southern parts of what became Arizona and New Mexico settled questions about the borders set by the Treaty of Guadalupe-Hidalgo and pleased supporters of a southern route for a transcontinental railroad. Young Americans had designs on the Sandwich Islands, now known as Hawaii, but settled for claims on Pacific islands with supplies of dung, which southerners needed for fertilizer—a gain for slave society, perhaps a metaphor for the country during and after Pierce's term, but no source of controversy.

Other overseas adventures created far more agitation at home and abroad. When Cuban officials seized a U.S. boat for violating harbor regulations, Pierce assured Congress that he would tolerate no assaults on American sovereignty. Giddings warned, "We are to have war with Cuba, not on account of the seizure of the cotton on the *Black Warrior*, but to forestall emancipation, to stay the progress of liberty there." Whatever their motives, Pierce and Marcy saw that northerners were wary of expanding slavery southward and resolved the matter with Cuba peacefully. But when Marcy informed Soulé that he still hoped to buy Cuba, the minister suggested a meeting with his diplomatic colleagues, and Buchanan came from England and

John Y. Mason from France to Ostend, Belgium, to work toward that end. They issued the Ostend Manifesto, declaring, "Cuba is as necessary to the North American republic as any of its present members, and that it belongs naturally to that great family of states of which the Union is the Providential Nursery." They suggested paying $120 million for the island, and Soulé sought war with Spain if it declined the offer. But the ensuing brouhaha over acquiring slave territory populated by people of color prompted Marcy to back away, angering southerners and expansionists but pleasing antislavery forces, who rarely found anything pleasing about the Pierce administration.[39]

Not that Pierce and Marcy gave up on Cuba—or other Latin American territory, thanks to an outbreak of filibustering. The term derived from the Spanish word for freebooting, referring to pirates and privateering, which aptly describes what William Walker and John Quitman did. Known as "the gray-eyed man of destiny," Walker led 200 followers into Mexico's Lower California peninsula in 1853, set up an independent republic, and announced the annexation of neighboring Sonora. Mexican leader Santa Anna disposed of him more easily than he handled Scott and his army, with Walker returning to the United States and winning acquittal for violating neutrality laws. In 1855, with broader support, Walker waded into a Nicaraguan civil war. When his side won, he named an ally president of the republic, declared himself commander-in-chief of the army, and won support from the U.S. minister there. But Marcy had no use for independent operators of this nature and refused to recognize Walker or his new government. In 1856, seeking support from southerners who backed Walker's efforts to expand American influence and slavery southward, Pierce recognized the Nicaraguan government. Unfortunately for Walker, Pierce's influence mattered less than that of Cornelius Vanderbilt, the shipping and railroad magnate, who worried about how Walker would affect his business in Central America and helped overthrow Walker's government.

Whereas Walker sympathized with the South, Quitman supported its secession. A former Democratic governor of Mississippi who had fought the Compromise, he wanted to detach Cuba from the shrinking Spanish Empire by filibustering, to the pleasure of southerners and Young Americans. Quitman complained, "The golden shore of the Pacific . . . is denied to Southern labor. . . . We are now hemmed in on the west as well as the north." A southern writer said, "The safety of the South is to be found only in the extension of its peculiar institutions, and the security of the Union in the safety of the South. . . ." But Quitman's plans interfered with Marcy's hopes for a diplomatic solution in Cuba. Worse, northern Democrats were nearly in revolt over southern expansionist efforts. When Pierce upheld American laws requiring neutrality in the spring of 1854, Attorney General Cushing followed by ordering Quitman's arrest. Quitman kept trying to free Cuba, but finally gave up the next year after a discouraging meeting with Pierce and Marcy. Although expanding slavery into the West remained a divisive issue for Americans, it turned out that was true of the expansion of slavery in any direction.[40]

THE LAW OF UNINTENDED CONSEQUENCES: THE KANSAS-NEBRASKA ACT

If the Mexican-American War and the Wilmot Proviso made the expansion of slavery into the West the cornerstone of American politics, the Kansas-Nebraska Act collapsed the nation's political edifice. Superficially, the measure had little to do with slavery. A senator who professed not to care about slavery introduced it. At the heart of the legislation was the future of the West, not slavery, but any discussion of that future proved impossible without discussing slavery. And, ironically, the issue of a transcontinental railroad—an internal improvement, the heart of Whig ideology, the core of Clay's "American System"—intersected with the slavery question and drove the final nail into the Whig party's coffin.

The trouble began with the effort to find a train route to the Pacific Ocean—the same motivation for the Gadsden Purchase. As a senator from Illinois, Douglas wanted to help potential investors in Chicago, including himself. As a presidential aspirant, he wanted to win friends. As chair of the Committee on Territories, he wanted governments organized in areas where a railroad might come through to encourage settlers and protect travelers, all of which presumably would be good for the country and, not coincidentally, his own political career. "How are we to develop, cherish and protect our immense interests and possessions on the Pacific with a vast wilderness fifteen hundred miles in breadth; and filled with hostile savages, and cutting off all direct communication?" he asked. "The Indian barrier must be removed. The tide of emigration and civilization must be permitted to roll onward until it rushes through the passes of the mountains, and spreads over the plains, and mingles with the waters of the Pacific." To achieve that would require votes—and if he wanted any from southerners, he needed to offer something in return.[41]

Just as one boardinghouse near Capitol Hill shaped the antislavery Wilmot Proviso, so did another one influence potentially proslavery legislation. Residing in the F Street Mess were Senators Andrew Butler of South Carolina, Hunter and James Mason of Virginia, and, most important to the Kansas-Nebraska Act, David Rice Atchison of Missouri—all powerful, all from slave states. Atchison and his longtime Missouri colleague, Benton, shared a desire for westward expansion, but whereas Benton believed in it for the United States, Atchison wanted it for both the United States and for slavery. Thus, Atchison shared Douglas's interest in western settlement and organization and encouraging construction of a railroad, but his goals went beyond Douglas's. Not only did Atchison think slavery would take root in the West, but he had the southern concern that free land would encourage slaves to rebel and migrate. The more room for slavery to grow, slaveholders reasoned, the likelier it was to survive where it existed. Atchison also shared southern resentment of the Compromise of 1820 because it imposed an artificial boundary for slavery and constrained southerners in a way that exempted northerners. As the *St. Louis Republican* put it early in 1854, "If Nebraska be made a free Territory then will Missouri be surrounded on three sides by free territory, where there will always been men and means to assist in the escape of our slaves. . . . With the emissaries of abolitionists around us, and the facilities of escape so enlarged, this species of property would become insecure, if not valueless, in Missouri."[42]

Introducing the Kansas-Nebraska Act on January 4, 1854, Douglas bowed toward the F Street senators and their southern colleagues. His bill would create one territory, Nebraska, "with or without slavery, as their constitution may prescribe at the time of admission." That provision ignored the Compromise of 1820, and might have slipped through as easily as the Compromise of 1850 did when it allowed Utah and New Mexico to decide the issue. But Atchison and his friends wanted more. Those territories were unlikely to enter the Union any time soon, but Nebraska was different, and letting the populace vote meant it could become an antislavery state. Reasoning that southern Whigs would benefit from taking a stand, and that amending the bill might kill it, Seward apparently encouraged Senator Archibald Dixon, a Kentucky Whig, to propose repealing the Missouri line. With the issue in the open, and under pressure from southerners, Douglas folded. Nearly three weeks later, his new bill set up two territories, Kansas and Nebraska, and deemed the Missouri Compromise "inoperative and void." Douglas predicted this would cause "a hell of a storm." That was an understatement.[43]

The storm began with the need to win Democratic support. Pierce had no use for the Missouri Compromise but even less use for tossing it, because he believed in the platform he ran on and wanted to avoid the disorder and displeasure its repeal would cause. For help, Douglas turned to Jefferson Davis, who fought him so hard in 1850 but had no objection to eliminating an artificial line restricting slavery. Closer to Pierce personally than any other cabinet member, Davis set up a meeting with southern senators who pressured the president; if as strong a personality as Douglas yielded, Pierce could be expected to cave in much more quickly, and he did. Thus, with Pierce approving and Douglas the driving force, the measure became not just a bill, but a Democratic bill, a test of party loyalty.

Northern antislavery Democrats either failed the test or decided that the party failed a test by imposing it. They not only opposed the Act, but proved cunning in their own right. Their leader was Salmon Chase, known as the "attorney general for fugitive slaves" for his many legal arguments in their favor, and soon to be better known for his ambition to become president. When Douglas introduced his revised bill, Chase asked for time to study it, and Douglas agreed. Douglas may have been the genius behind passing the Compromise of 1850, but in this case Chase outfoxed him and created what Eric Foner has called "the textbook of the conspiracy theory of the repeal of the Missouri Compromise."[44]

Giddings prepared the "Appeal of the Independent Democrats," which Chase revised and sent to the *National Era,* which had published the serial version of *Uncle Tom's Cabin.* The "Appeal" came out just after Chase won his delay. Promising to "resist it by speech and vote," the "Independent Democrats" decried the bill "as a gross violation of a sacred pledge; as a criminal betrayal of precious rights; as part and parcel of an atrocious plot to exclude from a vast unoccupied region immigrants from the Old World and free laborers from our own States, and convert it into a dreary region of despotism, inhabited by masters and slaves." They urged the public not to join "in extending legalized oppression and systematized injustice over a vast territory yet exempt from these terrible evils." They invoked the free labor ideology by warning, "The blight of slavery will cover the land. . . . Freemen, unless pressed by a hard and cruel necessity, will not, and should not, work besides slave. Labor cannot be respected where any class of laborers is held in abject bondage." They implored, "We beg you, fellow-citizens, to observe that it will sever the East from the West of the United States by a wide slaveholding belt of country, extending from the Gulf of Mexico to British North America. It is a bold scheme against American liberty, worthy of an accomplished architect of ruin." And they turned the tables on the argument for respecting southern rights: "Demagogues may tell you that the Union can be maintained only by submitting to the demands of slavery. We tell you that the Union can only be maintained by the full recognition of the just claims of freedom and man."[45]

The pressure on both sides proved enormous. The nastiness of the rhetoric paled in comparison with that of Clay, Webster, Calhoun, and Seward in 1850. But the fight lasted well over three months and enthralled the country. The only one of the four still alive, Seward announced, "We are on the eve of a great national transaction, a transaction that will close a cycle in the history of our country," and called it "an eternal struggle between conservatism and progress, between truth and error, between right and wrong." Representative Richard Yates, about to be superseded as the leading antislavery politician from Springfield, Illinois, told the House, "If slaveholders are permitted to take their slaves into Nebraska and Kansas, the inequality and injury are to the free white men of the North and South who go there without slaves. . . . The effect of slave labor is always to cheapen, degrade, and exclude free labor. . . . The Citizen of the North has a right to object, on the ground that the introduction of slaves will retard the prosperity of the state. Slave labor converts the richest soil into barrenness; free labor causes fertility and vegetation to spring from the very rock." One of the bill's opponents said, "The great object is delay. The bill must be kept in the Senate as long as possible. Meantime hell must be raised in the North. The ear of Congress is open. It must be deafened with a roar of condemnation." By contrast, in the South the *Charleston Mercury* said, "All is calm and easy indifference."[46]

A northerner and southerner belied the northern criticism and southern calm. With northerners barraging Congress with letters and petitions, Seward detected that "a steady but strong North wind was rattling through the country." Sumner, Chase, and Wade introduced amendments and claimed a conspiracy by the Slave Power, meaning slave owners and their sympathizers, prompted the bill. Chase assaulted Douglas's logic and Sumner his morality, the latter calling the Illinoisan "that human anomaly—*a Northern man with Southern principles.* Sir, no such man can speak for the North." But Douglas had strong support. Southerners had no use for popular sovereignty, but it was better than the Missouri Compromise ban, so they backed it. Pierce used the velvet glove (offers of patronage) and iron fist (threats of retaliation) to force reluctant northern Democrats into line, with varied success. Douglas kept his troops united despite scorching exchanges with Chase and Sumner. On March 4, the bill passed, 37–14, with a few northern Whigs and Democrats opposing it, along with one southern Democrat, the consistently contrarian Sam Houston of Texas, who declared that the Missouri Compromise should be left alone. In the House, Douglas played a role, but Alexander Stephens took charge and, as he wrote, "I took the reins in my hand, applied whip and spur, and brought the 'wagon' out at eleven o'clock p.m. Glory enough for one day."[47]

But the price of Stephens's glory proved steep. Although the bill passed the House, 113–100, on May 22, 1854, 43 northern Democrats defected, a blow to Pierce and party unity less than two years after antislavery Democrats abandoned the Free-Soilers for a doughface. Northern Whigs united against the bill and southern Whigs for it, and their electoral problems and sectional rivalry combined to make the prospect of reunion neither appealing nor possible. According to historian William Freehling, southern Whigs who voted for the measure "knew they could not prevail in southern elections if loaded down with the latest damning evidence of Northern Whigs' intransigence. The National Whig Party could be national no longer." The South celebrated the Kansas-Nebraska Act, but it guaranteed not that slavery would spread, just that it could—and for many, that was not enough. Even then, southerners showed signs of fissures: in Missouri, Benton challenged Atchison's reelection and lost, but Democrats were so divided that Atchison proved unable to gain enough votes to win, leaving the state with only one senator for the next two years. As Raymond wrote, the bill would "create a deep-seated, intense, and inerad-icable hatred of the institution which will crush its political power, at all hazards, and at any cost."[48]

The cost for Douglas was permanent damage to his reputation with antislavery northerners whose support he needed for the presidency, and the irony was that he had no love for slavery. Privately, he called it "a curse beyond computation to both white and black." But, just as Fillmore had expressed private reservations, he had no great moral commitment either way. Westward expansion mattered more to him. Four years before, marshalling support for the Compromise of 1850, he said, "We have a vast territory, stretching from the Mississippi to the Pacific, which is rapidly filling up with a hardy, enterprising, and industrious population, large enough to form at least seventeen new free states. . . . I think I am safe in assuming that each of these will be free territories and free states, whether Congress shall prohibit slavery or not."[49]

In 1854, that assumption was less clear. Douglas and his supporters misjudged the extent of northern anger over his actions and provoked a battle that would destroy the Democratic party as it existed and the Whig party as an entity. What Douglas and his fellow Democrats, antislavery northerners, and southerners thought about the spread of slavery into the West would lead to a complete overhaul of the American political system—and in the battles associated with that overhaul, blood would flow, literally and figuratively.

FOUR

※※※

BLEEDING PARTIES, BLEEDING KANSAS, BLEEDING SUMNER

In March 1854, Anthony Burns escaped from his master and found work in a Boston clothing shop. Two months later, as the final vote on the Kansas-Nebraska Act neared in the House of Representatives, Charles Suttle arrived from Virginia to claim Burns. When a federal marshal arrested Burns on a trumped-up robbery charge, local free blacks marched on the courthouse, hoping to free him. When a group of white abolitionists joined them, Thomas Wentworth Higginson became, as Henry David Thoreau said, "the only Harvard Phi Beta Kappa, Unitarian minister, and master of seven languages who has led a storming party against a federal bastion with a battering ram in his hands." They broke into the building, but marshals staved them off. President Franklin Pierce ordered Secretary of War Jefferson Davis to send troops. Suttle apparently offered to let abolitionists buy Burns's freedom, but federal officials said no. After legal wrangling, on June 2nd, troops marched Burns in chains to the dock to sail back to Virginia. Funeral crepe draped buildings and church bells rang. Amos Lawrence, a longtime conservative Whig leader, marveled that "we went to bed one night old fashioned, conservative, Compromise Union Whigs and waked up stark mad Abolitionists." Across the North, states passed or toughened personal liberty laws meant to enable citizens to refuse to help return fugitives to slavery. As it turned out, though the controversy over Kansas and Nebraska bubbled, the fighting over the Fugitive Slave Act was far from finished.[1]

A month after Burns's forced return to slavery, on the Fourth of July, abolitionists gathered outside Boston in Framingham, Massachusetts. William Lloyd Garrison, *The Liberator's* longtime editor, received the most notoriety for burning a copy of the Constitution. Thoreau also spoke, only a month before publishing a book, *Walden,* which detailed his return to nature. As Thoreau said, he left the wilderness and its simplicity because "I feel that my investment of life here is worth many percent less since Massachusetts . . . deliberately and forcibly restored an innocent man, Anthony Burns, to slavery." He added, "A government which deliberately enacts injustice, and persists in it, will at length even become the laughing-stock of the world. . . . What is wanted is men, not of policy, but of probity—who recognize a higher law than the Constitution, or the decision of the majority. . . ." For Thoreau, the moral high ground on slavery was nothing new. In response to the Mexican-American War, he wrote *Civil Disobedience,* advocating the non-violent resistance that influenced such leaders as Mohandas Gandhi and Martin Luther King. Then and later, Thoreau objected to accepting slavery—its power and its expansion.[2]

Whereas Thoreau advocated non-violent protest, others like Higginson acted violently. The mid-1850s were a bloody period for the United States, literally and figuratively. In Kansas, John Brown and others committed to their cause fought over whether slavery would spread into new territory. In Congress, Preston Brooks proved more violent than his colleagues, but he was not alone in using force to act on behalf of slavery and its growth. Meanwhile, the two major political parties, Democratic and Whig, bled to death over the Kansas-Nebraska Act, Democrats reconstituted themselves as an increasingly proslavery party, and Whigs merged into either the antislavery Republican party or the anti-immigrant American or Know-Nothing party. If the Compromise of 1850 had been no more than a truce, the cease-fire had ended.

THE BLOODY BILL

Returning home after the Kansas-Nebraska Act's passage, Senator Stephen Douglas wrote, "I could travel from Boston to Chicago by the light of my own effigy. All along the Western Reserve of Ohio I could find my effigy upon every tree we passed." When he had warned his southern allies that the bill would create "a hell of a storm," Douglas proved more prescient than he could have imagined. Repealing the Missouri Compromise created not merely a storm, but the political equivalent of a perfect storm: it tore apart a Democratic party barely held together and meant the end of an already crumbling Whig party.[3]

Making the blow especially bitter for conservative northern Whigs hoping to rebuild the party, the bill destroyed the remnants of two of their illusions: that the Compromise of 1850 drove slavery from the national debate, and that southern Whigs and unionists shared their desire to keep it that way. To those Whigs more interested in promoting economic development and a Protestant culture, slavery was simply a cause for disagreement with southerners. Late in the debate over the measure, Washington Hunt, who moved in and out of Seward's and Weed's orbit while disputing their antislavery views, wrote, "I have not believed till within a few days that the moderate and honest members from the South would consent to accept the dishonorable advantage which Douglas offers them." Disappointing as this awareness was, it also instilled some Whigs with what proved to be excessive hopes for salvaging Whiggery, even after some of their number pronounced it dead two years before, after the 1852 election. They realized, a conservative Whig editor wrote, that repealing the Compromise of 1820 would "surely produce an immense agitation throughout the North" against slavery and its defenders—and might create the radical change and radical response that went against the cautious approach to policy, politics, and national unity for which conservative Whigs long had stood. Thus, one of them, David Davis of Illinois, later one of Abraham Lincoln's Republican managers and a Supreme Court justice, spoke for many when he said, "Try to save the Whig party. I don't fancy its being abolitionized—although no one can be more opposed to Nebraska than I am."[4]

Antislavery Whigs doubted that conservatives like Davis outdid their opposition to the bill. But the issue's complexities were clear to them, especially Seward. He remained committed to the ideas of unionism, nationalism, and progress that Whigs inherited from Clay and Webster. He also saw his party as a better means of attacking slavery than the Democrats with their states' rights orientation. But Seward was torn over whether to count on the South or its sympathizers for party loyalty. Touring the South, he found in Virginia "a universal impress of poverty stamped on all around me" and in the potentially prosperous port of New Orleans that "the city is secondary, and the state unimportant. . . . Commerce and political power, as well as military strength, can never permanently reside, on this continent, in a community where slavery exists." None of what he saw fit his vision of what Whigs represented and the nation should be. Other Whigs agreed, especially as they assessed the Kansas-Nebraska Act's impact. As the *Ohio State Journal* said, the bill caused "the ultimate disruption and *denationalization* of the Whig party." How could Seward and his allies hope to rebuild the party on an antislavery foundation when the party included southerners with different beliefs not only in slavery, but also in the idea of human and economic progress?[5]

The answer was that they could not, but other questions came first. Seward hoped southern Whigs were gaining ground against their section's extremists whereas Thurlow Weed, his mentor and partner in New York politics, described northern Whigs as "on all occasions, and in every emergency, the most efficient and reliable organization both to resist the aggressions of Slavery and to uphold the cause of Freedom." But the two had other concerns. In fall 1854, New Yorkers would elect their legislators, who would decide the fate of Seward's Senate seat. With New York Whigs split as usual between

Sewardites and Silver Greys, Democrats more divided over slavery, and newer issues such as temperance and nativism, neither Seward nor Weed considered this an opportune time for political experimentation. Other northern Whigs, as strongly antislavery and less so, still hoped Democratic divisions over slavery would give their party the chance to resurrect itself, and thus were reluctant to change. Others were leery of fusion with Free Soilers or those devoted to a particular issue, such as banning liquor sales or restricting immigrants—two movements gaining political significance as the effects of the Kansas-Nebraska Act became clearer.[6]

Other Whigs shared Seward's and Weed's opposition to slavery expansion but evinced less desire to find common ground with the other side. Horace Greeley, the squeaky third wheel of their political operations and about to break with them, again declared the party dead, but this time he blamed southern Whigs and predicted that a sectional party would replace it. Others excoriated southern Whigs. Senator Benjamin Wade of Ohio, calling himself "an *Abolitionist* at heart," said, "We certainly cannot have any further political connection with the Whigs of the South." Normally moderate Whigs may have surprised even themselves with their anger. "No man has . . . struggled as I have to preserve it as a national party," wrote Senator Truman Smith of Connecticut, a conservative and the closest thing Whigs had to a national boss. Yet he called the Kansas-Nebraska Act "atrocious" and said, "I shall have nothing to do with any Southern Whig who joins Stephen A. Douglas in introducing into Congress & into the country another controversy on the subject of slavery." Resigning his Senate seat, Smith warned that "the break is final. We could not heal it if we would & would not if we could."[7]

For their part, southern Whigs faced a mirror image of the problem vexing northern Whigs. While northerners wondered how they could ally with supporters of slavery and its expansion, southern Whigs pondered how they could belong to a party that opposed the South's political, economic, social, and cultural foundation. Although their votes provided the margin of victory in the House, southern Whigs had split over the Kansas-Nebraska Act, citing such problems as opposition to popular sovereignty and doubts that slavery could spread into the new region. According to Whig Senator John Bell of Tennessee, southern Whigs felt a sense of obligation to the "patriotic and noble Whigs at the North, who . . . have acquiesced in the compromises of 1850—those who are opposed to the plan of the abolition organization, and entertain no purpose of pressing their antislavery feelings to the point of disunion." But his appreciation of northern attitudes was not found in most southern politicians at the time. Southern Whigs also hoped that if, as seemed likely, Millard Fillmore ran for president in 1856, putting a northern Whig with southern sympathies atop their ticket might salvage the party. Massachusetts Cotton Whigs and New York's Silver Greys, already loathe to tie themselves to the likes of Seward and Charles Sumner, feared that their opponents would take control and effectively make the Whigs a northern antislavery party in order to control their states. They had reason for their views: Seward had told his wife, "We no longer have any bond to Southern Whigs," and Weed concluded, "This Nebraska business will entirely denationalize the Whig party." The Whigs were proving that reports of their death in 1852 had not been greatly exaggerated: the party remained divided over slavery and its expansion into the West.[8]

As usual, efforts to salvage the Whig party depended on their opponents, and Democrats had managed to impale themselves on their own legislation. While southern Democrats basked in their success, Douglas told a friend his bill would "form the test of Parties," forcing Democrats "either to stand with the Democracy or rally under Seward, John Van Buren & co.," meaning the leaders of New York's antislavery Whigs and Democrats—and his bill would show that Douglas might sympathize more with proslavery forces than he let on. Northern antislavery Democrats and party elders had to decide whether to fight or switch. After the act passed, Francis Preston Blair, Andrew Jackson's old confidant and a living contradiction—one of the few border state Democrats opposed to spreading slavery, and a slave owner—told Martin Van Buren, John's father, "We are to have a renewed contest for the ascendancy of slavery over freedom." Preston King, an antislavery New Yorker, believed that "past lines of party will be obliterated with the Missouri line," then helped make it so by leading antislavery delegates in a walkout from the state Democratic convention after the defeat of a platform plank critical of the bill. But such longtime Democrats as the Van Burens, Thomas Hart Benton, and, for the moment, Blair, shared the concern of Whigs with whom they normally hated to agree: a sectional party, formed to oppose the spread of slavery, would further divide the country and garner limited support, even in the North.[9]

While old Jacksonians fretted, antislavery Democrats such as King were in a bind. One of them wrote, "All democracy left the democratic party, and every democrat that was too intelligent to be cheated by a name deserted its ranks." New York's Democratic party was simply a mess. King's efforts and walkout reflected a three-way division between other antislavery Barnburners and two other party factions: Hardshell Hunkers (who opposed any compromise with or forgiveness for antislavery forces), led by former Senator Daniel Dickinson, and Softshell Hunkers, led by Secretary of State William Marcy and John Dix, who had no use for slavery but viewed it as one of many issues and therefore hoped for some accommodation. In Illinois, Lyman Trumbull and John Palmer—loyal Democrats, but outside of Douglas's orbit and therefore used to being on the outside looking in—opposed the bill and still claimed to belong to the party, although their only hope for future political influence was to cooperate with Douglas or destroy him. Instead, they discovered, Douglas hoped to destroy them. Trumbull wrote, "I am astonished at their bitterness," and "there is no making terms or getting along in harmoney [sic] with such men"—and Douglas and his backers felt similarly about Trumbull and those like him. In Indiana, a Douglas ally on this issue, Senator Jesse Bright, abandoned any sign of a velvet glove in favor of an iron fist toward any Democrat doubtful about the Kansas-Nebraska Act, tightening his grip on the Hoosier State's party. Northern Democrats, already buffeted on slavery, seemed marginalized.[10]

But what could antislavery forces do outside of their existing parties? A sectional, antislavery party would require Democrats and Whigs to work together in a different way, and in greater numbers, than did the Free-Soilers of 1848. That prospect disturbed not only those who opposed the spread of slavery as one of many strands forming their ideology, but also those who put antislavery above all else. As dedicated as Salmon Chase was to antislavery, he believed the Founding Fathers intended for slavery to die out, with the federal government helping by not letting slavery grow or protect itself. This led him to a stricter, Jeffersonian view of the Constitution and a commitment to Democratic party ideals—at least, as he understood them. By contrast, Seward and the Whigs were in many ways intellectual heirs of the Federalist party, which celebrated property, believed in the idea of an elite, and envisioned a more expansive federal role in encouraging industry and business than Democrats could swallow. The two sides could agree on slavery, and would, because Seward and Chase were among the Republican party's co-founders. But first, they hoped to repair their existing parties. Only when those efforts failed would antislavery Democrats and antislavery Whigs come together. Meanwhile, southerners and conservative northern Whigs wrestled with the same problem: they had spent too long agreeing that slavery was an important issue and disagreeing with Democrats on everything else—and they even disagreed on just how important slavery was—to ignore decades of competition.

By the mid-1850s, Democrats and Whigs found the issues that once separated them had declined in importance. Canal and railroad building, both crucial to the northeast's development, proved controversial in the Old Northwest. Douglas and other Democrats shed some of their Jacksonianism to encourage federal support for projects that would help Illinois, and Whigs had long advocated such projects. With a spate of such projects in this period, what DeWitt Clinton intended with the Erie Canal more than a quarter of a century before had become a reality: East and West had become more connected economically, and thus socially and culturally, than ever before. Tied together, they could unite beyond party labels. Their merging interests and emerging power worried southerners who were also divided between urban and rural, large-scale planter and yeoman farmers, and deep southerners dependent on slavery and upper southerners less committed to fighting pitched battles to protect and spread it. These changes, and the ideological and political exchanges they produced, contributed to the party system's evolution and the debate over whether slavery would inevitably march westward.

"I KNOW NOTHING"

The process of creating a political party has never been neat and clean. The first party system, pitting Federalists against Republicans, grew from philosophical divisions and required both sides to overcome their antipathy to political parties and to plot strategy and tactics. After the Federalist party died, the second party system's birth required a similar combination of ideologies and organizing skills. Again, Democrats, who considered themselves Jefferson's heirs, proved better at the latter than their opponents, the Whigs. Yet their birth in the 1820s and 1830s followed a battle involving another party, the Anti-Masons, who feared Masonic lodges were a secret society with diabolical plans. Many Anti-Masons wound up being Whigs. That party began, as Michael Holt has written, "simply as a collection of the disparate foes" of Andrew Jackson's expansive view of presidential power, which they saw as "just as great a threat to republican institutions as Masonic power." In turn, the third party system, born in the 1850s, survived a difficult birth that included concern—even paranoia—about sinister forces—some overt, some covert. If Whiggery was doomed, how drifting Whigs would replace their party and what role disaffected Democrats might play proved less clear-cut and involved issues less divisive than slavery. As Douglas groused, the "anti-Nebraska movement" consisted of "a crucible into which poured Abolitionism, Maine liquor law-ism, and what there was left of northern Whiggism, and then the Protestant feeling against the Catholic and the native feeling against the foreigner."[11]

The first of what Trumbull called "side issues" was temperance, the movement to limit or ban alcohol sales. As early as the 1830s, Whigs backed laws to regulate social behavior and enjoyed support from other reformers, especially from the revival movements of the Second Great Awakening, whereas Democrats dismissed such measures as bigoted and infringing on individual freedom. Whig or not, temperance advocates began pushing harder for anti-alcohol laws in the late 1840s and early 1850s, coinciding with the arrival of Irish and German immigrants more open to drinking. The movement's first great success came in Maine, no hotbed for immigration, where legislators outlawed liquor sales in 1851. Across the North, especially in Maine, Connecticut, and Ohio, prohibitionists gained ground within the parties; the already fluid party system became even murkier.

Neither Democrats nor Whigs knew how to respond to the issue. Although anti-alcohol forces won support from Free-Soilers committed to social improvement (which abolitionism and temperance exemplified), antislavery Democrats and Whigs disagreed over whether reformers should stick together or remain separate lest one movement outshine the other. Whigs worried that backing temperance would open them to more charges of bigotry against immigrants and Catholics. Democrats feared appeasing prohibitionists would drive away their urban immigrant voters, especially Irish and German Catholics. Thus, capitalizing on a potential advantage would be difficult. Worse for Whigs already divided over slavery, their antislavery members seemed more willing than their Democratic counterparts to abandon their party for a cause, whatever it might be. Worse for both parties, voters had grown disgusted with leaders refusing to confront the issue, pro or con.

Complicating these party divisions and the temperance movement was a rising anti-immigrant tide, expressed in the 1850s in anti-Catholic sentiment as old as America itself. Early colonists participated, willingly or not, in an English political and cultural fight pitting Protestants against Catholics. After the War of 1812 and the Napoleonic Wars, more Europeans began crossing the Atlantic, peaking when nearly three million immigrants arrived between 1845 and 1854. For the first time, significant numbers of them were Catholic, victims of the potato blight, and, as an Irish-American journalist described them, "a different race of the Irish ten, 15, or 20 years since. . . . Dire wretchedness, appalling want and festering famine have tended to change their characters." Already inclined toward conservatism and traditional Protestant culture, Whigs dallied with the anti-Catholic American Republican party in the 1840s but backed away when its members rioted and destroyed Catholic churches. Beyond the possibility and reality of violence, another barrier between Whigs and nativists was Seward, who, as governor of New York, had fought anti-Catholic bias in public education. More crucially, many leading nativists wanted nothing to do with either major political party: though Democrats struck them as worse for toadying to Catholics, one nativist editor proclaimed his group's desire to "free our government from the . . . hordes of political leeches that are fattening their bloated carcasses in the people's money."[12]

Between increased immigration, battles over efforts to enact temperance laws, and divisions within the traditional parties, nativist groups grew. By 1850, New Yorker Charles Allen founded the Order of the Star-Spangled Banner, a nativist fraternal organization like the Masons in its love for secrecy, ceremony, and limited membership. In November 1853, the *New York Tribune* reported on candidates on "a mongrel ticket termed the *'Know-Nothing,'*" although the name's origins remain uncertain. The story persists that it resulted from a premium on secrecy: if asked about their activities, order members were to respond, "I know nothing." More importantly, whether called the Order of the Star-Spangled Banner, the American party, or the Know-Nothings, they flexed their political muscles. In several cities, Catholics resented the lack of religious instruction—or emphasis on Protestantism—in public schools, and sought state financing of Catholic schools, prompting a rise in nativist sentiment and candidates. Pierce's appointment of Catholic James Campbell to his cabinet annoyed Protestants in both parties, especially because as postmaster general, he controlled so much patronage.[13]

But the Know-Nothing party barely existed until June 1854, when membership skyrocketed, increasing twenty times by the November election. An economic downturn helped, but timing was critical: the Kansas-Nebraska Act and the response to it were affecting the nation greatly. The Kansas-Nebraska Act's opponents in both parties—and foes of alcohol and immigration—shared unhappiness with traditional parties, which were supposed to act on these issues or find a way to make them unimportant, and did neither. Know-Nothings benefited from the antislavery sentiment dividing the two parties and politicians willing to use any opportunity to get ahead, especially if those opportunities were lacking elsewhere. One example was Henry Wilson, known as the Natick Cobbler for rising from poverty to prosperity and disdained by Whigs on both sides of the debate for his humble origins. Referring to papal opposition to the revolutions of 1848, he argued that Catholicism "instinctively sympathizes with oppression in the Old World and the New." Others, including Anson Burlingame of Massachusetts, developed the same theme: "Slavery and Priestcraft . . . seek Cuba and Hayti and the Mexican States together because they will be Catholic and Slave. I say they are in alliance by the necessity of their nature,—for one denies the right of a man to his body, and the other the right of a man to his soul. The one denies his right to think for himself, the other the right to act for himself."[14]

These antislavery attitudes made the Know-Nothings at least a temporary haven for antislavery Democrats and Whigs who wanted out of their parties in the short term but had yet to figure out what to do in the long term. Not all of them planned to abandon long-standing political affiliations, and those who did had trouble agreeing on what a new party would stand for. Fusion conventions met in several states during the summer of 1854 but accomplished little. Even antislavery men debated whether to demand an end to the spread of slavery or just the restoration of the Missouri Compromise. George Julian, who already had bounced between the Whig and Free-Soil parties, saw reverting to the compromise as "halting, half-way, equivocal," but conservative Ohio Whig Thomas Ewing suggested that "we should frame our opposition so that wise and conservative southern men could unite with us on it." And what other positions would their parties take? Democrats and Whigs began hemorrhaging voters to the Know-Nothings because they avoided taking stands, and had enough trouble uniting on slavery, let alone other issues.[15]

THE BIRTH OF THE REPUBLICANS

One solution was a new party, which was no simple matter. "The passing of the Whig party and the rise of the Republicans was like a motion picture 'dissolve,' in which one scene slowly fades from view while another gradually takes its place," Don Fehrenbacher observed. As Fehrenbacher also stated, "These two complex events were not merely connected but inseparably part of one another, and for many men like Lincoln there was no exact moment of ceasing to be a Whig and becoming a Republican." After the Kansas-Nebraska Act passed, some of its Democratic, Whig, and Free-Soil opponents in Congress met. Israel Washburn of Maine suggested taking the name Republican, and the others agreed to oppose letting slavery expand westward rather than just seeking to restore the Missouri Compromise. Gathering at about the same time in Ripon, Wisconsin, opponents of Douglas's bill—some from the National Reform Association, a land reform movement whose egalitarianism and goal of homesteading the West appealed to some abolitionists—also suggested a new party, to be called the Republicans and designed to stop the spread of slavery. In Michigan, antislavery forces gathered in Jackson (whose name probably was not lost on Democrats or Whigs), heeded Greeley's suggestion that antislavery men unite in a new Republican party, and wrote a platform focusing entirely on slavery as "a great moral, social, and political evil." In both states, the anti-Nebraska group defeated the Democrats in the fall elections.[16]

Anti-Nebraska sentiment in Illinois fed bumpy efforts to form the Republican party. With the state divided between the Whiggish, antislavery north and the Democratic south, downstate politicians feared a new party or fusion movement that appeared too radically antislavery. In response, Owen Lovejoy, politically more realistic than many fellow abolitionists, engineered resolutions calling for the federal government to stop slavery from spreading into new territories. But the party ran no one for office, partly because one of its nominees, Lincoln, refused. He shared Republican animosity toward slavery and exceeded it in disdain toward Douglas. In an 1854 speech at Peoria, his first major step toward his political revival and joining the Republicans, he said of the bill's opponents, "We rose each fighting, grasping whatever he could first reach—a scythe—a pitchfork—a chopping axe, or a butcher's cleaver." Thus, "our drill, our dress, and our weapons, are not entirely perfect and uniform." But Lincoln moved cautiously out of concern about Know-Nothings' popularity and hopes of preserving the Whig party—enough to allow Whigs to put his name forward for the state legislature and campaign for the incumbent Whig congressman, Richard Yates.[17]

That fall, Illinois elected legislators to choose a U.S. senator. Douglas backers won most of the available seats, but the 1855 legislature would have an anti-Nebraska majority, spelling trouble for Democratic incumbent James Shields, a Douglas ally who had had the distinction of meeting Lincoln for a duel before cooler heads prevailed. Lincoln ran for the Senate as a Whig while Douglas Democrats maneuvered and Know-Nothings had representation but remained silent about who belonged to the group. On the first ballot, Lincoln nearly won, with Shields close behind, but fell short because anti-Nebraska Democrats refused to back a Whig. Finally, on the ninth ballot, to assure defeat for Douglas and an anti-Nebraska victory, Lincoln threw his support to Trumbull, who won. Lincoln admitted that "he could bear defeat inflicted by his enemies with a pretty good grace—but it was hard to be wounded in the house of his friends." More importantly, Douglas took a beating in Illinois, the antislavery Trumbull went on to a distinguished Senate career, and Lincoln would be back.[18]

In New York, Weed had to figure out how to reelect Seward with the Whigs perhaps permanently unglued, but amid the rise of Know-Nothings who despised Catholics and politicians such as Seward, who sympathized with them. What ensued showed Whig uncertainty about migrating to a new party, especially when a leading advocate of doing so was Greeley, and Weed's talent for legerdemain. Whereas some Seward supporters attacked the Know-Nothings, others joined them in hopes of taking over from within and enjoying some success. Weed swallowed hard and backed Myron Clark—antislavery and seen as a pawn, but a prohibitionist tied to the Know-Nothings—for governor. That began the chaos: Silver-Greys bolted to their own candidate, Know-Nothings were suspicious of "wets" (as opponents of the temperance "drys" were known) over their links to Catholics, and Democrats remained split between Hardshells, Softshells, and the remaining Barnburners. Clark won a four-way race by 309 votes, mainly on a temperance platform and with so little attention to slavery that Greeley likened his campaign to a performance of "Hamlet, with Hamlet not only omitted, but forgotten." At the next legislature, patronage and old animosities helped Weed divide and conquer Seward's opponents, who could unite on no one against him. Seward's victory also foreshadowed the Know-Nothings' dissolution over slavery: as one of them said, "a refusal to return *him* would be a concession to the slave power that could not be countervailed by the election of any other individual."[19]

In Massachusetts, Wilson combined antislavery ideology, nativism, and political savvy—or questionable principle. In 1854, the state's antislavery forces divided over whether to fuse as Republicans or remain split, with Wilson urging coalition and most Conscience Whigs hoping Whiggery had a future. Republicans ran Wilson for governor, but he grasped that Whigs were spiraling downward and Republicans too new and weak. Therefore, he quietly joined the Know-Nothings, backing their candidate for governor, Henry Gardner, in return for their support for the U.S. Senate—and waiting until just before the election to withdraw from the governor's race. Drawing from Democrats, Whigs, and Free Soilers, Gardner won and the legislature rewarded Wilson, who teamed with other opponents of slavery in Massachusetts to gut the Know-Nothing organization and build the new Republican party. Nor was Wilson alone: taking a similar path was Nathaniel Banks, a onetime factory worker called the "Bobbin Boy" who opposed slavery and joined the Know-Nothings en route to the Republicans.

In other states, the fall 1854 voting and early 1855 Senate elections revealed a party system in evolution. Whiggery had withered and Democrats had divided, but where the disaffected would go depended on their ideology and local alliances. Whether Know-Nothings or Republicans seemed likely to become the Democrats' main opposition and whatever the roots of antislavery ideology, slavery was the issue driving politics. Know-Nothings offered a pit stop for antislavery Pennsylvania Democrats who were led to nativism by Simon Cameron, a boss notorious for his corruption and political somersaults. The legislature ultimately elected no one after Cameron won the American party caucus with one more vote than the number in the room, somehow leading to accusations of "shameless and wholesale private bribery" and further divisions. But Cameron and other Democrats opposed the

Nebraska bill, as did Whig leader Andrew Curtin. While Cameron and Curtin fought for power in Pennsylvania, with ex-Whig Thaddeus Stevens maneuvering between them, their shared antislavery views drove them toward Republicanism.[20]

Antislavery Democrats and Whigs benefited from fusing with Know-Nothings elsewhere. John P. Hale, the Free-Soil presidential nominee in 1852 and Pierce's mortal enemy in New Hampshire, won a Senate seat with nativist support, but no one doubted his antislavery credentials. In Ohio, Chase won the governorship by migrating during the campaign from anti-Nebraska Democrat to Republican with Know-Nothing support. In Indiana, Know-Nothings made their presence felt by appealing to nativist sentiment and providing the only organized alternative party for unhappy Democrats and Whigs. The result was a Know-Nothing sweep that temporarily broke the back of Indiana's Democratic party and buried the state's already weak Whig party. The Democratic *Indiana State Sentinel* lamented, "We had to fight the church, the flesh, and the devil; the church in the temperance question; the flesh in the Old Whigs and the Devil in the Know-Nothings."[21]

For the Know-Nothings, the devil might have been in the details: remaining unified against immigrants when the dominant national political issue remained the expansion of slavery into the West. Know-Nothings wanted to translate their local success to the national level, but they were divided over what stand to take on slavery or, as southern and conservative northern ex-Whigs suggested, whether to take any stand. In a move that seemed ominous for their southern branch, in 1855, Virginians elected Democrat Henry Wise governor after he spent most of his campaign charging Know-Nothings with being in league with Massachusetts abolitionists—the kind of criticism that could just as easily have been directed against southern Whigs who tried to find common ground with northern Whigs. Meanwhile, antislavery forces debated whether to unite with Know-Nothings, preferably relegating them to secondary status within the nascent Republican party, or try to destroy them. Toward the latter end, Ohio editor Joseph Medill created a new group, the Know-Somethings, who emphasized stopping slavery's growth westward and appealed to Protestant immigrants.

Furthermore, for antislavery nativists, joining the Republican party would require a small step, not a leap. Granted, the strongest antislavery Republicans saw the Know-Nothings as an irritant, an obstacle to northerners awakening to what they considered the real threat: slavery and the Slave Power. But Republicans and Know-Nothings shared a dislike, if not for the immigrants themselves, then for what they represented and where they ended up politically. Most Irish Catholic immigrants of the 1840s and 1850s lived in cities and became part of the local Democratic machines, which both Republicans and Know-Nothings fought. Worse, as Eric Foner has written, "Many Republicans feared that the influx of immigrants was threatening to destroy the free labor ideal of an open society." If they remained poor, those immigrants would contradict the Republican belief that the North's free labor economy offered the social mobility lacking in the South's slave-based society. Whatever the roots of anti-immigrant feeling, Republicans and nativists could agree on the existence of a threat—just not on its extent or what to do about it. And anti-slavery men such as Seward and Chase had too long a record of advocating liberty to join an organization—the Know-Nothing party—that opposed it for some. As he so often did, Lincoln put it best when he tried to explain his political affiliation to his friend Joshua Speed: "I am not a Know-Nothing. That is certain. How could I be? How can any one who abhors the oppression of negroes, be in favor of degrading classes of white people?"[22]

When Know-Nothings held a National Council meeting in June 1855, they proved just as susceptible to intraparty disputes over slavery as Democrats and Whigs had been. Southern members won approval of a plank declaring it "the best guarantee of common justice and of future peace, to abide by and maintain the existing laws upon the subject of Slavery, as a final and conclusive settlement of that subject, in spirit and in substance." Although that aroused the ire of antislavery northerners who broke with their old parties over the Kansas-Nebraska Act, it enabled Republicans to attack Know-Nothings as proslavery, or at least supplicants to the Slave Power. Not that Know-Nothingism was dead—far from it; and the party remained a force in the North, thanks to anti-immigrant sentiment and conservative Whigs unwilling to join an antislavery party. But concerns about the Know-Nothing approach to slavery fostered divisions in Ohio, New York, and Pennsylvania, costing the party the antislavery support it needed to succeed in the North, and contributed to Republican growth and development.[23]

In addition to Know-Nothing divisions, Republicans helped themselves—and received help—from several developments. One reenacted the fight over electing a speaker of the House, which delayed the Congress that met in 1849 and 1850. Another fierce competition developed after the 1854 voting. Democrats supporting Pierce belonged to the minority, their delegation from non-slave states falling from 93 to 22 while antislavery congressmen won about 100 seats. But anti-Pierce, anti-Nebraska members had trouble agreeing on whom to support—indeed, on whether they were Democrats, Republicans, Whigs, Know-Nothings, or none of the above. The front-runners to manage the House and appoint committees were antislavery Ohio Whig-turned-Know-Nothing Lewis Campbell; Alexander Pennington, a long shot, who was a New Jersey Whig not formally aligned with a party; and Nathaniel Banks, a Massachusetts Democrat who joined the Know-Nothings because they offered the best opportunity for advancement and called himself "neither . . . pro-slavery nor anti-slavery." Banks later became a Republican, but for the moment his appeal lay in his support among fellow anti-Nebraska Democrats. For speaker, pro-Pierce Democrats ran a Douglas supporter from Illinois, William Richardson, then turned to South Carolinians in hopes of attracting southern Know-Nothings who might be more loyal to proslavery ideology than their new party. These efforts failed, and finally the House agreed to accept a victory by plurality instead of majority. After 132 ballots, Banks eked out a win—a significant step because he did it with Republican support and clearly leaned toward the new party, which gave the House a decidedly antislavery hue. One of Banks's supporters called it "the first victory of the North . . . since 1787," when the Constitution had been written.[24]

The next step was to organize a national Republican party. Hoping this would be the first step toward the presidency later in 1856, Chase suggested working with antislavery Know-Nothings in what Wilson called a "union for freedom." But most preferred to await the outcome of the Ohio governor's race, the other item on Chase's agenda, and planned to meet in Pittsburgh on February 22nd. First, though, came an important meal: Christmas dinner at Francis P. Blair's house in Silver Spring, Maryland. Although the old Jacksonian wanted to remain a Democrat, his priority was to wrest control of the party from Pierce, proslavery southerners, and northern doughfaces—and if he failed, he had to decide his best course of action. Claiming that he intended to plan how the anti-Nebraska forces could unite, and to learn more about party planning, he invited several leading antislavery politicians to his home: Seward, Chase, Banks, abolitionist Gamaliel Bailey, Sumner, and King. Seward, the only one who declined, told Weed that he could join no group that might unite with Know-Nothings. When the others deemed unity necessary, the two New Yorkers grasped that this marked a turning point in uniting the political antislavery movement and agreed to join.[25]

When Republicans met in Pittsburgh on George Washington's birthday—a date chosen for symbolic reasons and because Chase hoped winter weather might discourage travel by anyone who could block his presidential aspirations—it was not a formal convention. Possible candidates like Seward and Chase were nowhere to be found, befitting the political etiquette that the office sought the man. Most importantly, Blair presided, despite his old Democratic loyalties and, as abolitionist Lewis Tappan complained, "Think of an anti Slavery convention being presided over by a slaveholder!" Attendees ran the gamut from abolitionist to moderate and conservative. But their presence, especially Blair's, suggested the new party could reach across the political spectrum, except the Deep South—that even border state and northern conservatives could unite with Greeley and abolitionists Joshua Giddings and Owen Lovejoy. A Seward follower, *New York Times* founder Henry Raymond, drafted what his rival Greeley called a "bore of an Address." Delegates agreed, though, to support "the repeal of all laws which allow the introduction of Slavery into territories once consecrated to freedom" and "resist, by every Constitutional means, the existence of Slavery in any of the Territories of the United States." More importantly, what made it boring to Greeley was that it was more moderate on slavery than he would have liked, although that was important for drawing broader support for what could be perceived as a group of radicals.[26]

At that moment, as Republicans seemed to be rising, Know-Nothings revealed cracks in their political edifice. Across the state in Philadelphia, an American party convention demonstrated little brotherly love. The Know-Nothings decided to nominate candidates for the presidential election—former President Millard Fillmore and Tennessean Andrew Jackson Donelson, named for his uncle and thus from good Democratic stock. But Know-Nothings divided over seating convention delegates from heavily Catholic Louisiana and again proved unable to agree on whether slavery could expand into western territories. Within a few days in Pennsylvania, the third party system might not have achieved its final form, but it began to assume a recognizable shape. To the west, though, the idea of slavery expansion that divided Know-Nothings and united Republicans was a stark reality.

BLEEDING KANSAS

A conservative Whig, Orville Browning, told Supreme Court Justice John McLean, "Every free State in the Union has now declared against the violation of the Missouri Compromise, but notwithstanding all this Kansas will yet be a slave state." For his part, Seward restated his position on slavery, denouncing it to the Senate as "not only an evil, but a local one, injurious and ultimately pernicious to society wherever it exists, and in conflict with the constitutional principles of society in this country. I am not willing to extend nor to permit the extension of that local evil into regions now free within our empire." Seward also threw down a gauntlet: "Come on, then, gentlemen of the slave States. Since there is no escaping your challenge, I accept it on behalf of the cause of freedom. We will engage in competition for the virgin soil of Kansas, and God give the victory to the side which is strongest in numbers as it is in right." As historian Sean Wilentz noted, "Discerning God's will would be a gruesome business."[27]

First came competition for and among emigrants. Within a year after the law's passage, almost half of the 8,000 settlers in Kansas came from Missouri, and another one-third of the settlers were Midwestern or from the Mid-Atlantic states. Fewer than five percent were from New England, where abolitionist sentiment was strongest, but many of them were part of the New England Emigrant Aid Company. Poet John Greenleaf Whittier wrote, "We cross the prairie as of old/The pilgrims crossed the sea, / To make the West, as they the East, / The homestead of the free!" Funded by former Cotton Whig Amos Lawrence, whose name graced the first town they founded, these emigrants were supposed to bring free-soil principles to what might end up slave country—that is, if David Rice Atchison had his way. The senator led more than 1,000 fellow Missourians into Kansas in hopes of assuring that popular sovereignty would come out on the side of slavery. "We will be compelled to shoot, burn & hang, but the thing will soon be over," he said. Atchison argued that "the prosperity or the ruin of the whole South depends on the Kansas struggle," and "if we win we carry slavery to the Pacific Ocean." Losing would make slave property in Missouri "not merely unsafe but valueless, if Kansas is made the abode of an army of hired fanatics, recruited, transported, armed and paid for the special and sole purpose of abolitionizing Kansas and Missouri." Harkening to the late 1830s, when Missourians drove out newly arrived Mormons over their antislavery views and different ways, Atchison wrote, "We intend to 'Mormonize' the Abolitionists." Small wonder that some Missourians became known to Kansans as "Border Ruffians" present only to affect local affairs and then return home, or less kindly as "pukes," apparently based on Missourians who had settled on the California Gold Rush being described as "vomited forth" from their home state.[28]

Border Ruffians or not, proslavery supporters were rough. Not to be outdone by New Englanders, and unwilling to show any signs of being cowed, southerners formed emigrant groups. After Kansas opened to settlement, an Atchison follower started the Platte County Self-Defensive Association. Its members convicted two residents of "abolitionism," shaved half of the hair off of one's head and gave him two days to move elsewhere, and gave the other twenty-four lashes and a similar invitation to leave. In turn, Eli Thayer, the New England emigrant group's founder, told supporters that "it might be well for the Emigrant to be furnished with his Bible and his rifle; and if he were not protected in his rights according to the principles of the first, let him rely upon the execution of the latter."[29]

The deck proved to be stacked in slavery's favor. Pierce named Pennsylvania lawyer Andrew Reeder governor of Kansas territory. He scheduled an election for a territorial delegate to Congress in November 1854, and the "Southern Rights candidate" won easily—in numbers and in intimidation. One Kansan reported that "hordes of ruffians from Missouri . . . took entire possession of the polls in almost every district, brow-beat and intimidated the Judges . . . and crowded out and drove off all who were suspected of being in favor of any other candidate." The following March 30 brought the election of a proslavery territorial legislature with violence rare but the threat of it so widespread that many antislavery election officials stayed home. Some southerners doubted the wisdom of intimidation and violence, but others felt necessity dictated their use, with Atchison proclaiming that "we can send five thousand—enough to kill every God-damned abolitionist in the Territory." Indeed, two sensibilities were at work. Southerners feared that a slave state, Missouri, would be surrounded by free states that might shelter runaways. Northerners, especially New Englanders with more than two centuries of experience at conducting elections, were shocked that voting could be so violent—a cultural difference between East and West that may help explain the importance the older region attached to determining the younger one's future.[30]

The territorial legislature demonstrated the sway of proslavery forces. Reeder sought Pierce's support for new elections, but the president was lukewarm. When Reeder asked lawmakers to pass laws to "temporarily prohibit, tolerate or regulate" slavery until Kansans voted whether to allow it, the legislature imposed penalties of two years of hard labor for writing or distributing antislavery literature and death for causing a rebellion or stealing slaves. Even Lewis Cass, the father of squatter sovereignty, branded some of these laws "a disgrace to the age and the country." Although the Kansas version of the congressional gag rule, which banned abolitionist petitions, never was prosecuted, the measure put free-soilers in a difficult position if they criticized slavery. At one point, Reeder vetoed every bill the legislature passed and finally lost his job, partly over his moderate views, partly due to land speculation that gave Pierce (with support from southern Democrats) an excuse to oust him. After his removal, he remained in Kansas and switched to help lead antislavery forces. His successor, Wilson Shannon, was no improvement: he owed his job not to competence but to his party loyalty and proslavery views.[31]

Free-soilers took steps to arm themselves for political battle. In September 1855, at a convention near Lawrence, they developed a party and platform with help from Reeder and former anti-Nebraska congressman James Lane. The next month, they met in Topeka to write their own constitution in response to the proslavery version, which they blamed on intimidation and force, although theirs reflected their prejudices, too. Indulging in a kind of racism more common in the west than in the east, they proposed to exclude both slaves and free blacks from Kansas because, a *New York Times* reporter noted, they were "terribly frightened at the idea of being overrun by negroes. They hold to the idea that negroes are dangerous to the State and a nuisance. . . ." For the rest of that year and early into the next year they formed militias, partly with funding from the recently converted Lawrence and such abolitionists as Higginson and Henry Ward Beecher. In turn, slavery's supporters constituted themselves the Law and Order party, with one of their leaders announcing, "I would rather be a painted slave over in the State of Missouri, or a serf to the Czar of Russia, than have the abolitionists in power." Later in 1855, violence on both sides prompted Shannon to call out Kansans to protect their state, although antislavery forces faced graver dangers, especially in Lawrence, which needed the protection from Missourians besieging it. Nor did it ease tensions when Pierce chimed in with a special message in February 1856 that attacked "propagandist emigration" from New England and described the free-state effort in Topeka as possibly "treasonable."[32]

Pierce's comments signaled that, at the national level, both sides were becoming as entrenched as the Kansans. At Douglas's behest, the Senate Committee on Territories issued a report condemning New England emigrants and the Topeka constitution, with a Republican minority declaring "the subjugation of white freemen may be necessary, that African slavery may succeed." Congress sent a committee to investigate election fraud. Mocking Douglas's report, Seward likened Pierce's behavior toward Kansas to that of George III toward the American colonists in 1776. Vowing to introduce a bill to admit Kansas under the Topeka constitution, Seward declared Kansas "subjugated and prostate at the foot of the President of the United States; while he, through the agency of a foreign tyranny established within her borders, is forcibly introducing and establishing slavery there, in contempt and defiance of the organic law." When Lane brought the constitution to Congress and Douglas questioned its legitimacy, Lane challenged him to a duel and, when refused, called him a coward.[33]

Accordingly, Kansas soon began to justify its nickname: "Bleeding Kansas." Territorial officials wanted to assert their leadership and stop antislavery forces from undermining it. When the county sheriff sought to arrest an antislavery leader in Lawrence, he returned with a posse, and territorial judge Samuel Lecompte requested that a grand jury indict all Topeka "free state" officials and raze the buildings housing Lawrence's antislavery press and the Free State Hotel, whose name reflected its purposes and sympathies. When free-staters found out and some tried to leave the territory, more than 500 Missourians surrounded their town. In what became known as "The Sack of Lawrence," they burned those buildings, the homes of antislavery leaders, and their books and papers.

In turn, this news prompted a response that shocked and inspired the country. Following his father's example as an abolitionist but increasingly doubtful about the movement's non-violence, John Brown joined his sons in migrating to Kansas late in 1855. One of his sons had been active in politics and the free-state militia. Tired of "broken-down politicians," Brown said, "Something must be done to show these barbarians that we, too, have rights," and joined some of his sons on a rampage late in May 1856. One night, they went to three homes and, with guns and knives, murdered five members of proslavery families in the Pottawatomie area. Brown neither admitted nor denied a role. As Nicole Etcheson has written in her study of Bleeding Kansas, "Whether Brown was a hellfire and brimstone Calvinist bringing the judgments of the Lord down on the unrighteous, or a product of the millennialist Second Great Awakening seeking perfectionism and a society cleansed of sin, the result was to push the free-state movement to use the violent means they had threatened but had not yet implemented."[34]

That violence continued in Kansas throughout the year, although cooler heads could and did prevail. When the free-state legislature met in Topeka on July 4, the U.S. Army dispersed them without a fight, but with ample jostling and criticism on both sides. Later that summer, the arrival of new territorial governor John Geary, a Mexican-American War veteran and former San Francisco mayor, gave Kansas a leader who strove for fairness. He tried to remove the proslavery slate of territorial officials, whom he accused of "a virulent spirit of dogged determination to *force* slavery into this Territory," but proved unsuccessful: the Senate refused to confirm their replacements. That left Geary stuck between supporters of slavery who resented him and antislavery leaders with little faith in him. Kansas remained the battleground for trying to settle the question of whether slavery would indeed expand into the West, but under his leadership for the rest of 1856, it proved to be a more peaceful battleground. The same could not be said for the nation's capital, where the issue of slavery and its growth bred violence that stunned northerners and pleased southerners far more than events in Bleeding Kansas.[35]

BLEEDING SUMNER

The rhetoric in Kansas paled in comparison with what was said elsewhere about Kansas. For Brown, the last straw before his assault at Pottawatomie had been an assault of a different kind in Washington, D.C., after a lengthy speech that offended defenders of slavery and popular sovereignty, and produced even more offensive results. But, like Brown's mutilations, the crime against Charles Sumner over "The Crime Against Kansas" had a long history.

While Sumner seemed to exemplify the description of the "idealist in politics," that oversimplifies both him and politics. Born in Massachusetts in 1811, Sumner went to Harvard, toured Europe, and returned home to become bored with his law practice and more interested in foreign affairs and legal scholarship. Active with the Conscience Whigs, he joined the Free-Soilers in 1848, and he later won a Senate seat in 1851 through a coalition with Democrats. Thomas Hart Benton told Sumner that he "had come to the Senate too late. All the great issues and all the great men were gone. There was nothing left but snarling over slavery." Sumner's abolitionism won him no friends among northern colleagues who hoped that the Compromise of 1850 had settled the slavery issue for all time. A Chase friend and admirer, he found that though he shared Seward's and Hale's antislavery views, and genuinely liked the New Yorker, they were too political for his taste. As Sumner said in his first Senate speech on slavery, demanding the Fugitive Slave Law's repeal with the theme of "Freedom National—Slavery Sectional," "For this I willingly forget myself, and all personal consequence. The favor and good will of my fellow-citizens, of my brethren of the Senate, sir—grateful to me as it justly is—I am ready, if required, to sacrifice. . . . Sir, I have never been a politician. The slave of principles, I call no party master."[36]

Yet that speech reflected political realities in several ways. The coalition that elected him had become so upset with his failure to attack slavery that Seward interceded with abolitionist editor William Lloyd Garrison to ease his criticism of Sumner. Sumner prepared the speech, but parliamentary maneuvering kept him from delivering it at first. And the Senate's response revealed that the South tolerated no such criticism. Jeremiah Clemens of Alabama announced, "I rise to express the hope that none of my friends would make any reply to the speech which the Senator from Massachusetts has seen fit to inflict on the Senate. . . . I shall only say, sir, that the ravings of a maniac may sometimes be dangerous, but the barking of a puppy never did any harm." Responding to Sumner's claim that the founding fathers opposed slavery, North Carolina's George Badger said, "He applied the term abolitionist to such a great and good man as George Washington. Sir, in the Senate in which that word is now used, it is impossible that a greater calumny could be perpetrated upon the memory of that great man, than to call him an abolitionist." What may have surprised Sumner about the criticism was that his southern colleagues had been more congenial than most northerners: he called pro-slavery Louisianan Pierre Soulé, later the driving force behind the Ostend Manifesto, his best friend in the Senate, and he enjoyed the company of the senator in the seat next to his, South Carolinian Andrew Butler, a leader of the F Street Mess who helped pressure Douglas into repealing the Missouri Compromise.[37]

Thus the irony in what was to come. By the spring of 1856, Sumner was upset over what he read in letters and newspapers about Kansas. Politically, he felt displeased and threatened: Know-Nothings in Massachusetts still wielded influence among antislavery forces, and Governor Henry Gardner hoped to win his Senate seat. The Senate, already nasty and at times verging on violence over slavery, had long since degenerated into personal criticism during debate, with Sumner calling Washington "a godless place" and privately belittling Douglas as "a brutal vulgar man without delicacy or scholarship [who] looks as if he needed clean linen and should be put under a shower bath." For Sumner to "pronounce the most thorough philippic ever uttered in a legislative body," a speech he called "The Crime Against Kansas," to inveigh against efforts to expand slavery into the West, and to criticize colleagues personally, should have been nothing unusual.[38]

But it was. He addressed the Senate for the better part of two days, May 19th and 20th, 1856. He spent most of that time lecturing on history and current events, concluding—predictably—that Kansas had been wronged, and criticizing the policies of Pierce and his supporters. As his biographer, David Herbert Donald, wrote, "If the address had contained nothing more, it could hardly have been reckoned among the senator's more notable productions." But Sumner declared that "the wickedness which I now begin to expose is immeasurably aggravated by the motive which prompted it. Not in any common lust for power did this uncommon tragedy have its origin. It is the rape of a virgin Territory, compelling it to the hateful embrace of Slavery; and it may be clearly traced to a depraved longing for a new slave State, the hideous offspring of such a crime, in the hope of adding to the power of Slavery in the National Government."

That kind of statement might offend in an era of Victorian sensibilities that avoided overtly sexual language in public. The theme reappeared when he repaid two colleagues for their personal criticism:

> But, before entering upon the argument, I must say something of a general
> character, particularly in response to what has fallen from Senators who have raised
> themselves to eminence on this floor in championship of human wrongs; I mean
> the Senator from South Carolina, [Mr. Butler,] and the Senator from Illinois,
> [Mr. Douglas,], who, though unlike as Don Quixote and Sancho Panza, yet, like
> this couple, sally forth together in the same adventure. I regret much to miss the

elder Senator [Butler] from his seat; but the cause, against which he has run a tilt, with such activity of animosity, demands that the opportunity of exposing him should not be lost; and it is for the cause that I speak. The Senator from South Carolina has read many books of chivalry, and believes himself a chivalrous knight, with sentiments of honor and courage. Of course he has chosen a mistress to whom he has made his vows, and who, though ugly to others, is always lovely to him; though polluted in the sight of the world, is chaste in his sight—I mean the harlot, Slavery. For her, his tongue is always profuse in words. Let her be impeached in character, or any proposition made to shut her out from the extension of her wantonness, and no extravagance of manner or hardihood of assertion is then too great for this Senator. The frenzy of Don Quixote, in behalf of his wench, Dulcinea del Toboso, is all surpassed. The asserted rights of Slavery, which shock equality of all kinds, are cloaked by a fantastic claim of equality. If the slave States cannot enjoy what, in mockery of the great fathers of the Republic, he misnames equality under the Constitution in other words, the full power in the National Territories to compel fellowmen to unpaid toil, to separate husband and wife, and to sell little children at the auction block then, sir, the chivalric Senator will conduct the State of South Carolina out of the Union! Heroic knight! Exalted Senator! A second Moses come for a second exodus!

Dismissing Douglas as "the squire of Slavery, its very Sancho Panza, ready to do all its humiliating offices," he returned to Butler as having "overflowed with rage at the simple suggestion that Kansas had applied for admission as a State; and, with incoherent phrases, discharged the loose expectoration of his speech, now upon her representative, and then upon her people."[39]

Sumner saw no problem with his words. "I mean to keep absolutely within the limits of parliamentary propriety. I make no personal imputations; but only with frankness, such as belongs to the occasion and my own character, describe a great historical act . . . ," he said. Nor was the response—supportive from the antislavery side, critical among Democrats and southerners—unpredictable. Cass called the speech "the most un-American and unpatriotic that ever grated on the ears of the members of this high body." Douglas, a tiger in debate, attacked the "depth of malignity that issued from every sentence" and the "classic allusions, each one only distinguished for its lasciviousness and obscenity—each one drawn from those portions of the classics which all decent professors in all respectable colleges cause to be suppressed, as unfit for decent young men to read." When Douglas mocked his style and preparation, Sumner responded in kind: " . . . no person with the upright form of man can be allowed, without violation of all decency, to switch out from his tongue the perpetual stench of offensive personality. . . . The noisome, squat, and nameless animal, to which I now refer, is not a proper model for an American Senator. Will the Senator from Illinois take notice?"[40]

Others took notice. Seward had advised him to remove the personal comments, Wilson feared for his safety, and even Wade, known for his bluntness, thought he went too far. To criticize Butler's support for slavery was one thing; to use sexual overtones and invoke his speech impediment, the result of a stroke, was another thing entirely. A violent response was a real possibility. Douglas asked, "Is it his object to provoke some of us to kick him as we would a dog in the street, that he may get sympathy upon the just chastisement?" During the speech, Douglas reportedly said, "That damn fool will get himself killed by some other damn fool."[41]

Preston Brooks hardly seemed like a fool. The second-term congressman from South Carolina struck colleagues as level-headed and some of his home state's fire-eaters as too moderate. Sumner's insulting remarks about his home state and his cousin, Butler, still in South Carolina recovering from his stroke, required a response. This issue marked another distinction between the cultures of the North and South. Under the southern code of honor, a lawsuit was unworthy, making an action for libel or slander out of the question. So was a duel: Sumner never would accept, and because a duel was supposed to be between equals, it would be beneath Brooks and elevate the abolitionist from Massachusetts to a level unworthy of him. Smaller and thinner than Sumner, Brooks suffered from a limp and used a cane, the scars of an earlier duel, so he wanted to avoid giving Sumner an opportunity to strike him. Southerners believed punishing an inferior for an insult required a thrashing with a cane or whip. Brooks decided on a gutta-percha cane with a gold head. He hoped to meet Sumner on the street outside Capitol Hill and demand a proper apology. As his anger built up the next day, Brooks intended to take action on the Senate floor, but then chose to wait because a woman was present.[42]

On May 22nd—two days after the offending speech, two years to the day that Congress had passed the Kansas-Nebraska Act—Sumner sat at his desk, sending out copies of his speech. Brooks approached him and said, "Mr. Sumner, I have read your speech twice over carefully. It is a libel on South Carolina, and Mr. Butler, who is a relative of mine." Sumner looked up, puzzled because he did not know Brooks, and seemed about to rise. Brooks hit Sumner with the end of his cane. Sumner threw up his arms to protect himself. Brooks began beating him as hard and as fast as he could. Sumner tried to rise from his desk, which was bolted to the floor. His adrenalin rushing, Sumner pulled the desk, bolted to the floor, from its moorings and tried to get away, unable to see through the blood streaming from his head. Brooks followed him, beating him with the cane, which broke as he did so. "I . . . gave him about 30 first rate stripes. Towards the last he bellowed like a calf. I wore my cane out completely but saved the Head which is gold," Brooks said.[43]

While history records what went on between Sumner and Brooks, others were involved. Lawrence Keitt, another South Carolina congressman, accompanied Brooks in case he required protection from Sumner or others. As the beating unfolded, John Crittenden, the old Kentucky Whig, approached, admonishing Brooks. Keitt raised his cane at the aged senator and yelled, "Let them alone, God damn you." Robert Toombs of Georgia told Keitt not to attack Crittenden but said of the beating, "I approved it." Douglas had been beside Toombs outside the chamber, heard about what was happening, and said, "My first impression was to come into the Senate Chamber and help to put an end to the affray, if I could; but it occurred to my mind, in an instant, that my relations to Mr. Sumner were such that if I came into the Hall, my motives would be misconstrued, perhaps, and I sat down again." Others aided Sumner as he staggered into the anteroom and Wilson helped take him home. That night, Sumner said, "I could not believe that a thing like this was possible." Long afterward, Sumner would "ask his secretary with perfect simplicity what it was in the speech on Kansas that Butler's friends objected to, what part of it they considered insulting."[44]

Sumner's obtuseness aside, the response to Brooks was telling. As William Freehling has written, "While many southerners privately thought that, as usual, South Carolina had gone a little too far, most of them publicly castigated Charles Sumner for pushing oratorical insults way too far." Toombs wrote, "Yankees seem greatly excited about Sumner's flogging. They are afraid the practice may become general." Southerners sent Brooks dozens of canes to replace the broken one, including one inscribed, "Hit him again," and asked for the pieces that snapped off the original during the assault. Both houses of Congress investigated the incident, with the Senate claiming it lacked jurisdiction and the House falling short of the two-thirds majority required for expulsion. But Brooks resigned his seat anyway, returned home to seek election and vindication, and won both. When Wilson assailed him for a "brutal, murderous, and cowardly assault," Brooks challenged him to a duel, which Wilson declined as "the lingering relic of a barbarous civilization, which the law of the country has branded as a crime." A local court fined Brooks $300, which southerners sent him the money to pay. But Brooks had little time to enjoy his fame: he died early the next year of the effects of a virus.[45]

The northern response also ran deep. A conservative who deplored Sumner's speech, Edward Everett, described by antislavery Democrat William Cullen Bryant as a "polished icicle," observed "an excitement in the public mind deeper and more dangerous than I have ever witnessed. . . . If a leader daring and reckless enough had presented himself, he might have raised any number of men to march on Washington" from Boston. Democrats and conservative ex-Whigs could be critical—Fletcher Webster, Daniel's son, still resenting Sumner's battles with his father over slavery, groused that if he "would indulge in such attacks . . . he ought at least to take the precaution of wearing an iron pot on his head." But the immediate reaction mingled horror, anger, and a renewed commitment, if not to antislavery ideals, then to the dangers of the South and the Slave Power. As Bryant wrote, "The friends of slavery at Washington are attempting to silence the members of Congress from the free States by the same modes of discipline which make the slaves unite on their plantations." In Massachusetts, criticism was muted and, notwithstanding Webster, support came from all sides, enough to bolster what had been Sumner's questionable prospects for reelection—which he won despite making only a couple of appearances in the Senate for three years while he recovered from the trauma of the assault. Secretary of State Marcy, no sympathizer with Sumner's views but a shrewd political operator, predicted that the attack would cost Democrats 200,000 votes in the 1856 elections.[46]

That remained to be seen, but in Kansas and in the Senate, northerners had seen how far some southerners would go to defend slavery. Southerners had long since concluded that northerners would go too far and needed to be taught a lesson. At the core of the battle was the nation's future, which was in neither the North nor the South. More northerners turned toward a sectional, antislavery political party while southerners dug in their heels. Seward expected new states in the West "to finally decide whether this is to be a land of slavery or of freedom. The people of the northwest are to be the arbiters of its destiny. . . ." As a Whig, he found little common ground with a Jacksonian Democrat such as Francis Preston Blair, Jr., or even as devotedly antislavery a Democrat as Chase. But in 1854, Blair predicted, "The wealth and political power of the country will in a little time reside at its Geographical centre," which meant the West, and Chase anticipated that a West free of slavery would mean "freedom not serfdom; freeholds not tenancies; democracy not despotism; education not ignorance . . . progress, not stagnation or retrogression." After Bleeding Kansas and Bleeding Sumner—whose bleeding followed, after all, a speech about Kansas—the North and South would try to decide which vision of the future would triumph.[47]

FIVE

❦

A NEW PRESIDENT,
A NEW PARTY, A NEW
CONSTITUTIONAL CLASH

Throughout its history, the *National Intelligencer* had been the Whig newspaper in Washington, D.C. That created a problem for its editors in 1856: they had no party. Their organization no longer existed, except in the minds of a few, mostly northern holdouts hoping that concerns about the Union's future would bring back those who had given up on the Whigs. They refused to back Millard Fillmore because his nomination came from the nativist Know-Nothings. Democrats never had been acceptable, and Republicans represented the sectionalism and antislavery views that moderate and conservative Whigs long had found wanting.

In one issue, the *Intelligencer* captured the gulf separating the parties and the sections. A Virginia newspaper said, "We have got to hating everything with the prefix *free,* from free negroes up and down through the whole catalogue—*free farms, free labor, free society, free will, free thinking, free children, and free schools.*" A South Carolina counterpart chimed in, "The great evil of Northern *free* society is that it is burdened with a *servile class of mechanics and laborers,* unfit for self-government, and yet clothed with the attributes and powers of citizens." Across the ideological spectrum on slavery, Indiana abolitionist George Julian called the 1856 election "not alone a fight between the North and the South; it is a fight between freedom and slavery; between God and the devil; between heaven and hell." The *Intelligencer's* point in publishing these comments was to show that political campaigns produced heated rhetoric, and this one was no different. Everyone involved, the Whiggish editors agreed, would calm down.[1]

How much they calmed down is open to debate, especially from the perspective of the people of Lawrence, Kansas, and Senator Charles Sumner. Elections rarely turn out as originally anticipated, and 1856 fit that mold. When the campaign jockeying began in 1855, Know-Nothings seemed likely to be the Democrats' strongest competitor, with Republicans relegated to the margins as a sectional third party. By the late spring of 1856, though, the presidential election began to take shape as a two-section race: Democrats vs. Republicans in the North, Democrats vs. Know-Nothings in the South. Thus, it should have been the Democratic party's race to lose, and that would happen only if either of the other parties was fortunate and Democrats proved totally disorganized. Either was possible; neither happened.

"PENNSYLVANIA'S LAST CHANCE"

In 1856, Democrats should have had no chance of victory. Their northern wing split in 1854, costing them a substantial number of congressional seats and state offices. Events in Kansas had divided them even further. President Franklin Pierce sought renomination, reelection, and vindication, and in the unlikely event that he achieved the first of those, neither of the other two seemed probable and either of them could create further divisions. But although Democrats had no other clear-cut choice, they were fortunate in their opponents. Unless the Republicans and Know-Nothings somehow came together, they would keep fighting to be considered the leading opposition party. Both were new, meaning the Democratic organization was far superior, even after the party came apart over Kansas. The Republican opposition to expanding slavery kept southern support beyond their grasp, but northern and southern Know-Nothings proved unable to resolve that issue to mutual satisfaction. And both the Republican and American parties were coalitions whose members had yet to break the habit they had formed in their previous political incarnations of fighting with one another. Thus, if Democrats could find a candidate who could carry most of one section and pick off votes in the other, victory could be theirs.

Pierce's greatest liabilities were his policies and himself. The Kansas-Nebraska Act, which he made a test of party loyalty, split Democrats and upset advocates of free soil in general, and his subsequent handling of the territorial government in Kansas pleased no one. Southern Democrats generally liked him, but still harbored doubts that he was trustworthy, being a northerner and being Pierce. His efforts at territorial expansion and diplomatic influence had gone nowhere. Because he had left his candidacy to others to manage in 1852, and that had been his only try for national office, he had no organization to speak of and no experience at pulling his own wires on the national level. His efforts to build a base through patronage had been halting and, given his failure to mollify any wing of the party, unsuccessful. As his former secretary put it, he was "in rather bad odor, and he will stink worse yet. . . . The Kansas outrages are all imputable to him, and if he is not called to answer for them here, 'In Hell they'll roast him like a herring.'"[2]

Recovered from an illness and finally willing to make his plans known, Douglas was interested in the nomination and ready to fight for it. One of his managers wrote to the *Richmond Examiner* that rumors he would forego the race suggested "that he has raised an excitement in the country which has given strength to free-soilism, and that now, when in appearance his party is environed by difficulties, he wants to skulk and dodge the blows that might be struck at him if standing at the head of his party in a national political battle. . . ." For his part, Douglas said, "We must make no compromise with the enemy—no concession to the allied isms," meaning abolitionism (as he defined the Republicans) and nativism. His concern was that the "isms" would cooperate with each other.[3]

Douglas suffered from one of the problems that had plagued Henry Clay and Daniel Webster when they sought the presidency: as a Senate and party leader, he had been at the center of most storms, becoming controversial in the process. If Democrats wanted to win, they would be better off with someone who had been nowhere near the debates over Kansas and related issues, and Douglas had been in the middle of things. By contrast, James Buchanan had felt sidelined as minister to England, but was fortunate to be far from political battles back home. No Democrat could question his party loyalty or service—representative, senator, twice a diplomatic representative, secretary of state. Democrats could expect most of the southern vote if their nominee was properly deferential on slavery, but they needed someone to attract moderate and conservative northerners—especially in a vote-rich state like Pennsylvania, and Buchanan was a Pennsylvanian. He was 65, and thus it might be not just his last chance but, his supporters said, "Pennsylvania's last chance"—and the Democrats' best chance.[4]

That spelled trouble for Pierce and Douglas. Buchanan already had help from old friend and Pierce enemy John Slidell of Louisiana. Senator Jesse Bright, Indiana's boss, seemed a likely Douglas ally, but backed Buchanan when he realized the Little Giant would outshine him politically in the Old Northwest. Other Democrats blamed Douglas for impaling the party over Kansas or wanted to repay him for real or perceived slights. New York Democrats divided predictably: Secretary of State William Marcy's Softs saw Pierce had no chance and supported Douglas, prompting Daniel Dickinson's Hards to oppose him. Forced to choose between Pierce and Douglas, southerners tended to prefer Pierce because he aided in spreading slavery whereas Douglas's popular sovereignty might yet restrict it.

While Democrats seemed badly divided, Buchanan benefited from a superior organization and base of support, and from backers with an appetite for vengeance. Joining Slidell were Bright, Delaware's James Bayard, and Louisiana's Judah Benjamin, three senators who despised Pierce, were southerners or sympathized with the South, and combined talents for cunning and tyranny. Buchanan also had backing from Governor Henry Wise of Virginia, New York financier August Belmont, and Philadelphia editor

John Forney, a superior operative when sober and still shrewd on the frequent occasions when he was not. Former Senator Thomas Hart Benton of Missouri resented Douglas for capitulating to his longtime rival David Rice Atchison on the Kansas-Nebraska Act and Pierce for going along with them, so he backed Buchanan and helped recruit old Jacksonians.

The ride through the Democratic convention in Cincinnati was bumpy before it turned smooth. Two delegations arrived from Missouri and New York, and the convention handled both wisely: it refused to seat the Missourians, whose leader, Benton, refused to abandon the party, and accepted both New York groups. In turn, Buchanan's managers kept his loyalists in line and in the lead while Pierce gradually lost strength to Douglas. After 16 ballots, Douglas's managers saw he had peaked and pulled out a letter he had sent them in which he wrote, "If the withdrawal of my name will contribute to the harmony of our Party or the success of the cause, I hope you will not hesitate to take the step." They took the step and Buchanan won the nomination on the next ballot. His managers accepted the Douglas group's request that one of the Illinoisan's supporters, young Kentuckian John Breckinridge, join Buchanan on the ticket.[5]

Yet Douglas and his views—especially the issue he was most closely associated with, the expansion of slavery—left footprints everywhere. Whether that influence was permanent was yet to be resolved. Given Buchanan's age and Douglas's youth, the Little Giant could wait: he could expect to influence how the administration unfolded, then coast to the succession, although Buchanan distanced himself from the younger senator throughout the campaign and ignored Breckinridge. The party endorsed popular sovereignty, but in terms that made it what one Democrat called "an elastic platform susceptible of double reading," with the Kansas-Nebraska Act deemed "the only sound and safe solution of the 'slavery question.'" It backed the "Young American" foreign policy of using muscle in Latin American countries and standing up to Great Britain, then the world's superpower. It assailed the Know-Nothings as inimical to the "spirit of toleration and enlarged freedom" and Republicans as "a sectional party, subsisting exclusively on slavery agitation." And the other parties danced to Douglas's tune: Republicans fought popular sovereignty and Know-Nothings sought to win the votes of southerners convinced that the other two parties were out to get them. Buchanan agreed with a conservative platform; Douglas was in the shadows and out front, in a campaign with harbingers of his future dealings with Buchanan and the opposition.[6]

FREEDOM AND FRÉMONT

For Republicans, the road to a presidential nomination required them first to put together a party. The anti-Nebraska groups of 1854 and 1855 had been loosely knit, but their laxity varied across the country. Republicans agreed on stopping the spread of slavery into the West, the issue that brought them together in the first place. Beyond that, they were in flux. Perhaps that issue was enough: Salmon Chase suggested, "It seems to me that we can only carry the next Presidential election by making the simple issue of Slavery or Freedom. We shall need the liberal Americans and we shall also need the antislavery adopted citizens." Chase proved right, but to varying degrees in each state as Republicans navigated such issues as nativism, temperance, internal improvements, and the tariff. With new Governor James Grimes pulling strings, Iowa Republicans approved a platform that simply stated "freedom is alone national" and "all national territory *shall be free*," avoiding all other subjects and asserting the primacy of the one they discussed. In New Hampshire, Know-Nothings exercised most of the power in the party, yet the platform and preferred candidates adopted Republican principles. Indiana's anti-Nebraska convention waffled enough on slavery, immigration restrictions, and temperance to please supporters of each position and anger hard-line advocates, as in Julian's complaint about "trimming, temporizing, diluting, and *surrendering.*" Illinois Republicans benefited from taking conservative positions (Abraham Lincoln helped write the platform, which called for restoring the Missouri line), as well as Know-Nothings moderating their stances and both sides realizing that the only issue they could unite on was what had happened in Kansas.[7]

The tenuous nature of these coalitions made finding a standard-bearer difficult. Although the new party's most prominent member was Seward, his prominence came mainly from stands against slavery and nativism, and Republicans needed to attract conservative supporters on the former and crack the Know-Nothing base on the latter. Greeley said, "I shall go for the man who can secure the most strength outside our regular ranks, and let earnest Anti Slavery men come in when they get ready." He joined many Republicans in supporting expediency over principle, but did not reveal that his break with Seward and Weed motivated his effort to derail the New Yorker's presidential hopes. For different reasons, Weed agreed with Greeley. Despite Seward's desire for the nomination, and support from former Whigs and a significant number of radical Republicans, Weed questioned the timing. The party was new: if it lost, Seward would receive more blame for the defeat than he deserved. Besides, an alliance with Know-Nothings might prove necessary, and Seward's hatred for nativism made a coalition improbable. Writing in his *New York Times,* Henry Raymond, who made few political moves without Weed's approval, declared the need for "a *new man,*—one not identified with the political struggles and animosities of the past," explaining that "in all the Western and the New England States, the Republican party owes its strength in a very great degree to its alliance with Americanism." Seward resented that decision, but the party seemed unlikely to turn to him without a clear signal from him and Weed.[8]

Next to Seward in prominence among Republicans was Chase, who wanted the nomination even more but had even greater problems. Chase had been antislavery earlier and more notably than Seward, which made him feel more entitled to the nomination. But could Republicans attract conservatives if Chase headed the ticket? On the one hand, his alliance with Ohio Know-Nothings elected him governor and showed his ability to work with that party. On the other hand, his eagerness for that fusion unnerved Republicans trying to reduce nativist influence and attract German voters—the Republican faithful knew they might have to work with nativists, but they had no plans to enjoy it. Nor did Chase have well-organized supporters— certainly no one resembling a Weed to maneuver pieces around the political chess- board. Ohio's delegation divided over him, a bad sign for a new party going into a convention.

The other Ohio aspirant, John McLean, the Supreme Court's senior associate jus- tice, drew conservative and nativist support. Greeley, a Chase admirer then and later, declared, "If McLean is the man for Pennsylvania and New Jersey, then I am for McLean," and Lincoln thought McLean's ties to conservative Whigs would be a boon for Republicans. Unfortunately for them, McLean fit the description that John Quincy Adams had written in his diary years before: he "thinks of nothing but the Presidency by day and dreams of nothing else by night." McLean had flipped between parties according to where his chances looked better. He served in Adams's cabinet but sup- ported the campaign of his opponent, Andrew Jackson, then switched to the anti-Jack- son Whigs after his appointment to the Supreme Court. Republicans also had cause for concern that he never said outright that he opposed slavery in the territories, upheld the Fugitive Slave Act, and refused to say whether he was actually a Republican or a Know-Nothing. He claimed judicial propriety kept him from making a public decla- ration. When he saw his candidacy turning to ashes, he issued public letters professing Republican sympathies and prepared a dissent for a case not yet argued that might enable him to prove his antislavery views. Small wonder that Weed privately called him a "white-liver'd hollow-hearted Janus-faced rascal."[9]

Increasingly, Republicans leaned toward imitating the Whigs and looked to a mil- itary hero: John Charles Frémont. His western explorations and best-selling reports on them made him a household name; his nickname was "The Great Pathfinder." His wife, Jessie, was the daughter of Thomas Hart Benton, who declined to leave the Democrats for a sectional party he saw as a "motley mixture of malcontents with no real desire in any of them to save the Union," even if his son-in-law led its ticket. Indeed, Democrats discussed nominating Frémont, but that went nowhere, and Frémont opposed slavery, although he had been publicly quiet on the subject.[10]

Frémont's first promoter was Nathaniel Banks, whose maneuverings between Republicans and Know-Nothings suggested intrigue behind supporting a politi- cal neophyte. Amid signs of Republican interest, Jessie Frémont turned to one of her father's oldest friends, Francis Blair, who had toyed with the improbable idea of a Benton-Seward ticket before becoming committed to nominating Benton's son-in-law instead. Blair told Martin Van Buren in January 1856, "I think of

Frémont *as a new man*. He is brave, firm, has a history of romantic heroism . . . & has no bad political connections—never had—no tail of hungry, corrupt hangers on like Buchanan who will I think be the [Democratic] candidate." As the old Jacksonian gathered Republican support for Frémont, *New York Evening Post* editor John Bigelow observed, "Thurlow Weed says he is contented with Frémont, and, if so, of course Seward is," which could not have been more wrong. Greeley preferred Frémont, although he was "the merest baby in politics," because "we have had enough of third-rate lawyers and God knows what rate generals." But his political freshness attracted those hoping to influence him or figuring, as Ben Wade of Ohio put it, that he had "no past political sins to answer for." As Schuyler Colfax, an Indiana Republican with Know-Nothing tendencies, observed, Frémont became "the favorite of those who desire to *win*."[11]

Yet Frémont's path to the nomination showed both the difficulties of seeking the prize and the fluid political structure of the mid-1850s. Greeley waffled over Frémont's inexperience, and others agreed that in a time of crisis over the Union and slavery, someone with no record might be too weak an anchor to which to tie the country's fate. Party leaders fretted when Frémont issued a public letter to Charles Robinson, leader of the Kansas free-state movement, sympathizing with his cause without making clear just what he thought about the expansion of slavery. Northern Know-Nothings opposed to both immigrants and slavery showed interest in nominating him because Frémont's silence on the issues raised the possibility in their minds that he would be acceptable on both counts. That prospect would eat at the Republican party from within or deprive him of the support of all anti-nativist Republicans. Either way, his managers wanted to avoid it.

When Republicans met in Philadelphia on June 17, 1856, they filled the meeting hall and produced a more radically antislavery platform than had seemed possible, given their tentative beginnings and concerns about holding the coalition together. The platform committee, mostly former Democrats led by David Wilmot, echoed Chase's constitutional argument that the Founding Fathers had been antislavery. The party declared, "We deny the authority of Congress, of a Territorial Legislature, of any individual, or association of individuals, to give legal existence to Slavery in any Territory of the United States." It announced that Congress had "sovereign power" over territories and "the right and the imperative duty . . . to prohibit in the Territories those twin relics of barbarism—Polygamy, and Slavery." Republicans agreed on admitting Kansas as a free state, building a Pacific railroad, and giving federal aid to internal improvements, reflecting the Whig spirit infecting the party. Such antislavery leaders as Chase and Joshua Giddings were thrilled, especially because the platform reflected the "freedom national" idea that the old Liberty party and Chase had long advocated: that slavery is a creature of local law, limited to states where it existed. Democratic and Whig refugees were happy that the platform avoided such economically divisive issues as the tariff, a homestead law, and a national bank.[12]

Nominating a candidate proved easier than Republicans might have expected, but problems still surfaced. On the first day, delegates went wild at the mention of Seward, prompting more debate about his candidacy. He could be nominated, but Weed still doubted that he would win and feared a loss would taint him forever. At first upset over Weed's opposition, then torn asunder over conflicting advice, Seward finally took himself out of the running. His New York supporters then backed Frémont, making The Pathfinder's nomination all but inevitable beneath a banner of "Free Speech, Free Soil, Free Men, Frémont." Finally, Frémont won the nomination by acclamation, despite Thaddeus Stevens's warning that his state of Pennsylvania, so vital in any national race, would go Republican only if McLean was the nominee. He might have been right, but Buchanan's nomination gave Democrats a strong chance of winning the Keystone State anyway.

Pennsylvania remained at the center of controversy over choosing Frémont's running-mate. Republicans sought nativist support with their vice-presidential candidate. North Americans—the Know-Nothing party's northern branch—wanted Pennsylvania's William Johnston, but Stevens and other Republicans from that state deemed him unacceptable. Frémont wanted Simon Cameron, whose slipperiness would have balanced the political naiveté atop the ticket, but he was so corrupt that his selection would have driven away other voters. Befitting the fractious nature of Pennsylvania politics, Republicans and northern Know-Nothings could agree on no one from that state. Finally, the convention turned to William Dayton, who came from neighboring New Jersey and was a conservative ex-Whig backing McLean—as close to a nativist as the Republicans would accept, but not enough of one to mollify North Americans.

For Republicans, the issues were less clear-cut than their opponents thought. For all of Douglas's talk of "isms" and accusations of abolition, most Republicans said little during the campaign about slavery on purely moral grounds. They felt that it threatened white labor: Gideon Welles argued that slave owners "look upon and despise all labor as servile and degrading," and therefore, he reasoned, "If slavery is established in Kansas, free labor must be expelled. It is not the cause of the negro, but that of the free laboring white man that is involved in this question." Worse, they warned, the Slave Power wanted to spread northward and "wield the General Government against freedom—not only in Kansas, but every where else." If they succeeded, Republicans warned, that would mean the spread of southern society, too, which was still worse because it would also mean the spread of aristocratic tendencies, opposition to progress, and threats to the government as the Founding Fathers created it—not to mention, Republicans were quick to claim, more sacks of Lawrence and canings like Sumner's. Not only did these arguments have the virtue of representing the party's attitudes, but they also deflected charges of radicalism and diverted party members from having to discuss economic and other issues that divided the North and themselves.[13]

Unsurprisingly, though, Republicans proved unable to escape divisions and criticism. Some feared their party attacked the South too much. Even Republicans questioned whether Frémont had the experience needed in a president, especially running against veteran politicians like Buchanan and Fillmore, and it did his cause no good when his father-in-law, Benton, came out for Buchanan. Frémont's candidacy suffered from allegations that he belonged to the Catholic Church, which were untrue and refutable, but hard to combat once they were in circulation. Indeed, Seward pointed out, "Frémont, who was preferred over me because I was not a bigoted Protestant, is nearly convicted of being a Catholic." Democrats also made Jessie Frémont an issue because she was active behind-the-scenes—a different and unpopular role for a woman to play. They also made the most of any untrue rumor they could—that Frémont owned slaves and was an alcoholic—while Republicans were slow to counter them. Republicans had the advantage that their argument against expanding slavery into the West resonated with voters. But they still had to learn how to reach those voters.[14]

"AMERICANS SHOULD GOVERN AMERICA"

Although Know-Nothings had begun to come apart over slavery, they had neither gone away nor given up. With their ticket of Millard Fillmore and Andrew Jackson Donelson, the late president's nephew, they hoped to capture nativists, southern and conservative northern Whigs adrift in the political system, and the occasional lost Jacksonian. But they were in trouble from the start. In theory, they were better organized than the Republicans, having existed longer as a group, but the Republicans learned and moved fast. Two of their Massachusetts leaders, Nathaniel Banks and Henry Wilson, used their Know-Nothing affiliation to advance themselves with the Republican party—and Banks's power as speaker enabled him to reward Republicans and ignore nativists in distributing committee memberships, which helped the antislavery party build support in Congress.

As their problems in Massachusetts suggested, Know-Nothings made the other parties look unified in comparison. Southern remnants of the Whig party could generally come together as Know-Nothings, but even that was risky. Wise had made political capital in Virginia by accusing nativists of wanting to disenfranchise white voters and working in the kind of secrecy normally associated with slave conspiracies, ringing alarm bells with those who recalled Nat Turner's rebellion of 1831, among others. But while southerners outside of the Democratic party had few options, northern Know-Nothings seemed hopeless. "Moderates" hoped to counter antislavery and doughface Know-Nothings by restoring the Missouri Compromise line. "National Americans," mostly conservative ex-Whigs, wanted to stress Union above all else and hoped their prominence in border states and the lower northern states would appeal to southern party members. The "fusionists," antislavery, anti-Catholic, and potentially comfortable in either party, expected to join the Republicans or hoped to use the Know-Nothings' continued existence to force the antislavery party to adopt them by offering policy changes or patronage.

Worse still, Fillmore proved disastrous as a presidential candidate. First, he vacillated about running and spent most of his time deciding in Europe. That kept Know-Nothings from starting early and they never really caught up. Nor did he appeal to his own constituency. That he was no nativist—indeed, his daughter attended a Catholic school—bothered true believers, and Fillmore's emphasis on the Union instead of immigrants angered them even more. Northern members of the American party—the North Americans—had no reason to trust him on slavery. As the *Albany State Register* put it, "All political action, all political principles, all political policy, every political movement, begins and ends with Slavery. It is the Alpha and Omega of every sect, every part, and every creed. It controls every Southern vote, is the burthen of every Southern speech, the guide of every Southern man's footsteps; and we of the North must be, are compelled, whether we will or not, to be for it or against it. There is no longer a middle course—no neutral ground," and antislavery Know-Nothings became convinced that the ground they had to stand on was Republican. That was even truer as the events of May—the sack of Lawrence and, especially, Sumner's caning—sank in. Fillmore wrote, "Brooks' attack on Sumner has done more for Frémont than any 20 of his warmest friends . . . have been able to accomplish. . . . The Republicans ought to pension Brooks for life."[15]

Thus, grasping that "the cursed question of *slavery* is at the bottom of all our troubles," the Know-Nothings tried to work their way around the issue. They stressed Fillmore's experience: in troubled times, he was the only candidate who had been president and therefore was most qualified to deal with whatever plagued the country. They accused Republicans of overstating the problems in Kansas and the extent of Sumner's injuries. They made sure to distribute such Fillmore comments as, "Americans should govern America," signifying his commitment to the party's reason for being, while charging that Frémont belonged to the Catholic Church. They also insisted that only Fillmore could defeat Buchanan: with the South closed off to Republicans, Frémont could never win an electoral majority.[16]

They may have been right about Frémont, but they proved less prescient about their own prospects. Working with Republicans, Gardner negotiated Know-Nothings out of any chance they might have had in Massachusetts. In Fillmore's New York, the party overrated their supporters' loyalty to both their cause and their candidate, and underrated their opposition to slavery. In late summer elections in the South, Fillmore ran weaker than expected, costing him support across the region, and Know-Nothings began to lose hope. "By failing to rally most ex-Northern Whigs, Millard Fillmore became uninteresting to most ex-Lower South Whigs," William Freehling has written. "A Yankee who could rout the

Northern Democrats on a sectionally neutral nativist program might have been intriguing. But if the North had to be lost anyway, a vigorous proslavery campaign could better combat Lower South Democrats." As southern Know-Nothings gravitated to Democrats and North Americans to Republicans, American leaders even opened talks with Republicans about a fusion ticket. But Fillmore and his advisers remained convinced that if they won enough votes, they could throw the election into the House of Representatives, where lightning might strike.[17]

In the end, Republicans won even more votes than they should have hoped for, Know-Nothings fared worse than they imagined, and Democrats won the White House with deceptive ease. Winning every slave state but Maryland, Buchanan carried the key swing states: Pennsylvania, Illinois, Indiana, New Jersey, and California. Fillmore gained most of the southern Whig vote and nearly threw the election into the House, as he hoped, but barely registered in the North. Frémont carried the rest of the North and gave Republicans cause for optimism: if they could find a way to win the lower northern states that Buchanan had carried, they could win in 1860. Better still, for the moment, they swept enough states to control most northern legislatures, which sent Republican senators to Capitol Hill. Other Republicans thought they did well enough for a first campaign, but future success depended on finding a moderate candidate. Frémont believed he might have won if Republicans had given in to his desire to share the ticket with Cameron. He may have been right: because Buchanan ended up with 174 electoral votes, Frémont 114, and Fillmore 8, carrying Pennsylvania and another swing state might have won Frémont the White House—if Cameron's presence did no damage elsewhere.

Among Know-Nothings, recriminations flew. Southerners blamed both fellow southerners piqued at northerners dallying with Republicans and northerners who did the dallying. North Americans felt they could have won if Frémont ran with one of their own—Weed even told a Pennsylvanian that "the first, and as I still think fatal error, was in not taking a Vice President in whose nomination the North Americans would have concurred cordially." Although North Americans knew Fillmore's bows toward the South repulsed many northerners, nativists north and south agreed that the issue of slavery and its expansion proved its primacy by harming their movement. Few discounted the Know-Nothings—*The New York Times* noted that "no sentiment, or conviction, which has the power to create such a party in so short a time, can perish or lose its vital force so suddenly"—but Republicans from Wilson in Massachusetts to Lincoln and Trumbull in Illinois pushed their party to avoid adopting nativist views. They saw slavery as the issue of their time, and concerns about immigrants and Catholics resonated less with voters, especially with southern Know-Nothings dominating the nativist movement. This would enable Republicans to attract Know-Nothings by emphasizing the common enemy.

What Eric Foner has written about Pennsylvania applied to the North in general: "The defense of northern free labor against competition from foreign cheap labor was a goal both groups could support."[18]

NEW PRESIDENT, OLD PROBLEMS

Unlike Pierce, whose national experience had been limited, Buchanan took office with far more confidence and ability—but only to an extent. First, as he left the White House, Pierce did Buchanan no favors. He could have devoted his final annual message to healing the sectional divide and paving the way for his successor. Instead, he assailed those who abandoned his party or remained and fought his renomination. He blamed northern "agents of disorder" for Bleeding Kansas and Republicans for endangering the Union "by appeals to passion and sectional prejudice, by indoctrinating its people with reciprocal hatred, and by educating them to stand face to face as enemies rather than shoulder to shoulder as friends." While Republicans struck back and southerners defended Pierce, northern Democrats seemed to wish he would go away. For the short remainder of Pierce's term, members of Congress accomplished little, but overcame their animosities long enough to pass a new tariff designed to promote free trade and reduce federal revenues, which antagonized industrialists in Buchanan's Pennsylvania but pleased most Democrats—for the moment.[19]

Buchanan faced another problem: his cabinet proved little better than Pierce's. Like his predecessor, he had trouble choosing anyone without antagonizing some branch of his party, and his reluctance to do much about it foreshadowed the problems that afflicted his presidency. Because his support was overwhelmingly southern, he found it impossible to please the North. While his experience counteracted some of the cabinet's weaknesses, Buchanan also took too much on himself. This was especially true of diplomacy. For secretary of state, he chose Lewis Cass, by then a party elder of 75 who agreed to let the president name his deputy, meaning Buchanan would involve himself in most diplomatic affairs. Worse, as Cass originated popular sovereignty and proved willing to accept abuses of it, his presence did nothing to mollify Democrats already wary of Buchanan's doughfaced tendencies.

The rest of the cabinet made little impression. Most of Buchanan's prominent choices—Wise, Slidell, and Bright—preferred to stay where they were and probably would have just contributed to sectional tension anyway. The Treasury went to Georgian Howell Cobb, who felt that he deserved State and was too moderate for both fire-eaters and Douglas Democrats. For the War Department, Buchanan accepted Wise's suggestion of fellow Virginian John Floyd, whose loyalties were to the South and to filling his pocketbook and those of his friends with ill-gotten gains. Secretary of the Interior Jacob Thompson, Postmaster General Aaron Brown, and Secretary of the Navy Isaac Toucey brought no political strength to the cabinet. A Pennsylvania friend, Jeremiah Black, took the attorney general's office, giving Buchanan a shadow of himself nearby, but no one different enough from the president or close enough to Douglas to appeal to his branch of northern Democrats or to represent their interests.[20]

Buchanan's inaugural address reflected that tone-deafness. He assured each citizen of Kansas the right to "the free and independent expression of his opinion by his vote," but would demonstrate that preserving that right mattered less to him than appeasing proslavery forces—or, as Charles Francis Adams said with partisan displeasure and accuracy, "The next four years are to be more industriously employed than ever to uphold a tyranny which the progress of the age is doing its best to undermine and destroy." Buchanan was willing to spend federal money on a transcontinental railroad, a controversial topic for North and South alike, but planned to cut the federal surplus without "extravagant legislation" and "wild schemes of expenditure." More crucially, he hoped for the end of "the long agitation" over slavery and "that geographical parties to which it has given birth . . . will speedily become extinct . . . ," a process he expected a pending Supreme Court decision to hasten. He managed to be both wrong and disingenuous, and his words would scar his presidency and his historical reputation.[21]

THE DRED SCOTT CASE

As reviled as the Supreme Court was for *Dred Scott v. Sandford,* it remains among the Court's least understood rulings. The implications and interpretations of what the Court said on March 6, 1857, helped elect Lincoln president and destroy Douglas's candidacy. The majority opinion showed that even perhaps the country's most conservative institution could lose its sense of proportion in the battle over slavery and its expansion westward. Many observers, both then and since, dismissed Chief Justice Roger Brooke Taney's words as both legal propaganda and a short-lived aberration when, in fact, they were neither—for him or the Court.[22]

Born sometime in the 1790s in Virginia, Dred Scott had been a slave in Peter Blow's St. Louis home. After his master died, Scott wound up in Dr. John Emerson's household. When Emerson joined the Army, he moved from Missouri to Fort Armstrong in Illinois, a military post in a free state. Then he transferred to Fort Snelling, then in Wisconsin Territory, where the Missouri Compromise forbade slavery. When Emerson was transferred—he constantly hectored the Army for new assignments, claiming health problems—he hired out Scott and his wife, Harriet, to another officer at Fort Snelling. Later, he brought the Scotts with him to Florida, back to St. Louis, and then to Iowa. There Emerson died in 1843, leaving his estate to his wife and appointing as an executor his brother-in-law, John F.A. Sanford, whose name was misspelled in the official reports on the case.

On April 6, 1846, the Scotts sought permission in a St. Louis court to sue Emerson's widow for their freedom. When the judge agreed, they sued her separately, claiming to be free and charging that Irene Emerson "beat, bruised and ill-treated" Dred Scott two days before. Whether the suit was Scott's idea remains a mystery, but he was hardly the first slave to initiate such a suit. He also had help from Taylor Blow, his late master's son, on his trek through the courts.

The legal labyrinth Scott followed was slow and tortuous. In his first trial, problems with witness testimony led to a verdict for Emerson, but Scott's attorney won a motion for a new trial—and with Emerson's departure for a new home, Scott also had a new defendant, Sanford. At the retrial in January 1850, the Scotts won their freedom. But when Missouri's proslavery politicians heard about the case, they helped Sanford appeal to the Missouri Supreme Court. Its proslavery majority held that the Scotts remained slaves.

But Dred Scott was far from finished. The Blow family hired him out from Sanford and turned to a new attorney with a new strategy. Because Sanford moved to New York, the case involved two states and could be heard in federal court. After Scott's lawyer filed suit, Sanford's attorneys countered that as a descendant of slaves of "pure African blood," Scott could not be a citizen of Missouri and thus had no right to sue. Although from a slave state, the federal judge ruled that Scott could go to trial, reasoning he met the standard for a federal lawsuit: whether or not he enjoyed the rights of citizenship, he lived in Missouri and the defendant lived in another state. The ruling was no guarantee of success. Scott then lost at this trial, and his attorney sought new counsel and funding for an appeal to the U.S. Supreme Court. He found his man in Montgomery Blair, the son of Jacksonian editor and Maryland resident Francis Blair, and a former slave owner who disliked abolitionists but believed strongly in stopping the spread of slavery. Sanford's side brought in Henry Geyer, a Whig senator from Missouri, and Reverdy Johnson, a legendary lawyer from Maryland and former attorney general.

Thus, when *Dred Scott v. Sandford* reached the Supreme Court for argument in February 1856, it was no longer a legal question about one man's freedom, if that was all it had ever been. The case might well decide where slavery stopped and freedom began. It pitted Democrat against Whig, and antislavery Missourian and Marylander against proslavery Missourian and Marylander. It began before the Wilmot Proviso and appeared on the Supreme Court's docket in December 1854, after the repeal of the Missouri Compromise, which had been one of the issues in the case. It came before the justices during the political regrouping that followed the Kansas-Nebraska Act and as a presidential election approached. The lawyers' arguments reflected the changing political scene. Besides emphasizing Scott's residence in the state of Illinois instead of in a federal territory, Blair concentrated on defending Scott's right to sue. That would settle a question involving the rights of free and enslaved blacks and, if decided for Scott, gut the Fugitive Slave Law—a noble cause but a sign that Scott was, as Don Fehrenbacher wrote in his study of the case, "more clearly a pawn in the political game."[23]

For the moment, the Court decided not to decide. The justices asked the lawyers to reargue the case and planned to focus on whether Scott could sue and, if so, what should they say about a black man's right as a citizen to file a federal lawsuit? Blair added a co-counsel, George Ticknor Curtis, a Massachusetts Cotton Whig-turned-Democrat, but the arguments were predictable. Scott's attorneys pressed for his legal right to sue and congressional power to regulate slavery in the territories. Sanford's lawyers denied black citizenship, defended slavery, and claimed the Missouri Compromise had to be unconstitutional because Congress had no right to impede slavery's expansion. Afterward, Blair told Martin Van Buren, "It seems to be the impression that the Court will be adverse to my client and to the power of Congress over the Territories."[24]

Blair had good reason for that impression. Only two of the nine justices had any antislavery tendencies: John McLean had sought the Republican presidential nomination and had a long history of political intrigue, and Benjamin Curtis was a New Englander, but endorsed enforcement of the Fugitive Slave Act and thus might not be dependable on the subject. The two other northerners—Samuel Nelson of New York and Robert Grier of Pennsylvania—were Democrats with doughface inclinations. The other five justices provided a majority for the slave states: Taney, James Wayne of Georgia, and John Catron of Tennessee, all Andrew Jackson appointees; Peter Daniel, a Virginian named by Jackson's successor, Van Buren; and John Campbell of Alabama, Pierce's lone appointee.

The ninth justice, Taney, seemed more contradictory and more of a potential Scott sympathizer than he was. A Marylander born in 1777, he freed his slaves when he was young, and as a Catholic he had no use for nativism, which might have suggested that Scott had a chance. But as Jackson's attorney general, Taney wrote an unpublished opinion denying blacks had any rights as citizens, and his rulings as chief justice upheld slave owners' rights while doing little to benefit the cause of black freedom. Taney was less determined than his predecessor, John Marshall, to produce unanimity and avoid concurrences that blunted the main opinion or dissents that gave the losing side hope. But Taney never hesitated to use his power as chief justice in assigning opinions and controlling the issuing of the Court's rulings, as he would do in this case.

A states' rights Jacksonian, Taney could have kept the federal government out of an ostensibly local issue. But Jackson put the Union first when Calhoun and South Carolina claimed the right to nullify a federal law, and as president acted in accord with Chief Justice Marshall's declaration that the federal government, "though limited in its power, is supreme within its sphere of action." That led to two other issues. One, Taney wanted to end the slavery debate, much as Jackson settled the nullification controversy. Two, did the Constitution protect slavery? Taney's rulings leaned that way. As a southerner who saw northerners as attacking both slavery and southern society, Taney had moved toward Calhoun's view of slavery as a positive good and the South as deserving special protection. For northerners, Republicans or abolitionists—and to many southerners they were the same—to attack slavery was to attack all of the premises on which Taney had lived his 80 years when the time came for him to decide Dred Scott's fate.[25]

By the sensibilities of the time—and certainly those of a later era—the ruling was tainted. Each justice approached the issues differently. Taney, Wayne, Catron, Daniel, and Campbell—the five southerners—all wanted to decide against Scott, but the question was how. Nelson wrote an opinion with which they and Grier agreed, holding Scott remained a slave under Missouri law. But at Wayne's suggestion, the majority decided that Taney should write the main opinion and address other matters linked to the case: the legality of the Missouri Compromise and the issue of black citizenship. Alexander Stephens encouraged Wayne, his fellow Georgian, because he wanted those questions settled and, given the southern majority, expected the decision to go the South's way. That kind of discussion with an outsider would be unethical today and was dubious at the time. But neither side was virtuous: one of Scott's lawyers was Justice Curtis's brother (today the justice would recuse himself), and McLean had hoped for a decision in time for him to use his dissent as the basis for a presidential run in 1856.

The ethical quagmire associated with *Dred Scott v. Sandford* would thicken. As Taney wrote his opinion in February 1857, President-elect Buchanan mulled what to say about slavery in the territories in his inaugural address. He asked Catron, an old friend, whether a decision was near. The justice replied that the Court would avoid the territorial question. He then updated Buchanan on the new developments, which he blamed on McLean and Curtis wanting to address other issues. Not only did Catron divulge internal business, but he had been at best wrong and at worst dishonest about the reasons for the change. Worse, he suggested that with Nelson staking out his own position and Grier joining him, the Court would divide 5-4 by region. He hoped Buchanan would lean on his fellow Pennsylvanian—"drop Grier a line," adding later, "I want Grier *speeded.*" When Buchanan complied, Grier reported, "I am anxious that it should not appear that the line of latitude should mark the line of division in the court. I feel also that the opinion of the majority will fail of much of its effect if founded on clashing and inconsistent arguments," and so he would concur with the chief justice.

Inauguration Day, March 4, 1857, seemed to foreshadow better times; it was a warm day after a bitterly cold winter. After conversing briefly with Taney, who then administered the oath of office, Buchanan referred to slavery in the territories, setting the stage for a chill in some and fiery anger in others. "A difference of opinion has arisen in regard to the point of time when the people of a Territory shall decide this question for themselves," he said. "This is, happily, a matter of but little practical importance. Besides, it is a judicial question, which legitimately belongs to the Supreme Court of the United States, before whom it is now pending, and will, it is understood, be speedily and finally settled. To their decision, in common with all good citizens, I shall cheerfully submit, whatever this may be." But he already knew what their decision would be.[26]

Two days later, Taney delivered his opinion. The Court's decision denied blacks could be citizens and invalidated the Missouri Compromise or any other effort to limit the spread of slavery. He hoped to use the Court's prestige to end an increasingly violent debate. He failed; his task was impossible and his legal logic execrable. Taney's most infamous line was that blacks "had no rights which the white man was bound to respect," but his argument was even worse than his rhetoric. When the Constitution was written, he said, blacks were "considered as a subordinate and inferior class of beings, who had been subjugated by the dominant race, and, whether emancipated or not, yet remained subject to their authority," although free blacks could own property and vote in some states. By redefining what it meant to be a citizen of a state, he claimed Scott might be a citizen of Missouri but not of the United States. Free blacks had been citizens before and after the writing of the Constitution, but Taney contended they had been so few in 1787, they were "regarded as part of the slave population rather than the free." That was untrue, as was his proof: the clauses addressing the slave trade and fugitive slaves, which had nothing to do with free blacks. Referring to "the language of the Declaration of Independence and of the Articles of Confederation," Taney claimed they said something that they did not. He cherry-picked federal and state laws and executive actions, ignoring any that disproved his argument.[27]

More crucially, Taney wanted to decide whether Congress could interfere with the expansion of slavery—specifically, that it could not. To do so, he had to redefine the Constitution further. Article IV empowered Congress "to dispose of and make all needful rules and regulations respecting the territory or other property belonging to the United States." But according to Taney, that was true only of what belonged to the United States when the Constitution was ratified in 1789, meaning the federal government could regulate no territory it acquired afterward, including the Louisiana Purchase and the Mexican Cession. Besides, federal power over that territory would reduce its residents to the status of "mere colonists, dependent upon the will of the general government" when they were "on the same footing" as residents of states, and therefore Congress had no right to force them to do much of anything. Not only would that conclusion have surprised Taney's predecessors on the Supreme Court, not to mention the framers of the Constitution, but he also had just declared the already-repealed Missouri Compromise, the Republican party platform, and Douglas's popular sovereignty unconstitutional. Taney had tried to undo in one opinion what nearly 70 years of constitutional law had created.[28]

Understandably, Taney's majority was divided. Nelson's opinion more subtly echoed Taney's proslavery biases and arguments. Grier concurred with Taney's opinion. Other than Wayne, who joined Taney's ruling "without any qualification of its reasoning or its conclusions," the southern members disputed some of his conclusions. Daniel, so bitterly proslavery that he refused to cross the Mason-Dixon Line into the North, added that the Constitution gave slavery even more protection over other property than Taney claimed. Described in the *New York Tribune* as "a fire-eater of the blazing school," Campbell echoed Taney's views and unusual approach to legal argument and history by using arguments from Anti-Federalists to explain what the Constitution said and likening the Missouri Compromise to the measures the British passed in the years leading up to the American Revolution. Although agreeing with Taney's opposition to the Missouri Compromise and his decision in the Scott case, Catron contradicted the argument about whether Congress had power over territories—the most reasonable comment from the southern justices.[29]

If the majority's opinions proved controversial, the dissents created an uproar. McLean and Curtis agreed that Congress could regulate territories, and that slavery enjoyed no special protection, reversing Taney's argument by describing it as a creature of local law that could exist only with local action to protect it. To his claims "that a colored citizen would not be an agreeable member of society," McLean observed, "This is more a matter of taste than law." In turn, Curtis dismantled Taney's arguments. He noted that "in five of the thirteen original States, colored persons then possessed the elective franchise. . . . If so, it is not true, in point of fact, that the Constitution was made exclusively by the white race. And that it was made exclusively for the white race is, in my opinion, not only an assumption not warranted by anything in the Constitution, but contradicted by its opening declaration that it was ordained and established by the people of the United States, for themselves and their posterity." Because Scott wed in Wisconsin and Missouri had no right to ignore a lawful marriage, Curtis described the nuptials as "an effectual act of emancipation." Nor, McLean and Curtis agreed, could Scott's return to Missouri mean that he returned to slavery. Fehrenbacher noted the contradiction: southerners often accused northerners of stretching the law and politics to attack slavery and claimed to be constitutional conservatives, but McLean and Curtis had relied on the document and precedents whereas Taney and his majority simply did what they had to do to make the law suit their biases.[30]

Beyond the legal debate, controversy also followed publication of the opinions. Taney read his opinion aloud on March 6 but declined to submit it for publication. McLean and Curtis went ahead, and their opinions soon appeared in the northern press alongside blistering attacks on the chief justice. Then, Taney violated the Court's usual procedures by changing his opinion to answer the dissenters. When Curtis requested a copy of his opinion, Taney refused, accusing Curtis of wanting it for political purposes to use against him and the Court. The two exchanged bitter letters. Taney unquestionably changed his opinion from when he originally read it, adding text and footnotes to try to rebut Curtis. Already unhappy with his financial sacrifice in giving up his law practice to become a justice, Curtis considered their relationship and the Court's atmosphere so poisoned that he resigned and returned to Massachusetts. He later became a critic of the war powers exercised by Abraham Lincoln—joining in the criticism from, among others, Taney.

With the Blow family obtaining them, Dred Scott and his family became free anyway. Scott died the next year, but that attracted far less attention than his case. For the first time since Marshall's opinion in *Marbury v. Madison,* the high court overturned a federal law, and in doing so stood history and precedent on their heads. Taney's career as chief justice had excited little political comment, but instead of calming the waters, he now roiled them. Although the Court had yet to achieve exalted status as the final arbiter of all constitutional matters, it received widespread respect. Taney's actions harmed the institution enough that a senator later introduced a bill to abolish it, and attorneys—including Lincoln—argued more strongly than ever that the Court was an interpreter of the law, but not final or infallible. During the Civil War, Republicans passed legislation outlawing slavery in the territories without even referring to the case. Yet the Court retained enough public respect that Republicans sought the passage of the Thirteenth Amendment, and, during Reconstruction, the Fourteenth and Fifteenth Amendments, to overturn the decision and any possibility that it could curtail black Americans' rights.

Predictably, southerners hailed the opinion, Republicans excoriated it, and northern Democrats thought it best to accept it as the law of the land. On both sides of the debate, legislatures and party conventions passed resolutions and legal analysts poured forth pamphlets. But Fehrenbacher detected an oddity in the critiques: "The race question tended to unite Democrats and divide Republicans, whereas the slavery question tended to divide Democrats and unite Republicans." Republicans shared opposition to the growth of slavery but split on what rights African Americans should enjoy, whereas Democrats had no use for them as a race but varied in their feelings about slavery. Thus, the Republican assault on Taney's opinion concentrated on whether Congress could limit the institution's spread into the western territories, not the issue of black citizenship.[31]

One reason for Republican caution was that while the party dished out vitriol toward Taney, it also had to take it from his defenders. They claimed Republicans ginned up the case, especially after it turned out Emerson's widow had married a Republican congressman. They accused Republicans of proving through their criticism of Taney that they had no respect for the law and supported "revolution and anarchy." Worse, one critic claimed, "They hate the Constitution, the Bible and God." Senator James Mason of Virginia, the author of the Fugitive Slave Act of 1850, expected Taney's opinion to be "too strong for stomachs debilitated by the sickly sensibilities of a depraved morality."[32]

Republicans saw Taney, his majority, and their ideology as depraved, and made no effort to hide their feelings. Greeley's *Tribune* was especially important. Not only did it reach more readers than any Republican publication, but it also reduced Taney's influence by hammering his "wicked," "atrocious," "abominable," and "detestable" ruling and describing it as "entitled to just so much moral weight as would be the judgment of a majority of those congregated in any Washington barroom." Abolitionist clergy attacked the Court from the pulpit. William Cullen Bryant, the *New York Evening Post* editor who once shared Taney's commitment to Jacksonian Democracy, branded the majority "men who alter our constitution for us, who find in it what no man of common sense, reading it for himself, could ever find, what its framers never thought of putting into it, what no man discerned in it till a very few years since it was seen, with aid of optics sharpened by the eager desire to preserve the political ascendancy of the slave states."[33]

Republicans saw symbolic significance in the ruling, and their response affected their message and ideology. Some argued that because the Court denied Scott's right to sue, anything Taney said was *obiter dictum,* Latin for a statement made in passing—in other words, Taney's opinion had no legal standing. But others saw it as what Kenneth Stampp called "the last in a chain of sinister events . . . part of a conspiracy promoted by the southern Slave Power and assisted by its northern doughface allies." Lincoln perfectly expressed what Republicans saw as more possible than unlikely: "We shall *lie down* pleasantly dreaming that the people of *Missouri* are on the verge of making their State *free;* and we shall awake to the *reality,* instead, that the *Supreme* Court has made *Illinois* a *slave* State." Whether or not southerners really expected slavery to spread into northern states, the case armed Republicans against northern and southern critics alike. Republicans wanted to protect the country and Constitution as they were, party faithful said, but proslavery forces felt otherwise—and *Dred Scott* was the proof.[34]

These fears paled in comparison with the deeper meaning Republicans ascribed to the opinion. The *Cincinnati Commercial* said, "It is now demonstrated that there is such a thing as the Slave Power," and Republicans increasingly argued in favor of a slave power conspiracy, beyond the exchange between Buchanan and Taney at the inauguration. "We can not absolutely *know* that all these exact adaptations are the result of preconcert. But when we see a lot of framed timbers, different portions of which we know have been gotten out at different times and places and by different workmen—Stephen, Franklin, Roger, and James, for instance," Lincoln observed, "and when we see these timbers joined together, and see they exactly make the frame of a house or a mill . . . in *such* a case, we find it impossible to not *believe* that Stephen and Franklin and Roger and James all understood one another from the beginning, and all worked upon a common *plan* or *draft* drawn up before the first lick was struck." His workmen—Douglas, Pierce, Taney, and Buchanan—came from northern or border states, but that was the Republican interpretation: southerners promoting a slave power conspiracy that northern acquiescence made possible. Some northerners even feared the Slave Power would use Taney's ruling as a means of reopening the African slave trade.[35]

Leading the Republican charge even more ardently than Lincoln, Seward saw a clearer conspiracy between Buchanan and Taney. On inauguration day, with the public "unaware of the import of the whisperings carried on between the President and the Chief Justice," Buchanan "announced (vaguely, indeed, but with self-satisfaction) the forthcoming extra-judicial exposition of the Constitution, and pledged his submission to it as authoritative and final. . . . It cost the President, under the circumstances, little exercise of magnanimity now to promise to the people of Kansas, on whose neck he had, with the aid of the Supreme Court, hung the mill-stone of slavery, a fair trial in their attempt to cast it off." The day after the inauguration, the justices paid their traditional visit to the White House, Seward said, "without even exchanging their silken robes for courtiers' gowns. . . . Doubtless the President received them as graciously as Charles I did the judges who had, at his instance, subverted the statutes of English liberty." Democrats howled, and Taney was so offended that he later said if Seward had been elected president in 1860, he would have refused to administer the oath of office. But Seward was more correct than even he could have realized at the time.[36]

Lincoln and Seward were more certain about Democrats than Democrats were. They, too, denied that the opinion mattered, even if they failed to realize they were saying so. Douglas warned that "whoever resists the final decision of the highest judicial tribunal, aims a deadly blow at our whole republican system of government—a blow, which if successful, would place all our rights and liberties at the mercy of passion, anarchy and violence." But after assailing Republicans for questioning the decision's finality, he did it himself. Taking a slave into a territory "necessarily remains a barren and a worthless right, unless sustained, protected and enforced by appropriate police regulations and local legislation, prescribing adequate remedies for its violation. These regulations and remedies must necessarily depend entirely upon the will and wishes of the people of the territory as they can only be prescribed by the local legislatures," he argued. "Hence the great principle of popular sovereignty and self-government is sustained and firmly established by the authority of this decision," a conclusion he could reach only if he twisted the facts as much as Taney did, but in the opposite direction.[37]

Douglas's appearance prompted two Republican speeches in response. The more popular came from his Senate colleague, Lyman Trumbull, who declared, "I utterly repudiate this extra judicial, sectional opinion. . . . I appeal to a power higher and above even this court of last resort, whose name is 'The People,' and who will, I trust, in due time reform this sectional court by increasing the number of Judges, or otherwise placing upon the bench a fair proportion of Northern members." Less popular with more vocal antislavery Republicans was Lincoln's reply, which flayed

Douglas: "He denounces all who question the correctness of that decision, as offering violent resistance to it. But who resists it?" Enjoying the opportunity to skewer both Taney and Douglas, Lincoln pointed out that the Little Giant adored Andrew Jackson, who ignored the Supreme Court and doubted the constitutionality of the Bank of the United States, which the Marshall Court upheld as legal. Lincoln also tried to insulate Republicans against the common, politically vexatious Democratic claim that they believed in racial equality while appealing to those in his party who did feel that way. "I protest against that counterfeit logic which concludes that, because I do not want a black woman for a *slave* I must necessarily want her for a *wife*. I need not have her for either," he said. "I can just leave her alone. In some respects she certainly is not my equal; but in her natural right to eat the bread she earns with her own hands without asking leave of any one else, she is my equal, and the equal of all others."[38]

Dred Scott—the man and the case—became a pivot on which several politicians and issues turned, beyond the respect that Taney's abuse of history and power cost the Court. The opinion and the appearance of a conspiracy leading up to it ruined the already minimal chance that Republicans would support anything Buchanan did. The fate of Kansas remained as puzzling and troubling as before. The strained relations between Buchanan and Douglas, and their supporters, stretched even thinner. Republicans gained a new issue, Douglas faced new obstacles to the idea of popular sovereignty to which he had tied his national political future, and in Illinois, Lincoln was warming up for a campaign that eventually would help rocket him to the presidency.

Six

⤜⟡⤏

GREAT DEBATES AND GREATER DEBATES

On October 25, 1858, in the midst of congressional and state elections, William Henry Seward addressed a crowd in Rochester, New York. He said nothing new. His speech was antislavery and politically to the point; it was scholarly, demonstrating his learning and intellect but revealing none of Seward the political operator or convivial dinner guest. He traced the history of slavery around the world before turning to the origins of the northern free labor ideology and its superiority to the South's economic and social system. He condemned slavery for what it did not only to the slave, but also to "the freeman, to whom, only because he is a laborer from necessity, it denies facilities for employment, and whom it expels from the community because it cannot enslave and convert into merchandise also." Worse, the slave and free states and their "antagonistic systems are continually coming into closer contact, and collision results. Shall I tell you what this collision means?" he asked. His answer proved to be perhaps the most controversial words he ever uttered: "It is an irrepressible conflict between opposing and enduring forces, and it means that the United States must and will, sooner or later, become either entirely a slaveholding nation, or entirely a free-labor nation." Because so many refused to face these facts, their efforts at compromise proved "vain and ephemeral. Startling as this saying may appear to you, fellow-citizens, it is by no means an original or even a modern one."[1]

Indeed it was not. When southerners and their northern sympathizers flayed Seward for describing an "irrepressible conflict," he and his supporters had every reason to be surprised. Not only had he said much the same thing before, but other Republicans often implied the existence of such a conflict. That May, Philemon Bliss, a congressman from Ohio, had described the battle as not between North and South but as "between systems, between civilizations." Boston editor William Schouler distinguished between "two kinds of civilization in this country. One is the civilization of freedom, and the other is the civilization of aristocracy, of slavery." More memorably, only five months before, a less-known, less radical Republican said something similar in Illinois. On June 16, the Republican state convention having nominated him for U.S. senator, Abraham Lincoln declared, "'A house divided against itself cannot stand.' I believe this government cannot endure, permanently half *slave* and half *free*. I do not expect the Union to be *dissolved*—I do not expect the house to *fall*—but I *do* expect it will cease to be divided. It will become *all* one thing, or *all* the other."[2]

Believing that the Slave Power was in control of the government and determined to retain that control, Republicans had voiced conspiracy theories about slavery before and continued to do so. But Democrats showed signs of more cracks in their already crumbling foundation over the issues that Republicans described. By 1858, the battle over Kansas had soiled James Buchanan and further divided Democrats, providing Republicans with an opportunity for political gain but a dilemma over how much to emphasize the conflict between the sections. Where it would end was unclear, but at the end of his "irrepressible conflict" speech, Seward had said, "I know, and you know, that a revolution has begun. I know, and all the world knows, that revolutions never go backward." At least, so Republicans hoped. The question was how revolutionary they were, would be, and could be.

PANICS: MONEY AND A MASSACRE

While Buchanan tried to navigate the slavery issue, he faced an economic crisis not of his own doing—and did little about it. Not that that made him unusual at the time, politically or ideologically. While some northerners debated whether Congress could legislate against slavery in western territories, few saw any need for the federal government to impose itself on industry. When Salmon Chase, who considered himself a truer Democrat than those who stayed in the party, suggested railroad regulation in a gubernatorial message to Ohio's Republican-dominated legislature, his supporters ignored him while Democrats attacked him. Given their previous party's history, Whigs-turned-Republicans had no objection to federal involvement in the economy. But many preferred not to roil their new party when the coalition had started so successfully and seemed so tenuous. Meanwhile, Buchanan's southern constituents objected strongly enough to the federal government telling them what to do about slaves that they felt no differently about interference with the economy.

Over the past decade, while slavery and territorial expansion became the overriding issues, a variety of factors seemed to have assured American prosperity. In 1846, Great Britain had repealed its protective Corn Laws, promoting free trade that benefited the United States. In addition, the Mexican-American War aided economic and industrial growth, as wars often do. Immigration from Europe and emigration to California provided workers, making factories hum, and gold fields enhanced the money supply, international trade, and the banking industry. Unfortunately, those gold exports served mainly to make up for an unfavorable balance of trade, so more of it went toward paying debts than buying or making new products. The illusion and reality of prosperity inspired the opening of undercapitalized, under-regulated banks and a great deal of land and stock speculation. In 1854, a downturn drove down stock prices and forced dozens of banks out of business. In Europe, the Crimean War, pitting Great Britain and France against Russia, created an artificial boom for American products, but investments in Europe to fund the war harmed American markets already tied to British lenders and speculators, and created opportunities for overzealous American lenders and speculators.

In the spring and summer of 1857, the bubble began to burst. Speculation drove cotton prices so high that textile manufacturers and sellers were paralyzed. Planters bought as much cheap land as they could to produce as much as they could. On land values, North and South could agree: improvements in machinery and high food prices prompted northern farmers to speculate in land, just like their southern counterparts. Banks expanded so quickly that their debts far outran their assets. Then, in August, one of New York City's oldest grain and flour firms, N.H. Wolfe, collapsed, followed by the Ohio Life Insurance and Trust Company, which was not an insurance business but a major Wall Street bank. Within a month, bankruptcy claimed the Illinois Central Railroad, banks across the country stopped payments, and the problems in major western cities such as Chicago and St. Louis signified the ripple effect of the economic calamities afflicting the East.

Buchanan's administration was alternately responsive and muddled. Secretary of the Treasury Howell Cobb, usually a moderate states' rights southerner but hardening on slavery, had no problem redeeming federal bonds and minting more gold coins to combat the panic. His actions helped stem the tide but did little to turn it. When New York City's jobless overwhelmed relief agencies and assaulted federal offices in hopes of removing money from their vaults, Buchanan sent soldiers and marines to stop them, showing a decisiveness that seemed lacking when southern states seceded in 1860 and 1861. When some ex-Whigs called for a new national bank, Buchanan argued that the panic resulted "solely from our extravagant and vicious system of paper currency and bank credits, exciting the people to wild speculations and gambling in stocks," and fell back on Jacksonian ideology in demanding an end to all paper currency.[3]

The panic also affected the political parties. Local Democratic politicians, especially in New York City, responded vigorously to calls for help from the unemployed and earned loyalty, especially from recent working-class immigrants. The Democrats' response, combined with advocacy of white laborers and criticism of Republicans for seeming more concerned with black laborers, paid off for urban Democrats on Election Day for decades to come. In turn, Republicans thought more legislatively than socially and individually, perhaps a residual connection to the Whig party's difficulties in appealing to a wide spectrum. They pushed for a homestead act to encourage western settlement and farming, easing the pressure on cities and industries. They also relied increasingly on the thinking of economist Henry Carey, whose calls for a higher tariff might attract protectionist Pennsylvania to their party. Both of these positions, especially protectionism, had the potential to exacerbate internal party tensions and provoke southerners into stronger denunciations of the North and the rapidly expanding Republican party.

While the recovery had begun by the early spring of 1858, due mainly to gold pouring into eastern financial centers from Europe and California, the panic's impact extended beyond economics. Relying on slavery and plantation agriculture, southerners suffered less than the more industrial, free labor North, convincing them that their economy was strong and their system better than the North's—and that spreading that system would be better for all. As the North tried to recoup its losses, South Carolina's James Henry Hammond, already a leading architect of the South's defenses of slavery, rose in the Senate that March 4 and delivered a wide-ranging speech. He accused the North of breaking its pledges and viewing the South as a colony, and assured his listeners that they were in no danger because whenever the South "has seized her sword it has been on the point of honor, and that point of honor has been mainly loyalty to her sister colonies and sister States, who have ever since plundered and calumniated her." Besides, he continued, "you dare not make war on cotton. No power on earth dares make war upon it. Cotton is king."[4]

Although part of his argument was economic, Hammond sought mainly to counter the perception of the North's free labor society as superior to the South's, based as it was on slavery. He told the Senate that "the greatest strength of the South arises from the harmony of her political and social institutions. This harmony gives her a frame of society, the best in the world, and an extent of political freedom, combined with entire security, such as no other people ever enjoyed upon the face of the earth. . . . The South, so far as that is concerned, is satisfied, content, happy, harmonious, and prosperous." Beyond defending the South, though, he also aimed to spotlight the North's hypocrisy and failings. "In all social systems there must be a class to do the mean duties to perform the drudgery of life. . . . It constitutes the very mud-sills of society and of political government . . . ," he said. "The difference between us is, that our slaves are hired for life and well compensated; there is no starvation, no begging, no want of employment among our people, and not too much employment either. Yours are hired by the day, not cared for, and scantily compensated. . . . Your slaves are white, of your own race; you are brothers of one blood." Horace Greeley's *New York Tribune* dismissed his views as "the sentiment of all aristocracies," and Henry Raymond's *New York Times* said, "It would be easy to go on and show that nothing can be more fallacious than the idea that the wealth and production of Free States in modern times can possibly depend upon any single branch of industry, and so to disabuse the Cottonocracy of their natural but untenable delusion in regard to the importance of their pet staple to the perpetuity of the universe."[5]

The *Chicago Daily Tribune's* editors detected something else in the speech. Perhaps their different reaction was due partly to their westernness: although the westward expansion of slavery was central to Republican ideology, the party's leadership tended to be eastern in its orientation. "In the Northern or Free States, there are more than two millions of families, numbering at least twelve millions of people, whose avocation is farming. And taken as a whole, they are independent, wealthy, intelligent, and happy. They are the yeomanry of the land—the back-bone of the nation, either in peace or war," the *Tribune* said. "They own enough property to buy out all the plantations in the South, with their gangs of slaves on them. As a class they are far better educated than the slave holders themselves; they are more refined, moral and honest; they are self-reliant, self-supporting, brave, generous and free. It is this mighty mass of men— the finest specimens of the human race in the attributes of mind and manhood, whom the supercilious Carolina negro driver denominates the mud sills of society! . . ." The *Tribune's* editors defended the northern free laborer's honor, and with it a key component of Republican thought. They also had provided another means for their party to appeal to an electorate that might have lacked sympathy for the slave's plight or interest in weighty matters of governance and cultural analysis, but certainly resented the South's masters dismissing them as unimportant and enslaved.[6]

As the panic unfolded, Buchanan confronted an issue involving a panic of a different kind with a far less happy ending. When he took office, Utah's territorial governor was Mormon leader Brigham Young. According to Buchanan's annual message of December 1857, Utah's almost completely Mormon population obeyed "his commands as if these were direct revelations from Heaven. If, therefore, he chooses that his government shall come into collision with the Government of the United States, the members of the Mormon church will yield implicit obedience to his will." Any federal official who challenged or questioned him felt unsafe under his "despotism." As president, Buchanan said, "I was bound to restore the supremacy of the Constitution and laws within its limits. . . ." He considered Mormon practices "deplorable in themselves and revolting to the moral and religious sentiments of all Christendom," but they were, he said, not at issue."[7]

More accurately, neither Millard Fillmore nor Franklin Pierce considered Utah worth too much trouble, but soon after taking office, Buchanan dispatched Alfred Cumming to replace Young. How much Cumming exaggerated his problems is open to conjecture. Clearly, Mormons were used to obeying Young, whether he led the territorial government or their church, and they continued to do so. Federal appointees before Cumming's arrival believed that Young and his followers were in revolt against the United States and so informed Buchanan. Acting with what would prove to be unusual decisiveness, Buchanan sent the army west that summer to bring Mormons to heel. Neither side shed blood, but it took until the summer of 1858 before the so-called "Mormon War" ended. Cumming remained governor and Young acknowledged his power, except when he preferred not to do so.

Although politicians of all stripes—Democrat and Republican, northerner and southerner—regularly condemned Mormons as outlaws for their belief in plural marriage and seemingly clannish ways, the frayed nerves afflicting the country showed that Mormons and their critics had more in common than they might have liked to ponder. In the spring of 1857, a Mormon apostle traveling in Missouri and Arkansas died, the victim of vigilante justice. The circumstances differed, but the murder brought back unpleasant memories of the mob that killed church founder Joseph Smith in Illinois in 1844. The arrival of an emigrant party from Missouri and Arkansas convinced some Mormons that another invading army was on the way. Early in September 1857, dressed like Indians, they attacked the wagon train at Mountain Meadows in southern Utah. They killed approximately 120 adults and older children, took the younger children into the church, and tried to pin the blame on nearby Native Americans. It took 20 years of controversy and investigation before one of those involved, John D. Lee, went to the gallows for his role. Nevertheless, the Mountain Meadows Massacre remained controversial because Mormons claimed church leaders played no role in the massacre. Like the northerners and southerners they often condemned for their criticism, Mormons were not alone in suspecting the worst of others, or being suspected of the worst.

A book—less popular and controversial than *Uncle Tom's Cabin* but important in its own right—contributed to impassioned rhetoric between North and South. In *The Impending Crisis of the South,* North Carolina-born poor white Hinton Helper wrote, "Non-slaveholders of the South! Farmers, mechanics and workingmen, we take this occasion to assure you that the slaveholders, the arrant demagogues whom you have elected to offices of honor and profit, have hoodwinked you, trifled with you, and used you as mere consummation of their wicked designs." His "mixture of roaring polemics and plodding statistics," as Sean Wilentz has called it, claimed that slave owners sought to control both their slaves and southern yeomen, and that the solution was to emancipate slaves and return them to Africa. What proved most striking was not what Helper said, but what southerners did in response to him, Harriet Beecher Stowe, and other critics. By the late 1850s, every state that later

seceded in the winter of 1860–61 passed a law limiting the distribution of antislavery literature. Southerners decided to protect slavery at all costs, perhaps at the cost
of the freedom in which they professed to believe so strongly.[8]

BLEEDING KANSAS REVISITED

After the Sack of Lawrence and John Geary's arrival as governor, Kansas seemed
quiet in the spring and summer of 1856, and Buchanan hoped to keep it that way
after taking office. But the circumstances of his election—and Buchanan himself—
conspired against that goal. Without such strong southern support, he would have
faced the ignominy of losing to a brand-new political party in its first presidential
election. Accordingly, Buchanan proved more loyal to southern Democrats than to
his party in general, a trend that continued in his policies toward Kansas. Although
his reputation as a president has suffered more for his actions after the 1860 election,
what he did about Dred Scott in 1857 and Kansas in 1857 and 1858 helped seal his
and his country's fate.

At first, Buchanan seemed to move Kansas the right way. Having deployed an
iron fist to stop the fighting, Geary resigned in disgust when proslavery legislators
overrode his veto of a bill to keep control of the voting in the hands of proslavery
county sheriffs, which would have assured the proslavery constitution's passage. To
succeed him, the president turned to Robert J. Walker, who seemed likelier to use
the velvet glove. A Pennsylvanian like Buchanan, he moved to Mississippi, speculated
in slaves while freeing his own, and won a Senate seat. As secretary of the Treasury,
he served with Buchanan in James Polk's cabinet, where he pushed through a reduced
tariff and a subtreasury system to involve the federal government in the financial system without going as far as Whigs who were seeking the national bank's return. He
also maneuvered the financing of the Mexican-American War. Then he returned to
Mississippi, where he grew wealthier and more influential behind the scenes in the
Democratic party. A defender of slavery, he backed the Compromise of 1850—he
and Douglas had become close friends—and thought slavery had to end, albeit in
tandem with newly freed slaves leaving the United States. Walker's appointment
seemed inspired: a Jacksonian, a respected northerner gone south, proslavery yet conscious of the institution's evils. He accepted only after Buchanan assured him that he
wanted a fair vote in Kansas. They shared the goal the president hoped to attain with
the Dred Scott decision: eliminating slavery from national discourse. That first failure proved a harbinger of the next failure.

Walker was prepared when he arrived in Kansas in May 1857. He had met with
Democrats and Republicans en route from Washington, D.C., and voiced his desire
for a fair election. He delivered an inaugural address he ran past Buchanan and
Douglas, with the latter's influence perhaps explaining his declaration that "in no con-
tingency will Congress admit Kansas as a slave state or free state, unless a majority of

the people shall first have fairly and freely decided this question for themselves by a direct vote on the adoption of the Constitution, excluding all fraud or violence." As Thomas Jefferson and Daniel Webster suggested in different contexts, he noted that its climate and crops made Kansas unsuitable for slavery, which could "no more be controlled by the legislation of man than any other moral or physical law of the Almighty." He also warned Kansans to obey the Fugitive Slave Act of 1850. All of which suggested his desire for a middle ground and revealed how out of touch he was with the bulk of southerners, who increasingly believed slavery itself had to grow and found any middle ground unacceptable. After surveying his surroundings, Walker apprised Buchanan that he enjoyed majority support, except for "restless men on both sides who desire revolution." Hoping to make Kansas a balance wheel between proslavery and antislavery Democrats, he tried to keep those groups in Kansas from going too far. He assured them of his support from Buchanan, who told him that "the institutions of Kansas must be established by the votes of the people."[9]

The first sign of failure—or the buzzsaw Walker had walked into—came in mid-June 1857 with the election of a constitutional convention for Kansas. Walker demanded a fair election and claimed he could use his authority as territorial governor to assure it. With the South determined to spread slavery westward and protect its institution, Walker's requirement meant trouble. First, in southern minds, for the federal government's representative in Kansas to dictate any kind of behavior contradicted the notion of states' rights—never mind that Kansas was not yet a state. Also, for a Democrat to interfere in democracy was antidemocratic, even to assure fairness, and if that notion seemed ridiculous, it suggested how determined and contradictory southerners could be in their quest to expand slavery. Worse, antislavery forces declined to trust anyone who suggested fair treatment of or by the proslavery side. Thus, Kansas Free-Soilers refused to participate because the legislature set up the districts to assure a proslavery victory. Proslavery forces voted but assailed Walker, as did many southern politicians and editors, for impartiality in demanding fair and free elections and partiality in claiming that climate or anything else could constrain slavery. This had been the belief of earlier generations of southerners, and still represented the hope of those in the Upper South not completely reconciled to slavery. But to the Lower or Deep South, Walker threatened its prosperity, if not its social system. That was unacceptable.[10]

The October legislative election only made matters worse. The magnitude of the proslavery victory prompted Walker to investigate. During the 1850s, the growth of urban and immigrant populations contributed to increased corruption in cities across the country, but what Walker found was egregious. In one precinct of six houses, proslavery candidates received 1,628 votes, or 271 per home; one list of returns consisted of names copied from a Cincinnati directory, all in the same handwriting; and an area with 100 qualified voters cast nearly 1,300 ballots, almost all proslavery. When Walker tossed those results, Free-Soilers took control of the territorial legislature.

Combined with his earlier request for troops to deal with a minor incident—some Lawrence residents tried to form their own municipal government and he overdramatized the situation—Walker had proven his fairness and willingness to court controversy. Proslavery Kansans also dug in their heels: they wanted to send the existing Lecompton Constitution directly to Congress.

Buchanan and his cabinet wanted to avoid controversy, but this time they saw no choice but to seek it. In the summer of 1857, Democrats gained 10 House seats in elections in Kentucky, Tennessee, North Carolina, and Missouri, all slave states. For Buchanan and other party leaders, gains in Democratic legislative seats, whether filled by southerners or northerners, indicated that their pro-South policies were working and suggested that anything that made the South happy would benefit them politically. Between the outcry from Georgia and exchanges with relatives in Mississippi, Cobb turned against Walker. No cabinet member was closer to or more influential with Buchanan than was Cobb, unless it was Attorney General Jeremiah Black, who, as Allan Nevins put it, "regarded freesoilers much like rattlesnakes." One southerner described Buchanan as "thoroughly panic-stricken." If so, an editorial in the *Chicago Times,* widely known as Douglas's voice, gave him more reason to feel that way. It anticipated the pending constitutional convention in Kansas by declaring that "any attempt to force a pro-slavery constitution upon the people without an opportunity of voting it down at the polls will be regarded, after the recent expression of sentiment, as so undecidedly unjust, oppressive, and unworthy of a free people, that the people of the United States will not sanction it. . . . As Kansas must be a free State, even those persons in the Territory who are known as pro-slavery men must recognize in the late election a decision which must not be slighted. . . ."[11]

But it would be slighted. Proslavery delegates—"broken-down political hacks, demagogues, fire-eaters, perjurers, ruffians, ballot-box stuffers, and loafers," said an antislavery correspondent—rammed through the Lecompton Constitution, which any southern rights advocate could love. "The right of property is before and higher than any constitutional sanction," said the preamble, reversing Seward's pronouncement in 1850 of a "higher law than the Constitution" by making that higher law the protector of slavery, "and the right of the owner of a slave to such slave and its increase is the same and as inviolable as the right of the owner of any property whatever." The document excluded free blacks from Kansas (as did the Topeka free-state constitution), required the Fugitive Slave Act to be strictly obeyed, and banned legislators from emancipating slaves already in Kansas. It would go before the people for a vote, but not as Douglas and other believers in popular sovereignty would have done it: voters could choose between "the constitution with slavery" and "the constitution without slavery." The constitution would go directly to Congress for consideration, and where slavery already existed, it could continue—the South's fallback position on popular sovereignty.[12]

For the most part, the parties and regions responded predictably. Republicans assailed the constitution, its authors, and anyone associated with it. The deeper in the South they lived, the more ardently southerners endorsed the document and the prospective state, but the entire region seemed united in demanding a slave Kansas. Rumors spread that if Congress and the administration decided against them, several southern states might secede. Buchanan should have been worried that among northern Democrats, widespread criticism of the convention and its results showed the primacy of Douglas's approach to popular sovereignty. Worst of all for Buchanan, his old friend John Forney resented the president's failure to reward him for his support before and after the election. Able at both politics and propaganda, Forney decamped for Philadelphia, opened a new newspaper, and tore into the Lecompton Constitution, its authors, and anyone who dared to support it.

Buchanan dared. As Walker left Kansas for the East Coast on November 17, 1857, apparently for personal and health reasons and to lobby, the administration's organ, the *Washington Union,* endorsed the Lecompton Constitution. Southerners in the cabinet, led by Cobb, defended the document and its supporters. Reports spread that Cobb ordered a moderate editorial on Kansas removed from the *Union,* and he or fellow southerner Jacob Thompson, the secretary of the interior, leaked the news that Buchanan would remove Walker. The president may have been putty in Cobb's hands, or gambling that Cobb's comparative moderation would help him keep the most ardent states' rights Democrats loyal to the party or the Union, or simply in agreement with the proslavery forces. But, any which way, the president was boxed in, by design or accident, and seemed to have no interest in finding his way out. Any choice he made would alienate someone; the question was whom he could least afford to antagonize.

When Congress met that December, Buchanan's annual message revealed his choice. He took credit for restoring calm by overcoming a "revolutionary organization," he said, "whose avowed object it was, if need be, to put down the lawful government by force, and to establish a government of their own under the so-called Topeka constitution," but ignored the lawlessness of the border ruffians. Repeating his instructions to Walker in favor of a popular vote free from interference, he disclaimed any "intention to interfere with the decision of the people of Kansas, either for or against slavery. From this I have always carefully abstained," which was no longer true. The Kansas-Nebraska Act sought "not to legislate slavery into any Territory or State, nor to exclude it therefrom, but to leave the people thereof perfectly free to form and regulate their domestic institutions . . . ," which, he explained, "are limited to the family. The relation between master and slave and a few others are 'domestic institutions,' and are entirely distinct from institutions of a political character"—given the habits of some owners visiting slave quarters, a deliciously ironic comment. Ignoring how the constitution was written and the legacy of violence in Kansas, he proclaimed, "At this election every citizen will have an opportunity of expressing his opinion by his vote 'whether Kansas shall be received into the Union with or without slavery,' and thus this exciting question may be peacefully settled in the very mode required by the organic law." The election, he claimed, would thus be legitimate.[13]

The consequences of the vote were obvious. With antislavery forces staying home, the constitution passed, 6,266–567. Two weeks later, conducting their own vote, Free-Soilers turned it down, 10,226–162, meaning more than 60 percent of those who voted in Kansas opposed slavery. In March, southern, Democratic, and dough-faced senators voted 33–25 to accept the proslavery constitution, but the dissenters included two old Whigs from the upper South, Kentuckian John Crittenden and Tennessean John Bell. On April 1, the House voted down Lecompton, 120–112. While northern Republicans and just under half of northern Democrats were part of the majority, five border-state former Whigs swung the vote against the proslavery side. Southerners tried to pass legislation sidestepping Lecompton, but Kansas would remain a territory until after southern secession.

For the South, it was a horrifying moment. Deep southerners, aware of the North's growth, had counted on regional unity, and the border state votes showed them that even their region was divided. Worse, many Southerners believed that they needed to find new slave territory to the west, for new lands for crops and to expand and protect their slave investments. Accordingly, they looked longingly toward the Caribbean in hopes of acquiring more slave territory. William Walker, the "gray-eyed man of destiny" who had invaded Nicaragua, was the most famous filibusterer, but not the only one: a dozen times during the rest of the decade, southerners or their hirelings landed in Cuba and other Latin American countries in hopes of gobbling up land for a slaveholding empire. They failed, and probably were surprised to find little support even in pockets of the Deep South, where some of the most determined advocates of slavery and southern rights saw no reason to expand a Union they increasingly wanted to leave. They also talked more openly about reopening the African slave trade or even reenslaving free blacks in the South—which, some hoped, would repulse the North, divide Democrats still further, and promote disunion.

But the only disunion at that point was among Democrats. When Congress began its next session in December, Stephen Douglas arrived furious at Buchanan and his allies for perverting popular sovereignty, accepting anything less than a fair vote in Kansas, and attacking his friend Walker. Douglas had never shied away from a fight and was primed for another one. To his close friend, fellow Illinois Democrat John McClernand, he wrote, "We must stand on the popular sovereignty principle and go wherever the logical consequences may carry us, and defend it against *all assaults* from whatever quarter."[14]

To another Illinoisan, Douglas harkened to his withdrawal from the race for the Democratic nomination in 1856 and revealed that a Little Giant could have a big ego: "I will show you that I will do what I promised. By God, sir, I made Mr. James

Buchanan, and by God, sir, I will unmake him!" At a White House meeting, Douglas, the chairman of the Senate Committee on Territories and thus someone worth consulting on such matters, learned that Buchanan would support the Lecompton Constitution in his annual message. Douglas said, "If you do, I will denounce it the moment your message is read." Finally, Buchanan said, "Mr. Douglas, I desire you to remember that no Democrat ever yet differed from an Administration of his own choice without being crushed," which had the virtue of being untrue, and added, "Beware the fate of Tallmadge and Rives," two opponents of Andrew Jackson who achieved limited success in the Democratic party and did no better when they joined the Whigs. Douglas replied, "Mr. President, I wish you to remember that General Jackson is dead."[15]

The parallels were lacking—Douglas was no Tallmadge or Rives, both minor figures in comparison, and Buchanan was no Jackson—but past and present had met. Despite Buchanan's invocation of Jackson, Douglas saw himself as representing what the Democratic party had been: the embodiment of the Jacksonian ideal of rule by the people. Buchanan stood for what the Democratic party had become: a proslavery, states' rights party dominated by southerners and their willing accomplices in the North. When the House voted down Lecompton, Douglas won the battle. Whether he would win the war was another matter: he would be up for reelection in 1858, the president's side controlled the party and its patronage, and the real war was about to be fought in Illinois and across the nation for the Democratic party's future.

THE GREAT DEBATES

The 1858 Senate election in Illinois has become so legendary that what else happened politically that year often has become lost to memory. With northern Democrats divided over the Kansas-Nebraska Act of 1854, Lecompton split the remainder. In 1858, Democrats marched into an electoral disaster. In usually Democratic Indiana, the party lost the legislature and half of its House members, meaning that of 11 representatives, 7 were Republican, 2 were Douglas Democrats, and 2 were pro-Lecompton. In Pennsylvania, the state ticket and 11 of the 15 Democratic congressmen lost, including J. Glancy Jones, Buchanan's close friend and the party's floor leader. That left only 2 pro-Lecompton Democrats in a delegation of 25 that now included Thaddeus Stevens, a Whig-turned Republican who hounded Buchanan for most of their careers. Of Ohio's 22 House members, only 4 were Democrats, and 3 of them opposed the Lecompton Constitution. In New York, Republicans swept the governor's office and the Assembly, and 29 of the 39 House members opposed Lecompton. Making the message to Buchanan more obvious, every anti-Lecompton Democrat who ran for reelection had won.

These victories also confirmed the decline of Know-Nothing influence. Granting that nativist views retained some vitality, Republicans co-opted Know-Nothings or simply overwhelmed them. In Massachusetts, Nathaniel Banks, who glided between the two parties, won the governorship but cast his lot with the Republicans. In New York, Seward and Weed supported a longer registration period for new citizens but said nothing else about the nativist platform. When the Know-Nothing vote in New York in 1858 fell by nearly one-half, Weed proved Republicans could win without openly fusing with the group. In western states, the growing German immigrant vote prompted Republicans to avoid Know-Nothings like the plague, and as the sweep of 1858 showed, nativists had grown marginalized politically. The issue of slavery expanding westward trumped immigration.

In Illinois, the same could be said of the pro-Lecompton, pro-Buchanan forces. Republicans gained legislative and congressional seats. Although they lost the Senate race, Douglas's victory also marked a defeat for Buchanan, who deprived the Little Giant of funding for his campaign and removed several federal officeholders tied to Douglas. History has suggested that Republicans actually salvaged victory in Illinois in 1858, because their candidate won the larger battle. The campaign and the debates associated with it were a factor in Abraham Lincoln's nomination two years later, and scholars have devoted ample attention to the deeper meanings of what went on in 1858. Lincoln and Douglas fought for alternate visions of their parties, the country, and its future: what democracy meant, and whether slavery should expand westward.[16]

Because Douglas had had no problem creating controversy or facing down detractors over the compromise in 1850 and Kansas and Nebraska in 1854, his willingness to oppose Buchanan and Lecompton openly was unsurprising. In December 1857, introducing the usual resolution ordering copies of the president's annual message printed, Douglas fired a warning shot. After agreeing with most of it, he declared, "I totally dissent from all that portion of the message which may fairly be construed as approving of the proceedings of the Lecompton convention." He urged allowing Kansas residents to make their own decisions on territorial laws and regulations, prompting a long debate about Kansas, with Buchanan loyalists defending him and his message. For their part, Republicans enjoyed the dispute and tried to stoke it. While Seward deemed Buchanan's argument "very lame and impotent," Lyman Trumbull chimed in with excerpts from a speech that Buchanan had delivered two decades before that contradicted his position on Kansas.[17]

The next day, Douglas returned to the Senate floor to skewer Buchanan with his own argument. The president claimed to support a fair election, but the choice was a constitution with slavery or a constitution without it, a rush to statehood that struck Douglas as antithetical to democratic ideals. He accused Buchanan of using hair-splitting arguments over how Kansans should vote, intimating that he did so only to protect proslavery interests. He compared Buchanan's approach with how Napoleon "was elected first Consul. He is said to have called out his troops. . . . 'Now, my soldiers, you are to go to the election and vote freely just as you please. If you vote for Napoleon, all is well; vote against him, and you are to be instantly shot.' That was a fair election. . . . This election is to be equally fair." Believing that Buchanan was corrupting democracy and popular sovereignty, he said, "It is not satisfactory to me to have the President say in his message that that constitution is an admirable one. . . . Whether good or bad, whether obnoxious or not, is none of my business and none of yours. It is their business and not ours."[18]

Then, Douglas threw down a gauntlet to Buchanan. He concluded by saying, "If this constitution is to be forced down our throats, in violation of the fundamental principle of free government, under a mode of submission that is a mockery and insult, I will resist it to the last. I have no fear of any party associations being severed. I should regret any social or political estrangement, even temporarily, but if it must be, if I cannot act with you and preserve my faith and my honor, I will stand on the great principle of popular sovereignty. . . ."[19]

The Senate galleries roared in response. Virginian James Mason, architect of the Fugitive Slave Act of 1850 that Douglas helped turn into law, demanded the removal of the spectators—and even that led to a long debate. More crucially, Douglas defied Buchanan and the leaders of his southern-dominated party as openly as possible. He held himself up as a truer Democrat than any of them. And he did so in direct contradiction of the *Dred Scott* decision, which denied the right of Congress or the citizens of territories to legislate against slavery, which the theory of popular sovereignty allowed Kansans to do. At no time, then or in other public appearances, did Douglas take a stand on slavery. Privately, he claimed to dislike it, but in this speech he said what he always claimed to believe: it was for the public to decide. Further, by leaving the decision to the public, he hoped to accomplish here what he also had wished to do with the Kansas-Nebraska Act: remove slavery as a political issue and take control of the Democratic party from southerners and put it in the hands of northerners—more specifically, himself.

What Douglas planned for Democrats may have mattered less at that moment than whether he would even remain a Democrat. Some eastern Republicans preferred to think of the enemy of their enemy as their friend. Rumors spread that Douglas would join the new antislavery party, which seemed unlikely. Other Democrats who found a home with the Republicans had been longtime foes of slavery, not advocates of leaving the matter up to the people. Whether they had been vocal in their views depended on where they came from and the vitality of the issue there. In Illinois, Democrats had predominated politically from the second party system's beginnings in the early 1830s, when Lincoln went to the legislature and remained part of a Whig minority. Also, laws banned blacks from moving to the state, and even the emphatically antislavery Trumbull claimed to like it that way. Douglas seemed to have no reason to abandon his party, even if Buchanan was plotting an effort to make Douglas's party abandon him.

If Democrats did abandon Douglas, some Republicans wanted to offer him a safe haven, with Horace Greeley taking the lead. In the *New York Tribune* and, importantly, its national edition, Greeley hailed Douglas for standing up to the Slave Power whose bidding so many Democrats, especially Buchanan, seemed eager to do. Other Republicans dreamed of a grand alliance to destroy a Democratic party dominated by the Slave Power. Others saw that keeping Democrats divided could only help Republicans. They knew that Douglas had been considered a front-runner to succeed Buchanan. A party divided in 1858 was likely to stay divided in 1860. And Douglas was, as always, plotting: he reportedly sent out feelers to Republicans, offering to withdraw from the Senate race if they would back his slate of congressional candidates. The confusion that had been an inevitable part of the second party system's collapse was evolving with the third party system: Republicans and not Know-Nothings would become the main competition for Democrats, but how Democrats and Republicans would compete and change remained uncertain.

The ultimate problem with this political dance was that Illinois Republicans declined to join in. In 1855, with anti-Nebraska Democrats unwilling to support someone still claiming to be a Whig, Lincoln gracefully withdrew from the Senate race and enabled Trumbull's victory. Trumbull promised to help Lincoln in the future and, in 1858, anti-Nebraska Democrats and antislavery Whigs coalesced as Republicans, even if they remained mutually wary. Not only did they feel they had a good candidate of their own, but Illinois Republicans, particularly Lincoln, also felt they understood Douglas better than those who knew him as a senator. Indeed, from their days as young lawyers and political rivals in Springfield in the late 1830s, Lincoln had envied Douglas's success and considered him an opportunist. Douglas lacked a moral center, in Lincoln's view, and, as Harry Jaffa has written in his classic study of Lincoln and Douglas, at the heart of their battle was the role of morality in democracy and republicanism. Thus, with alarm and sarcasm, Lincoln asked Trumbull, "What does the New-York Tribune mean by it's [sic] constant eulogizing, and admiring, and magnifying of Douglas? . . . Have they concluded that the republican cause, generally, can be best promoted by sacrificing us here in Illinois? If so we would like to know it soon; it will save us a great deal of labor to surrender at once." The answer was yes, although Lincoln noted, "As yet I have heard of no republican here going over to Douglas. . . ."[20]

Illinois Republicans decided to send a message to eastern Republicans and officially nominate Lincoln for the Senate. This step, unprecedented for a state party convention at the time, led to two problems. First, Greeley and other would-be kingmakers viewed Lincoln less enthusiastically than the convention did. That contributed nothing to Lincoln's hopes for national party help, which put him in a lonely position akin to the one in which Douglas found himself. Second, Lincoln's "House Divided" speech created more trouble than it was worth politically by suggesting slavery had to end or become national. The Republican coalition included former Whigs like Lincoln who had made little noise about slavery but made clear their dislike for it—and other former Whigs who became Republicans simply because they saw nowhere else to go, especially on issues related to the economy, federal power, and states' rights. As far as they were concerned, the less Lincoln said about slavery, the Slave Power, and anything else that conjured visions of abolition or free blacks, the better.

While understanding their concerns, Lincoln disagreed. For him, it was a moral issue that had the virtue of being politically wise and distinctive. He sought to define how he and other Republicans differed from Douglas. His "House Divided" speech has stood out for that metaphor, his charges of a Democratic conspiracy to perpetuate slavery, and his warning that the Dred Scott case could spread slavery into states that had banned it. Lost in much of the discussion of that speech was his assault on Douglas's power and principles—or the lack of them. Without naming names, but aiming at eastern Republicans and undecided Whigs, Lincoln derided the idea that Douglas agreed with Republicans on anything. Douglas's supporters, he said, "remind us that *he* is a very *great* man, and that the largest of *us* are very small ones. Let this be granted. But 'a *living dog* is better than a *dead lion.*' Judge Douglas, if not a *dead* lion, *for this work*, is at least a *caged* and *toothless* one." Having suggested that Douglas could never achieve Republican goals, he explained why they should not expect him even to try. "How can he oppose the advances of slavery? He don't *care* anything about it. His avowed *mission is impressing* the 'public heart' to *care* nothing about it. . . . He has done all in his power to reduce the whole question of slavery to one of a mere *right of property*. . . ."[21]

When Douglas returned home from Washington to campaign, he knew he was in for a fight. Without the usual required contributions and campaigning by Democratic officeholders and support from the president, Douglas was on his own, except for his popularity and following in Illinois. That combination might not be enough against Lincoln, whom Douglas saw as wrong on the issues but as tough an opponent as he could find. He told Forney, another powerful Democrat who had broken with Buchanan, "I shall have my hands full. He is the strong man of his party,—full of wit, facts, dates,—and the best stump speaker, with his droll ways and dry jokes, in the West. He is as honest as he is shrewd. . . ." Douglas soon found that Lincoln planned to trail him around the state, vivisecting his speeches and record at each stop. Challenged to a series of debates, Douglas agreed. He felt they probably would help Lincoln as a challenger more than they would help him as a nationally known incumbent, but he also knew Republicans were accusing him of hiding from Lincoln—and even his worst critics would agree that Douglas had no fear of a political challenge.[22]

The Lincoln-Douglas debates stretched through seven Illinois towns. They were great theater, with supporters surrounding the candidates before, during, and after the exchanges, hurrahing and hissing. Making it more interesting, Lincoln and Douglas differed in every way imaginable. In physical appearance, as Allen Guelzo has written, "Douglas's stumpy legs and paunchy torso made him look like Humpty

Dumpty in a toupee, while Lincoln's height was entirely in his legs and gave audiences the impression of a scarecrow come to life." As speakers, they resembled the parties in which they grew up politically: Lincoln was whiggishly dispassionate and droll, Douglas democratically boisterous and fighting. What they said was not necessarily intended for the ages, although that is what it proved to be; they were engaged in an argument over whether the Founding Fathers intended slavery to survive, left it up to future generations, or put it on the road to extinction. It was for a campaign, meaning the debates came amid other speeches and appearances. Both engaged in demagoguery and tailored their message for their audience and to win votes, according to when and where they spoke and how reporters and stenographers conveyed their words and the audience reaction.[23]

Thus, Douglas was as thoroughgoing a partisan as ever and more openly a race-baiter than normal. In the first debate, seeking to win over former Whigs still on the fence, Douglas claimed that Democrats and Whigs agreed on slavery, which was somewhere between an oversimplification and a lie, and that Lincoln and Trumbull conspired to destroy the Whigs and create an abolitionist party, which really was a lie. He upheld popular sovereignty as the democratic solution to the country's problems—and a means of keeping free blacks out of Illinois and away from the ballot box. His constituents opposed black suffrage but Maine felt otherwise, so he endorsed popular sovereignty by saying, "Let Maine take care of her own negroes and fix the qualifications of her own voters to suit herself, without interfering with Illinois, and Illinois will not interfere with Maine." But Lincoln was like "all the little Abolition orators," he said, and told his listeners, "I do not regard the negro as my equal," while Lincoln would allow African Americans "to come into the State and settle with the white man . . . to vote on an equality with yourselves, and to make them eligible to office, to serve on juries, and to adjudge your rights."[24]

Lincoln's response laid out themes he would pursue for the rest of the debates and the campaign. He knew that Illinoisans had no use for black equality, but he also believed in the Republicans' free labor ideology. Reconciling these views, he declared that "anything that argues me into his idea of perfect social and political equality with the negro, is but a specious and fantastic arrangement of words, by which a man can prove a horse chestnut to be a chestnut horse." Beyond doubting that Douglas could be trusted, he also sought to dispel the notion that he believed in absolute racial equality, taking a mainstream Republican position. "I have no purpose directly or indirectly to interfere with the institution of slavery in the States where it exists. I believe I have no lawful right to do so, and I have no inclination to do so. I have no purpose to introduce political and social equality between the white and the black races," Lincoln said. "There is a physical difference between the two, which in my judgment will probably forever forbid their living together upon the footing of perfect equality, and inasmuch as it becomes a necessity that there must be a difference, I, as well as Judge Douglas, am in favor of the race to which I belong, having the superior position." Declaring that "there is no reason in the world why the negro is not entitled to all the natural rights enumerated in the Declaration of Independence," Lincoln said, "I agree with Judge Douglas he is not my equal in many respects—certainly not in color, perhaps not in moral or intellectual endowment. But in the right to eat the bread, without leave of anybody else, which his own hand earns, *he is my equal and the equal of Judge Douglas, and the equal of every living man.*"

Although Lincoln's views would hardly pass muster today, they were advanced for their time and, especially, their place. But those views posed a political problem: without using the specific words, he had distinguished between absolute equality and equality of opportunity. Winning conservative votes required Lincoln and other Republicans to go further, and not just join Douglas in a competition for the mantle of Henry Clay and the support of those who still worshiped his memory. Thus, at the fourth debate at Charleston, Guelzo has written, "he began with the words every Lincoln admirer since then wishes he had never uttered." There, Lincoln repeated his belief that racial equality was impossible. He assured his listeners that he opposed allowing blacks to vote, serve on juries, hold office, or marry whites. Indeed, "I have never had the least apprehension that I or my friends would marry negroes if there was no law to keep them from it, but as Judge Douglas and his friends seem to be in great apprehension that they might, if there were no law to keep them from it, I give him the most solemn pledge that I will to the very last stand by the law of this State, which forbids the marrying of white people with negroes."[25]

Also at issue was the question of popular sovereignty itself. Naturally, Douglas defended the idea as exemplifying democracy itself. Lincoln expressed doubts, observing that "my understanding is that Popular Sovereignty, as now applied to the question of Slavery, does allow the people of a Territory to have Slavery if they want to, but does not allow them *not* to have it if they *do not* want it." What Lincoln said in the second debate led to what became known as Douglas's Freeport Doctrine. He asked the senator whether a territory's residents could exclude slavery. Douglas replied that they could and that he had said so before. Lincoln's allies later claimed that his purpose in asking was to destroy any chance of southern support for Douglas's presidential campaign in 1860—that he claimed to be "killing larger game. The battle of 1860 is worth a hundred of this," meaning that Lincoln hoped to promote his chances while making it impossible for Douglas to win the southern Democratic votes he would need for the nomination and election. Whether Lincoln said that is doubtful—reminiscences of Lincoln evolved in proportion to his later martyrdom—and Lincoln's intent is unknown, "unless, of course," as Guelzo has posited, "the presidency Lincoln thought he was denying Douglas was not a Democratic one but a Republican one." Lincoln knew eastern Republicans still dreamed of capturing Douglas for their side, and that Douglas's ideology and scruples were far afield from their party.[26]

Their contrasting views of the Declaration of Independence were central to Lincoln's argument. In the fifth debate at mostly Republican Galesburg, Douglas resorted to the kind of language that John Calhoun had employed when he declared that this "doctrine of Lincoln's—declaring that the negro and the white man are made equal by the Declaration of Independence and by Divine Providence—is a monstrous heresy." Lincoln replied, "I believe the entire records of the world, from the date of the Declaration of Independence up to within three years ago, may be searched in vain for one single affirmation, from one single man, that the negro was not included in the Declaration of Independence." That was untrue: although southerners long had subscribed to that theory, Lincoln aimed more at Douglas's sponsorship of the Kansas-Nebraska Act and arguments for popular sovereignty than for the truth. Reminding the audience that Thomas Jefferson wrote that he "trembled" for the country's fate over slavery, Lincoln vowed to provide "the highest premium to Judge Douglas if he will show that he, in all his life, ever uttered a sentiment at all akin to that of Jefferson." In the final debate at Alton on October 15, questioning whether Douglas believed in true democracy, Lincoln sought to distinguish between them in explaining "the real issue":

> That is the issue that will continue in this country when these poor tongues of Judge Douglas and myself shall be silent. It is the eternal struggle between these two principles—right and wrong—throughout the world. They are the two principles that have stood face to face from the beginning of time; and will ever continue to struggle. The one is the common right of humanity and the other the divine right of kings. It is the same principle in whatever shape it develops itself. It is the same spirit that says, "You work and toil and earn bread, and I'll eat it." No matter in what shape it comes, whether from the mouth of a king who seeks to bestride the people of his own nation and live by the fruit of their labor, or from one race of men as an apology for enslaving another race, it is the same tyrannical principle.

A majority of Illinoisans agreed with Lincoln, whose candidates won more of the popular votes and legislative seats up for reelection. Thanks to the number of sitting incumbents and how legislative districts had been gerrymandered, Douglas already had several legislators ready to vote for his reelection to the Senate, and survived Lincoln's challenge. Still, Lincoln and his fellow Republicans could take heart from the results. First, the success of both Lincoln and Douglas meant Buchanan and his sympathizers clearly had lost big. Second, a one-term representative accustomed to life in the political minority had stood at center stage with one of the majority party's most powerful members—perhaps, next to the president, the most powerful—and won more votes. Third, the outcome was a sign of what might happen across the North in 1860, both for that party and for Douglas's hopes for the presidency, with the right Republican candidate. Fourth, when Douglas went back to Washington, his caucus stripped him of his chairmanship of the Committee on Territories, demonstrating that Democrats remained in the hands of increasingly uncompromising proslavery forces, and that Douglas and his ideas would have limited power in the party with which they were associated. All of which showed the contradiction at the heart of Douglas's argument. He tried to overcome the party's southern and doughfaced powers by appealing to the same kinds of base prejudices they expressed, and it neither won him a majority in Illinois nor helped him politically outside of Illinois.

Lincoln had reason for displeasure, too. In 1855, other anti-Nebraska forces denied him a Senate seat, but this time other former Whigs declined to help him or even opposed him. He and Douglas claimed to follow in Clay's footsteps as the great advocate of Union, but Douglas won a significant number of the votes of his old followers, thanks partly to Lincoln's refusal to sink any lower than he did to join in Douglas's race-baiting, and partly because John Crittenden, the Kentuckian who came closer than anyone to being Clay's protégé, had kind words for Douglas and none for Lincoln. In the end, Lincoln seemed to be simply a two-time loser, albeit through circumstances outside his control, with no chance at a Senate race for another six years, unless he chose the presumably suicidal course of challenging Trumbull's reelection. "I am glad I made the late race," he said. "It gave me a hearing on the great and durable question of the age, which I could have had in no other way; and though I now sink out of view, and shall be forgotten, I believe I have made some marks which will tell for the cause of civil liberty long after I am gone."[27]

Yet another option was open to him. Lincoln and Douglas both defended the Union. The differences in their defense were stark: Lincoln believed slavery poisoned it and contradicted the Declaration of Independence; Douglas saw no problem with enslaving people based on their skin color. In appealing to former Whigs and revealing his own views, Lincoln had turned in the first debate to Clay, "my beau ideal of a statesman," and echoed him in describing Douglas. "When he invites any people willing to have slavery, to establish it, he is blowing out the moral lights around us. When he says he 'cares not whether slavery is voted down or voted up,'—that it is a sacred right of self government—he is in my judgment penetrating the human soul and eradicating the light of reason and the love of liberty in this American people," Lincoln said. More northerners seemed to share Lincoln's concerns about reason and liberty, and the problem with allowing slavery to expand westward, but Republican victory meant attracting conservative voters in states like Illinois. During his Senate campaign, Lincoln told a visiting journalist that his wife had high hopes for him beyond even the Senate, that he would someday be president. "Just think of such a sucker as me as President," he said. After the 1858 election, more Republicans began to think it.[28]

SEVEN

❧❧

PURGING THE LAND
WITH BLOOD

During Abraham Lincoln's term in the House of Representatives, from 1847 to 1849, he became friendly with Alexander Stephens. They made an unusual pair: the lanky, spottily educated frontiersman blessed with what Stephens called "a very strong, clear and vigorous mind," and the southerner whom Lincoln described as "a little, slim, pale-faced, consumptive man." Both had been loyal Whigs who could analyze the past and present with cold logic, and both professed their unionism. Stephens remained a political force whether at home in Georgia or on Capitol Hill, merging both unionist and disunionist sentiment while encouraging a proslavery ideology. Lincoln returned home to Illinois and comparative anonymity after his stint in Washington before reentering politics with the opportunity to express his moral, yet cautious, opposition to the institution Stephens and his allies defended.[1]

After winning the presidential election of 1860, Lincoln exchanged letters with Stephens as they tried to gauge each other and their regions. Lincoln asked, "Do the people of the South really entertain fears that a Republican administration would, *directly*, or *indirectly*, interfere with their slaves, or with them, about their slaves? If they do, I wish to assure you, as once a friend, and still, I hope, not an enemy, that there is no cause for such fears." But he also said, "You think slavery is *right* and ought to be extended; while we think it is *wrong* and ought to be restricted. That I suppose is the rub. It certainly is the only substantial difference between us."

Stephens's response veered between radical, reasoned, and philosophical: "When men come under the influence of fanaticism, there is no telling where their impulses or passions may drive them. This is what creates our discontent and apprehensions, not unreasonable when we see . . . such reckless exhibitions of madness as the John Brown raid into Virginia, which has received so much sympathy from many, and no open condemnation from any of the leading members of the dominant party . . . ," which was untrue. He concluded, "A word fitly spoken by you now would be like 'apples of gold in pictures of silver,'" the kind of Biblical allusion that Lincoln would appreciate.[2]

Stephens's suggestion was neither unique nor limited to his region. One of many northerners asking Lincoln to reassure the South, Truman Smith, the onetime conservative Whig leader from Connecticut, did much to unify their old party. In that spirit, he thought a statement from Lincoln would help "to disarm mischief makers, to allay causeless anxiety, to compose the public mind . . . ," especially in the South. Although he thanked Smith, Lincoln declined. "To press a repetition of this upon those who *have* listened, is useless; to press it upon those who have *refused* to listen, and still refuse, would be wanting in self-respect, and would have an appearance of sycophancy and timidity, which would excite the contempt of good men, and encourage bad ones to clamor the more loudly," he wrote. Nor did Lincoln empathize with businessmen worried about the southern response to his election. "I am not insensible to any commercial or financial depression that may exist; but nothing is to be gained by fawning around the '*respectable scoundrels*' who got it up," Lincoln said. "Let them go to work and repair the mischief of their own making; and then perhaps they will be less greedy to do the like again."[3]

Southerners confirmed his judgment. The *New Orleans Daily Crescent* saw "no need for Lincoln to declare his policy. We know well enough what it is to be. The party that elected him would not have done so if they thought he would cheat them. . . . If Mr. Lincoln had gotten up and told the people that his Administration would protect the rights of the South as understood by the Southern people, he would have subjected himself to universal contempt, and made himself worthy of the brand of personal infamy and dishonor—because everybody knows that he was elected by a party organized upon the basis of hostility to those rights as universally understood by the southern people." While southerners detested the personal liberty laws designed to subvert the Fugitive Slave Act, fire-eater Robert Rhett of the *Charleston Mercury* suggested that another northern action was far more wicked: "What are these acts as indications of the hostility and faithlessness of the Northern people towards the South (and they are nothing more), when compared with the mighty sectional despotism they have set up over the South in the election of Messrs. LINCOLN and HAMLIN to the Presidency and Vice-Presidency of the United States?"[4]

With Stephens accusing Republicans of saying something they had not and fire-eaters claiming Lincoln threatened something he had not, the North and the South indeed seemed incapable of finding common ground. Stephens cited John Brown's raid, but events of the past decade—indeed, the past two centuries—had separated the economy and ethos of the two regions, even as they fought within and among themselves over the very issues that united them against each other. Lincoln was right: extending slavery was the rub, and the rubbing that had eroded the ties between the North and the South was about to wear them away entirely.

VIOLENCE AND VIGILANTISM: BOOTH, BRODERICK, AND BROWN

With the benefit of hindsight, the events of 1859 clearly led toward civil war. At the time, though, they were highly controversial in their own right and a sign of how the debate over slavery's growth westward had expanded beyond that issue and into other directions. Accordingly, a Supreme Court case, a duel in California, and an attempt to cause a slave insurrection may seem unrelated, and the three events did happen separately. But all revealed something about the issues dividing the United States. The obstacles to sectional peace were becoming insurmountable. Both sides had grown more extreme in their views and more willing to resort to violence in defense of them. Northerners and southerners were willing to be inconsistent, if not downright hypocritical, in pursuing their goals.

The case, *Ableman v. Booth,* gestated for five years. In March 1854, as Boston wrangled over fugitive slave Anthony Burns, a less provocative case proved equally entangled in law and sectional politics. U.S. Marshal Stephen Ableman arrested fugitive slave Joshua Glover in Racine, Wisconsin, one of several northern states that passed a personal liberty law to circumvent the Fugitive Slave Act by claiming states need not help capture or extradite fugitive slaves. Abolitionist Sherman Booth organized a mob that sprung Glover, who fled to Canada. Then began a round of arrests and lawsuits. Trying a new legal tack, abolitionists swore out a warrant to arrest Benjamin Garland, who claimed ownership of Glover, for assault. When a federal judge tossed that aside, Ableman arrested Booth and charged him with violating the Fugitive Slave Act. Booth countered that he could not be arrested because the law he was accused of breaking was unconstitutional, and the Wisconsin Supreme Court agreed. The federal court had him arrested again, tried him, found him guilty, and sentenced him to prison and a fine. Garland chimed in with a federal lawsuit and won a federal verdict that required Booth to pay him for Glover's value. The state high court ordered Booth released and repeated its opinion about the fugitive slave law's constitutionality. It also ignored U.S. Attorney General Jeremiah Black, who asked the court to back away from its position that a state had the right to defy the federal government.[5]

Again, Roger Taney and the United States Supreme Court entered the fray. As in *Dred Scott* two years before, *Ableman v. Booth* would address slavery, but from the opposite side of the spectrum. Just as South Carolina proposed to nullify a federal tariff in the 1820s and 1830s, and other states had claimed similar rights before, Wisconsin had passed laws to nullify the Fugitive Slave Acts of 1793 and 1850. Taney had been a Jacksonian before, but, as his *Dred Scott* opinion showed, his view of slavery had lurched toward Calhoun's. Would his Jacksonian or Calhoun side appear when it came to protecting slavery, and had he adopted Calhoun's ideas about nullification, too?

The answer was clear and constitutionally unassailable. This time, Taney stuck to the facts and the Jacksonian idea of states maintaining their power but deferring to the federal government when necessary. He argued that "the State of Wisconsin is sovereign within its territorial limits to a certain extent, yet that sovereignty is restricted and limited by the Constitution of the United States. And the powers of the General Government, and of the State, although both exist and are exercised within the same territorial limits, are yet separate and distinct sovereignties, acting separately and independently of each other, within their respective spheres"—a classic example of Taney's usual thinking on collisions between federal and state law. Taney granted that state governments had defined powers, but "the sphere of action appropriated to the United States is as far beyond the reach of the judicial process issued by a State judge or a State court, as if the line of division was traced by landmarks and monuments visible to the eye."[6]

The opinion both resembled and differed from *Dred Scott*. This time the Court was unanimous: joining the opinion were John McLean, a dissenter in *Dred Scott*, and Benjamin Curtis's successor, states' rights Maine Democrat Nathan Clifford, and the rest of Taney's majority in *Dred Scott*. *Ableman* was, according to constitutional historians Harold Hyman and William Wiecek, "one of Taney's monuments," part of a long line of cases upholding federal judicial supremacy against state and local lawlessness. That also was the problem. As Hyman and Wiecek have written, "It bore the millstone of slavery around its neck and was temporarily obscured because many read it only in terms of its immediate end, which was the preservation of slavery's expansionist power." Taney could not resist adding—unnecessarily—that the Fugitive Slave Act was constitutional. Asserting federal power and avoiding a major controversy in the process, Taney delivered as strong a statement on behalf of slavery as two years before and reinforced its protection against interference with its growth.[7]

Indeed, both sections could point to the case as reinforcing their arguments. As *Ableman* wended through the courts, radical Republican Horace Greeley's *New York Tribune* declared, "The example which Wisconsin has set will be as rapidly followed as circumstances admit. By another year, we expect to see Ohio holding the same noble course. After that, we anticipate a race among the other free states, in the same direction, 'till all have reached the goal of state independence"—a position that, on any other issue, Greeley found untenable. Meanwhile, the South had no problem with upholding federal supremacy at the expense of the states, which ran counter to its claims for protecting slavery, because in this case the federal supremacy upheld was over the issue of slavery.

Whereas the Court reached its decision without violence, two events that made more news in 1859 involved more violent results, but with the same relationship to sectional differences over slavery. The first took place in California, distant from the debate in miles but not in ideology or importance. Central to the Compromise of 1850 and expected to vote in a way befitting its absence of slavery, California defied easy political categorization. It elected mostly Democrats to national office throughout the decade, but reflected the battles dividing the party in the North and the South through the words and deeds of its two senators, David Broderick and William Gwin. Broderick had migrated from New York, where he fought the Tammany Hall Democratic political machine, and built his own network in California. Long active in Mississippi Democratic politics, where he was close to future Kansas territorial governor Robert Walker, Gwin came west when his opportunities for advancement at home dried up.

Both Broderick and Gwin won California's Senate seats in the mid-1850s, but not easily and with different political trajectories. Unsurprisingly, Gwin supported slavery. In New York, the labor leaders Broderick had been close to included George Henry Evans, an antislavery advocate of homesteads, and Mike Walsh, another anti-Tammany political infighter who took his views on slavery from Calhoun. In California, Broderick established himself as an advocate of free white labor without opposing slavery. Unsurprisingly, after arriving in the Senate he became a Douglas lieutenant and advocate of popular sovereignty.

The Broderick-Gwin relationship was even worse than it seemed on the surface. With Broderick controlling enough legislative votes to decide who was elected as his colleague, victory required Gwin to cede California's Democratic patronage to his colleague. But in Washington, Gwin quickly became popular with Buchanan and the southerners who dominated the Senate and the administration. Between those connections and the fight between Buchanan and Douglas, Gwin wound up with the patronage, despite the agreement. Amid the infighting, Broderick exchanged insults with Gwin backer David Terry, a southerner and California's chief justice, who challenged Broderick to a duel—by then a less common occurrence, especially outside of the South. They met near San Francisco, at Lake Merced, on September 13, 1859, and Terry shot Broderick. As he lay dying, Broderick said, "I die because I was opposed to a corrupt administration and the extension of slavery." His eulogist, the seemingly ubiquitous Edward D. Baker—a close enough friend for Abraham Lincoln to name a son for him, an early arrival in California, and soon to be a Republican senator from Oregon—declared, "His death was a political necessity, poorly veiled beneath the guise of a private quarrel."[8]

If Broderick died for southern Democrats to consolidate their control over California, his death was far more of a political sacrifice than the earlier beating of

Charles Sumner, but it was no less a part of the sectional conflict. Terry may well have been an assassin for California's southern Democrats, or he may have reflected the same southern sense of honor that had inspired Preston Brooks to attack Sumner, or he may just have been violent (he later died of gunshot wounds from the body-guard of a Supreme Court justice he was assaulting), or some combination of all three. Whatever their backgrounds, a Douglas Democrat and a southern Democrat tried to kill each other over political issues. It was another sign of the divisions over slavery and regional power, especially within a Democratic party already fatally divided over Kansas and the issues flowing from it.

If grasping what happened in California is hard, understanding John Brown's historically more famous and important actions at Harpers Ferry may be impossi-ble. What Brown did, in Kansas and later at the federal arsenal, has been subject to endless psychological and historical analysis, which has bred still more disagreement about what he did and why he did it. This much is clear: Brown decided to take violent steps on behalf of the abolitionist cause, to which he was devoted, with far-ther-reaching implications than the murders he and his sons committed in Kansas. He tried to involve abolitionists and Republicans, and succeeded only to a limited degree. Then he attacked the federal arsenal at Harpers Ferry, Virginia, hoping to attract slave followers. He failed, federal military forces captured him, and he wound up tried, convicted, and hanged for committing treason against the state of Virginia. Those details are complex enough, but simple in comparison with the rest of the story.

Early in 1858, Brown began outlining plans for an attack intended to start a southern slave insurrection. Eventually settling on Harpers Ferry, he sought help from a group of abolitionists that became known as "The Secret Six," including wealthy New Yorker Gerrit Smith and five New Englanders: Franklin Sanborn, a teacher and protégé of transcendental thinker Ralph Waldo Emerson; pipe manu-facturer George Stearns; minister Theodore Parker; Unitarian minister Thomas Wentworth Higginson, who had advocated such uprisings and led the throng that tried to free Anthony Burns; and doctor and reformer Samuel Gridley Howe. Brown tried to attract others, including Senators Seward and Henry Wilson, and Frederick Douglass, whom he viewed as crucial to leading the slaves he expected to rush to his side. Wilson was critical, Seward apparently dismissed the whole thing, and Douglass was skeptical, advising Brown that an assault on Harpers Ferry probably would fail and few would rally to his side. But the six abolitionists provided funding and moral support.

Whether noble of purpose or a murderous lunatic or both—opinions vary—Brown planned poorly. On the evening of October 16, 1859, a month after Broder-ick's death 2,500 miles away, Brown and 22 followers had no trouble capturing the arsenal—it had only one night watchman—and several hostages. He laid no groundwork with neighboring slaves, so the hosts he expected to help him never came. He had no escape route, and the weapons he had obtained for his expected followers had been pikes, because he reasoned that slaves had no idea how to handle guns—probably true, but begging the question of why he started by assaulting an arsenal. After cutting nearby telegraph wires so that neither he nor slave owners could reach reinforcements, he released hostages who could warn others of what he was doing. He brought no food, which made holding onto Harpers Ferry problematic. Instead of heading into the nearby mountains he had seen as vital to his plans for guerilla warfare, he sat and waited.

By the next afternoon, a detachment of United States Marines arrived under Colonel Robert E. Lee's command. Lieutenant J. E. B. Stuart, who had served in Kansas, peered through a door and recognized Brown. They led an attack that wounded Brown and killed 15, including two of his sons. Captured, Brown went to jail to await his trial for treason against the state of Virginia—another oddity, because he attacked a federal arsenal. A jury easily found him guilty, and he hanged on December 2, 1859, before soldiers and volunteers who had come to make sure no northern rescue attempt saved him. The crowd included fire-eater Edmund Ruffin; Virginia Military Institute professor Thomas Jonathan Jackson, later to be nicknamed "Stonewall"; and an actor who volunteered for the militia out of his eagerness to see Brown die: John Wilkes Booth. As he went to the gallows, Brown handed a message to an attendant: "I John Brown am now quite *certain* that the crimes of this *guilty, land: will* never be purged *away;* but with Blood." Whether or not he was insane, he was prophetic.[9]

Many Republicans grasped immediately that any connection to Brown would doom their chances for high office. "It was not a slave insurrection. It was an attempt by white men to get up a revolt among slaves, in which the slaves refused to participate," Lincoln said. "In fact, it was so absurd that the slaves, with all their ignorance, saw plainly enough it could not succeed." Calling Brown's execution "necessary and just," Seward deemed his actions "sedition and treason." But other Republicans considered Brown, in Massachusetts editor Samuel Bowles's words, "the bravest man of this generation" and "a true man and a Christian" who increased "the moral hostility of the people of the free states to slavery." Abolitionists felt even more strongly, with Emerson declaring that Brown would "make the gallows as glorious as the cross," ministers honoring him from the pulpit, and tributes across the North.[10]

Southerners developed two related, yet wholly different, views of him. They admired his courage. Ruffin marveled at his "complete fearlessness of & insensibility to danger and death." Governor Henry Wise of Virginia called him "a bundle of the best nerves I ever saw, cut and thrust and bleeding and in bonds," and later defended his bravery. But to many southerners, Brown just was more open in his treason and hatred for the South than other northerners: all of them wanted to free the slaves and help them kill their old masters, but Brown had the courage to try it. Thus, even in Virginia, an Upper South state more open to discussions of the spread of slavery than those in the Deep South, one editor reported "almost a complete revolution in the sentiments, the thoughts, the hopes, of the oldest and steadiest conservatives in all the Southern states," while another felt Brown had "advanced the cause of disunion more than any other event." Southerners did not fear Brown so much as what he represented: the prospect of future insurrections led by northerners who might be better planners and thus more successful. A congressional investigating committee headed by Senator James Mason of Virginia found no connection between Republican leaders and Brown, but that proved less important than the image embedded in southern minds of an antislavery northerner fomenting a slave insurrection. Robert Toombs of Georgia said, "Never permit this Federal government to pass into the traitorous hands of the black Republican party." As fate would have it, Toombs and his allies were about to make that very event possible.[11]

DIVIDED HOUSES

In late 1859 and 1860, the selection of a speaker of the House and presidential nominees highlighted and heightened sectional divides over slavery. When Congress convened in December 1859, its cast had changed considerably from the previous term. New House members included Whig-turned-conservative Ohio Republican Tom Corwin, a veteran of Millard Fillmore's cabinet and previously a governor, congressman, and senator; Charles Francis Adams, the Free-Soil vice-presidential candidate of 1848, from Massachusetts; and even more radical Thaddeus Stevens, elected from James Buchanan's hometown of Lancaster, Pennsylvania—a slap at the president and a boon to Republicans. Coming to the Senate were moderate Republican James Grimes of Iowa, unionist Tennessee Democrat Andrew Johnson, and Toombs, who seemed more willing to compromise than he actually was. But southerners had enough power in the Senate to name southerners or doughfaces to chair every committee, with southerners comprising a majority of each committee.

Exemplifying the split, the speaker's election began when Congress met on December 5 and took two months to resolve. No party had the majority of 119 needed to organize the House: Republicans had 109, Democrats 101 (13 of them anti-Lecompton and not party loyalists), and 27 identified themselves as Whigs, Americans, or nothing in particular. Republicans ran moderate Ohioan John Sherman, a future U.S. senator and secretary of state who had signed an endorsement of an abridgment of Hinton Helper's *The Impending Crisis of the South.* Democrats and southerners made that enough of an issue—Sherman dismissed it as "ludicrous"— to block him from gaining more votes. At the same time, Douglas and his supporters proved unable to win enough southern votes, from their party or the opposition to the Republicans, to elect any of their candidates. Finally, in late January, Sherman withdrew for William Pennington, a New Jersey Whig who dipped his toes in the Republican party without immersing himself. Pennington was little known enough to capture a bare majority, and promptly named all of the committee chairmen on Sherman's slate. The atmosphere in Congress was so bad, South Carolina's James Hammond said, that "the only persons who do not have a revolver and a knife are those who have two revolvers." When abolitionist Owen Lovejoy derided the South for refusing to allow discussions of the slavery issue, it led to threats of fighting and cocked pistols on the House floor.[12]

If they were willing to use guns, members of Congress used legislation to make their points, too. Coming from different parts of Mississippi, Democratic Senators Jefferson Davis and Albert Gallatin Brown showed the divide even in the Deep South. Brown carped that Davis sat "in an easy chair in Washington, getting his 8,000 a year and drinking champagne" while he was "riding through the pine woods with the heat at 90 degrees . . . and drinking rot gut." Although Brown was a wealthy slave owner in his own right, Davis undeniably was snobbish, especially in comparison. Serving in the Army and the cabinet, Davis developed a more national outlook than Brown had or, for that matter, had to. Thus, their views on slavery looked similar but differed in a crucial and, for Democrats, potentially fatal way. Early in 1860, Brown proposed a resolution that any territorial legislature had a "duty . . . to enact adequate and sufficient laws for the protection of all kinds of property . . . and that upon its failure or refusal to do so, it is the admitted duty of Congress to interfere and pass such laws." Two weeks later, Davis countered by defending slavery and slave owners' rights under the Constitution, and the Fugitive Slave Acts of 1793 and 1850. He also declared "That neither Congress, nor a Territorial Legislature, whether by direct legislation or legislation of an indirect and unfriendly nature, possess the power to annul or impair the constitutional right of any citizen of the United States to take his slave property into the common Territories; but it is the duty of the Federal Government there to afford for that, as for other species of property, the needful protection." He also wrote that "if experience should at any time prove that the judiciary and executive authority do not possess means to ensure adequate protection," and "if the Territorial government shall fail or refuse to provide the necessary remedies," the legislative branch would act. Further, a territory's residents could decide whether to permit slavery when they wrote their constitution for statehood—not at the beginning.[13]

Although this may seem like hair-splitting, the differences were stark. Brown proposed to follow *Dred Scott,* protect slavery everywhere, and jettison popular sovereignty. Davis wanted northerners to feel the South was reasonable and giving them room to make choices about slavery. Hoping to keep the party together, conscious of divisions even among southerners, and regretting the need to block his old friend Douglas from the Democratic nomination, Davis would allow for popular sovereignty to ban further slavery, albeit after slave owners established a beachhead for the institution and assured control of their human property. Davis's resolutions passed and Brown's failed. But the issue remained unsettled and proved critical to their party's future.

Just as these resolutions had an unexpected impact, so did the Democrats' earlier decision to hold their 1860 nominating convention in Charleston, South Carolina. Getting there from Washington, D.C., required six changes of train and the weather that April varied between steamy and rainy, worsening already frayed tempers. Rhett, the South Carolina editor, hoped for the "demolition of the party" to promote secession, and Democrats obliged with the help of Alabama fire-eater William Lowndes Yancey, who had walked out of the 1848 Democratic convention when it approved what was then called squatter sovereignty and had spoken, written, and plotted for secession for two decades. Yancey pushed what historian William Freehling has called "reasonable extremism," exemplified by the proposed Democratic platform. The platform committee's majority report, the work of southerners and northern sympathizers, called for the federal government "in all its departments, to protect, when necessary, the rights of persons and property in the Territories," as in Davis's resolutions. But whereas Davis sought unity, Yancey hoped to anger southerners enough to break up the convention and stop Douglas, whose claim of neutrality on slavery made him anathema to many southerners. In their minority report, Douglas's supporters still advocated popular sovereignty, their only hope of winning in the North. Addressing the convention, Yancey demanded protection for slavery and threatened that any southerner who would "ask the people to vote for a party that ignores their rights ought to be strung upon a political gallows higher than that ever erected for Haman." Douglas backer George Pugh of Ohio responded, "Gentlemen of the South, you mistake us—you mistake us—we will not do it." That refusal, and adoption of the minority report, prompted Mississippi and Alabama delegates to do as Yancey hoped: they walked out of the Charleston convention and took the Democratic party's hopes with them.[14]

Consequently, Democrats wound up with two tickets on two platforms. They met again in Baltimore, but delegates from the Deep South walked out and the rest nominated Douglas on a platform of popular sovereignty with Herschel Johnson, a Georgia unionist. Another group chose Vice President John Breckinridge, not yet forty, a Kentuckian who had almost completed four years of being ignored by Buchanan. As his running-mate, deep southerners picked a relocated one of their own, Senator Joseph Lane of Oregon, and essentially adopted *Dred Scott* as their position on slavery. Although Breckinridge had supporters in the North and Douglas in the South, each would be the Democratic candidate in his region—and neither could win enough electoral votes to capture the White House.

A new party made matters both worse and potentially better for Democrats. Composed mostly of old northern Whigs too conservative to join the Republicans, ex-border state Whigs unwilling to join Democrats or fire-eaters, and Know-Nothings with nowhere to go, the Constitutional Unionists were, in Sean Wilentz's phrase, "so aged and august that they gave the party the air of an over-the-hill gentlemen's club." They formed their organization in 1859, won local victories, and met in Baltimore after the Democratic disaster in Charleston. Henry Clay's protégé, John Crittenden, probably could have had the nomination but had no interest in it. Texan Sam Houston, who had dallied with almost every available political party in the past two decades and retained his unionism and popularity, wanted to run but lacked border state support. They pushed through John Bell, a Democrat-turned-Whig and former senator who had regularly battled James Polk for power in Tennessee. For balance, the Constitutional Unionists chose Edward Everett, the longtime Massachusetts conservative Whig, orator, educator, diplomat, and sometime politician. Their platform was "to *recognize* no political principle other than *the Constitution of the Country, the Union of the States, and the Enforcement of the Laws,*" which looked and sounded good but ultimately said nothing. Their best hope, which they shared with Democrats, was to assure that no one received an electoral majority, throwing the election into the House, where the battle over the speakership showed the deep divisions in that chamber. Then, southerners could hope the House would be unable to agree on a winner, sending the election to the Senate, which they dominated. But even southerners were split between unionists and potential secessionists—and if Republicans won outright, the issue would be moot.[15]

LINCOLN'S CONTRACT

Whether Republicans could win the electoral college depended on several factors. One of them was the Democratic crevice, opened in the fight over the Kansas-Nebraska Act, that had widened into a chasm when Taney handed down the *Dred Scott* ruling and Douglas waffled between ignoring it and openly repudiating it, then broke with Buchanan. Another was divisions in the South: if southerners could choose between at least two candidates, they would be less unified than they were in 1856 when Maryland was the only slave state not to give Buchanan its electoral votes. Better still for Republicans, the Lower South, the heart of secessionist thought, would be likely to support the most proslavery candidate, Breckinridge; the Upper South, committed to defending the institution but less inclined to think it worth breaking up the Union over, might go for Bell; and in the border states, where slavery was more limited anyway, Douglas and Bell probably would battle for votes. That left the other factor: nominating a candidate antislavery enough to hold Republican votes, but conservative enough to pick up antislavery Democrats upset with Douglas and conservative former Whigs and Know-Nothings unwilling to back either a Democrat or a former southern Whig.

Unintentionally, Republicans proved similar to modern twentieth- and twenty-first century political parties: they began their presidential campaign for 1860 even before the nomination in 1856, when Weed persuaded Seward not to run. Though he hardly could have anticipated how events would unfold in the South and the Democratic party, the New York boss correctly calculated that the new party was unlikely to win its first presidential campaign and needed to draw enough Know-Nothings into the party the second time around to elect Seward. From Ohio, where he won a second term as governor, Chase laid groundwork for a run of his own, hoping his deeper involvement in abolitionism and political antislavery—he had belonged to the Liberty and Free-Soil parties, precursors to the Republicans, whereas Seward avoided straying from Whiggery—and Democratic ties could help him overcome Seward.

If Republicans wanted to capture wavering ex-Whigs and conservatives, and carry electoral votes they had lost in 1856, they might seek a candidate from a key state. That made Abraham Lincoln a possibility. Although lesser known than Seward and Chase, he had achieved national notoriety for his work as a Republican in Illinois and especially for his challenge to Douglas in 1858. Lincoln worked hard at publishing an edition of the debates, which made his analysis of the history and constitutionality of slavery more readily available, especially to potential convention delegates when it came out in 1860. He issued warnings to fellow Republicans against trusting Douglas, telling Chase, "Had we thrown ourselves into the arms of Douglas, as re-electing him by our votes would have done, the Republican cause would have been annihilated in Illinois, and, as I think, demoralized, and prostrated everywhere for years, if not forever." He kept working with his Illinois allies and corresponded with Republicans elsewhere, discouraging Chase from supporting an effort in Ohio to demand repeal of the Fugitive Slave Act. He traveled to several states holding off-year elections, speaking in Indiana, Ohio, Wisconsin, Iowa, and Kansas on behalf of Republicans, restricting slavery, and the value of free labor. He also inveighed against "that insidious Douglas Popular Sovereignty," attacking a lengthy article the Little Giant had published in *Harper's Weekly* on his ostensibly Democratic beliefs. Declaring, "His explanations explanatory of explanations explained are interminable," Lincoln countered that what Douglas called popular sovereignty was something else entirely: "a principle, no other than that, if one man chooses to make a slave of another man, neither that other man nor anybody else has a right to object."[16]

Lincoln's desire to answer Douglas, make his own stand, and perhaps see his son at school in New England prompted him to accept a speaking invitation in Brooklyn in February 1860. This plan evolved into a speech at the Cooper Union in Manhattan before a group that included Greeley and William Cullen Bryant, Republicans who disagreed on many issues but agreed on one key point: anyone but Seward should be the party's nominee. The result, according to Harold Holzer, was "the speech that made Abraham Lincoln president." The few who knew much about Lincoln thought of him mainly as what he was not—an educated easterner prominent in the nation's higher councils—than as what he was. His performance that night, for which he prepared as never before, affected his and the country's future. Before a large audience accustomed to sophisticated political oratory, Lincoln provided not a frontier stump speech but a historical analysis of where the Founding Fathers stood on slavery, countering Douglas's claim in *Harper's Weekly* that they left the question to future generations. He tried to reassure southerners of Republican intentions not to interfere with slavery where it existed. Without disguising his sense of humor, he spoke in a far more scholarly manner than usual, announcing, "Let us be diverted by none of those sophistical contrivances . . . such as Union appeals beseeching true Union men to yield to Disunionists, reversing the divine rule, and calling, not the sinners, but the righteous to repentance—such as invocations to Washington, imploring men to unsay what Washington said, and undo what Washington did"—a plea intended in part to undercut what he saw as Douglas's usurpation and misrepresentation of the Founding Fathers.[17]

By then, Lincoln was interested in the presidency, and his eastern trip did nothing to hurt his chances and a great deal to help them. When Republicans gathered in May in Chicago, Lincoln had several advantages, and not just, as one of Greeley's reporters wrote, because "No man ever before made such an impression on his first appeal to a New York audience." For one, Republicans were on his home turf: his supporters packed the galleries, encouraging delegates to believe their native son enjoyed widespread support. He was a known quantity, thanks to attention from his battle with Douglas in 1858 and subsequent speaking engagements. He came from a battleground state: without Seward, Republicans undoubtedly would win New York, but Illinois might be another matter without Lincoln. He also was a respected and respectable moderate who could appeal to all sides of the party. And the confidence of his opponents and their supporters made it that much easier for his managers, led by Illinois operatives David Davis and Leonard Swett, to bargain for him to become their second choice if their favorite failed—which they knew to be impossible. As Weed told Seward—incorrectly, it turned out—"Lincoln's Friends started him only for the second place, for which I immediately accepted him."[18]

The Republican field's weaknesses played to Lincoln's strengths. Countering the Democrats' reputation for corruption—growing with their urban immigrant core and investigations of some of Buchanan's cabinet—would be easier with "Honest Abe" than with Seward, whose closeness to Weed called his probity into question; Chase, whose overarching ambition to be president made him susceptible to questions about his honesty; and Simon Cameron, a Pennsylvanian legendary for his ethical legerdemain. Attracting conservatives might prove impossible for Seward and Chase, and nominating a conservative like Edward Bates, the almost fossilized ex-Missouri Whig, might drive away radicals, but Lincoln stood a better chance of winning over both sides. Lincoln lacked Seward's and Chase's national and executive experience, but that also meant he had less of a record with which to offend undecided voters. All but Seward came from swing states, but Chase and Cameron seemed likely to drive away as many Ohioans and Pennsylvanians as they might attract, and Bates's appeal in the border states might work against him in devoutly antislavery areas. Not that Lincoln and his supporters could feel confident, but they had every reason to stay in the race.

Seward remained the front-runner, but with a daunting problem: an angry and avenging Greeley. The editor always backed Republicans, including Seward and Weed, but helping the New Yorker win the big prize was a wholly different matter. Partly to derail Seward, partly because he saw his problems as a candidate, partly in hopes of calming border state concerns about supposed Republican radicalism on slavery, Greeley looked to Bates, who never really left his old party or joined the Republicans, had owned slaves, and voted for Fillmore in 1856. Denied membership in New York's delegation, Greeley wangled a seat as a delegate from Oregon, enabling him to work the convention floor against Seward. Although few other than Greeley credited the editor with much political cunning, he had support in his effort for Bates from the Blair family, both the patriarch and his sons, Montgomery and Frank, Jr., all with ties to the border states, all convinced of the need for a unifying candidate—and to the resentful Greeley and old Democrats like the Blairs, Seward was no unifier.

In turn, Illinois Republicans outmaneuvered some of the party's shrewder maneuverers. Their goal was to stop a first-ballot nomination, which fit with what Greeley and the Blairs sought; working separately, they angled toward the same ends. With one exception: Indiana, whose leaders might have inclined toward Bates until Illinoisans reminded them of their state's German vote, which would be unlikely to go to a former Know-Nothing; Lincoln took Indiana on the first ballot. Before the convention, Lincoln told Davis, "Make no contracts that will bind me." One of Cameron's managers tried to bind him by demanding the Treasury Department for his boss. Davis apparently mumbled something about assuring Pennsylvania a cabinet spot and suggesting Cameron for it, which was either an endorsement or meaningless, but good enough to secure the delegation and reduce the second ballot to a race between Lincoln and Seward. On the third ballot, the remaining delegates kept shifting to Lincoln until Ohio switched from Chase. Seward's supporters then moved to make the nomination unanimous, which they did as Weed bawled and Greeley beamed.[19]

Lincoln and his vice-presidential running-mate, Democrat-turned-Radical Republican Hannibal Hamlin of Maine, had an excellent chance of victory for several reasons. First, as the campaign wore on, despite the chance that Lincoln might win, Democrats remained resolutely divided, demonstrating the depth of the party's regional and ideological split. Second, although Republicans increasingly opposed anti-immigrant legislation, Lincoln's care to keep his distaste for nativism muted may have cut the number of former Know-Nothings likely to vote against Republicans and for Douglas or possibly Bell. Third, while Lincoln had to follow custom and avoid playing much of a role in his campaign, he nonetheless soothed Seward's wounded feelings, helped broker peace among the always divided Pennsylvania Republicans, and kept his Illinois managers focused on the main prize.

The battle for that prize quickly became Lincoln vs. Douglas in the North and Breckinridge vs. Bell in the South. When Douglas saw that Lincoln would win, he ignored his failing health—due to overwork and overimbibing—and the precedent against campaigning. He traveled through border states to warn against the plans of Deep South fire-eaters, then into Alabama and Mississippi to hail the Union and harangue against secession. Douglas may have had an impact: the Constitutional Unionists won their 39 electoral votes in border slave states (Virginia, Kentucky, and Tennessee), and ran stronger in the Deep South than expected. Breckinridge won the rest of the South and its 72 electoral votes. Douglas barely won two states—New Jersey and Missouri—for 12 electoral votes. Lincoln carried about 40 percent of the popular vote nationally, but 54 percent across the North for 180 electoral votes. Crucially, the chances a combined ticket would have defeated Lincoln were slim: as of November 1860, a semi-united North with its more rapidly expanding population had the electoral votes to defeat all of the slave states. That the votes went for a Republican merely made matters worse; Breckinridge and Bell votes were rare enough in the North to make clear to southerners that Douglas's popular sovereignty was the best they could hope for. Even that, it turned out, would not be good enough.

"THE BETTER ANGELS OF OUR NATURE"

Great-grandson of one president, grandson of another, son of a Massachusetts congressman and ardent Free-Soiler, Henry Adams had a well-defined sense of history when he named the winter of 1860–61 "the great secession winter." Even that oversimplifies what happened between Lincoln's election on November 6, 1860, and the firing on Fort Sumter just over five months later. That southerners would leave the Union over Lincoln's victory struck most northerners at the time as unlikely, and southerners had mixed emotions.[20]

On learning of his victory, Lincoln made a list of possible cabinet members. Incredibly, most of them wound up in his administration, but not easily. Seward and Chase topped his list, but neither wanted to serve with the other. Their efforts to dislodge each other failed, and Seward wound up in the higher-ranking slot, State, with Chase in the Treasury, providing the previous parties—Whigs and Democrats—the cabinet's two leading posts. Bates became attorney general and Montgomery Blair of Maryland postmaster general, again balancing the old parties and assuring border states of representation. The reward for former Indiana Whig Caleb Smith's convention support was the Interior Department. Ex-Connecticut Democrat Gideon Welles went to the Navy Department. For the War Department, Lincoln wanted to thank Pennsylvania for its support but found himself in an unpleasant position:

Cameron seemed most deserving of his thanks and his state's fractious Republicans could agree on no one else, but his reputation for corruption and political gymnastics would prove deserved once he entered the cabinet. Lincoln had balanced his cabinet between old Democrats and old Whigs, and tried to include all states and stripes from the Republican coalition.

Lincoln also faced pressure to appoint a southerner—at least, from farther south than the border states. Weed and Seward thought that would send a helpful signal to the South—and might block someone they disliked, perhaps Chase, from the cabinet. They agreed at least on talking with unionist North Carolinian and ex-Whig John Gilmer. Lincoln had written a passage for a speech by Senator Lyman Trumbull of Illinois in which he said that "each and all of the States will be left in as complete control of their own affairs . . . as they have ever been under any administration." As Lincoln asked afterward of *New York Times* editor Henry Raymond, "Has a single newspaper, heretofore against us, urged that speech with a purpose to quiet public anxiety? Not one, so far as I know. On the contrary," he said, some "endeavor to inflame the North with the belief that it foreshadows an abandonment of Republican ground by the incoming administration" while others "hold the same speech up to the South as an open declaration of war against them." Thus, to the prospect of a southerner in the cabinet, Lincoln ghost-wrote an editorial asking, "Does he surrender to Mr. Lincoln, or Mr. Lincoln to him, on the political difference between them?" Lincoln assured Gilmer that he intended to leave the South alone but on whether slavery could enter new territories, "I am inflexible." Gilmer and most other southerners found that unacceptable.[21]

Nor would Lincoln tolerate more from them. "Let there be no compromise on the question of extending slavery. If there be, all our labor is lost, and, ere long, must be done again. The dangerous ground—that into which some of our friends have a hankering to run—is Pop. Sov.," he told Trumbull. "Have none of it. Stand firm. The tug has to come, & better now, than any time hereafter." Some of his allies felt when the tug came, nothing would snap. "We are not prophets if the result . . . is not a settler on the disunion movement," the *Chicago Tribune* unprophetically said. Whether radical like Chase or conservative like the Blairs, most Republicans had no doubt the South's threats of secession exemplified the line from Lincoln's favorite Shakespearean tragedy, *Macbeth:* full of sound and fury, signifying nothing. They were willing to call the South's bluff. Lincoln told Raymond, "The cause of that excitement is evidently an entire misapprehension, on the part of the Southern people, of the sentiments and purposes of the Republican party. That cause can only be removed by actual experience of a Republican Administration." By contrast, Justin Morrill, a Vermont Republican known for his protectionism and fiscal wizardry, said, "If we could legally let all the slaveholders go, I don't know but I would say amen." In numerous editorials, Greeley similarly suggested letting the South go in peace.[22]

Ultimately, Republicans and other northerners expected southerners to share their unionism and reasonableness. Because the North acquiesced when southerners and their sympathizers won, the South should do the same—or as Indiana's elected governor, Henry Lane, said, he did not "feel like apologizing . . . for being found in the majority once in twenty years." Seward forsook a reputation for radicalism while enhancing his reputation for shrewdness, sometimes to excess, by backing compromise proposals in Congress. Seward hoped to put the onus for any disunion and rebellion on the South and stall developments long enough for Lincoln to replace James Buchanan, but radicals worried that he had lost all principle. In the House, Seward's ally Charles Francis Adams endorsed statehood for New Mexico, which could have slavery under the Compromise of 1850. For that, some radicals railed at Adams, but they misunderstood that he expected the South to reject his plan, thereby making deep southerners look unreasonable and showing border state and upper southerners that Republicans could be reasonable. "I think I know the difference between surrendering unimportant points and sacrificing principles," Adams said.[23]

If Republicans were unsure of their ground and some of their members, southerners were less united than they appeared to northerners. When news of Lincoln's election reached the South, secession was far from the forefront. The *New Orleans Bee* had a one-word reaction: "WAIT." Most other southerners agreed: because they controlled Congress and the Supreme Court, a Republican president might have a limited impact. But southerners had enjoyed decades of freedom from abolitionist or antislavery literature in their mails, and whoever a Republican president named postmaster general—even an antislavery southerner like Blair—probably would end that policy. With Lincoln controlling patronage all the way up to the Supreme Court, any southerner he appointed might have some sympathy with his views. Whether Lincoln would interfere with slavery in the states was an issue, but states' rights mattered far less to southerners than their rights in the national government: it was the federal government that had forced the North to help return fugitive slaves and protect slave owners in other states and in territories. Thus, for many southerners, the gravest concern about Lincoln was that he would deprive them not of states' rights, but of national power. Those holding that power—large-scale planters, as opposed to yeoman farmers—feared Republicans would find a way to win over nonslaveholding southerners to the antislavery cause, perhaps by ending the gag rule and offering patronage. Not only could southerners be in danger from slave rebellions, but they also faced, if only in their own minds, the prospect of Republicans aiding a class war that would pit southerner against southerner.[24]

As Lincoln's election had approached, southern leaders exchanged ideas about how to respond. Fire-eaters like South Carolina's Rhett and Alabama's Yancey strategized. Even if South Carolina led the secessionist charge, the Lower South needed to leave with it. The Palmetto State's legislature stayed in session after choosing electors for Breckinridge, then voted to hold a convention on secession on January 15—a delay that worried fire-eaters because anti-Republican fervor might have time to die down or die out. Fortunately for them, a mass meeting of secessionist speakers prompted legislators to back up the convention to December 17 and hold the election of delegates to it as soon as possible. On December 20, the convention unanimously agreed that "the union now subsisting between South Carolina and other States, under the name of the 'United States of America,' is hereby dissolved," and that South Carolina was an "Independent Commonwealth."[25]

Across the South, other states followed. Mississippi went along on January 9, followed the next day by Florida and the day after by Alabama. By February 1, Georgia, Louisiana, and Texas seceded, but not unanimously or without debate. In Georgia, Stephens battled immediate secession, arguing that slavery in the territories mattered less for the moment than demanding the repeal of all northern personal liberty laws to protect the Fugitive Slave Act—but then Stephens retreated from the fray and Georgia acted. In Texas, Sam Houston fought hard to keep his state in the Union, but, despite his popularity and reputation there, to no avail. In Congress, Kentucky's John Crittenden proposed restoring the Missouri Compromise line to the Pacific and applying it to territory "hereafter acquired," and Toombs told his Senate colleague that because Georgia would accept it, he would go along. But Republicans rebuffed the Crittenden Compromise because it meant slavery in the territories and possible future efforts by the South to acquire Caribbean territory. Indeed, according to Toombs, the biggest foe of compromise on the Senate's compromise committee was that supposed sellout, Seward.

The problem became what William Freehling has called "the snowball effect." It began with South Carolina taking the step toward secession, other steps followed, and Buchanan was at the heart of them. That December, his annual message blamed Republicans for the sectional crisis and declared secession illegal. But he claimed to be powerless to stop it, prompting Seward to analyze his stand: "No state has the right to secede, unless it wants to. The Executive is bound to coerce a seceding state, unless the Executive be opposed in its efforts to do so." Under pressure, Buchanan finally forced out or accepted resignations from cabinet members from seceding states, replacing them with unionists like New York's John Dix and Pennsylvanian Edwin Stanton. In turn, Buchanan acted decisively, and perhaps too quickly, sending ships to reinforce forts in South Carolina and Florida in early January rather than waiting for events to unfold. His actions reassured northerners that at least he opposed secession, but convinced more southerners that still another northerner had turned on them, and that the rights of their states were indeed at issue, even with a Democratic administration. And when Republicans, now in control of Congress with dozens of southerners seceding with their states, admitted Kansas as a free state and passed a protective tariff, southerners still in the Union felt more isolated.[26]

All sides jockeyed for position. Representatives of the seven seceded states met in Montgomery, Alabama, hoping to attract states from the Upper and border South. They approved a constitution that drew heavily on the U.S. Constitution, banned the African slave trade, and chose as president and vice-president of the Confederate States of America Davis and Stephens. Neither resembled a fire-eater, and Davis claimed secession merely followed in the Founders' footsteps, but Stephens delivered a speech in Georgia declaring that the new Confederate government's "foundations are laid, its corner-stone rests upon the great truth, that the negro is not equal to the white man; that slavery—subordination to the superior race—is his natural and normal condition."[27]

For Republicans, the key remained keeping the Union as whole as possible until Lincoln could replace Buchanan. A peace conference, called an "old gentlemen's convention" for all of the aged Democrats and Whigs involved, met in Washington in February but produced nothing, and Republicans did their best to assure that outcome and buy time. Lincoln traveled east from Springfield, starting with a moving farewell to the townspeople, seemingly offering platitudes whenever he spoke along the way but making clear to those who took the time to read his statements that he would tolerate no violent action from the South, and crept into Washington, D.C., due to concerns about threats on his life. It was a decision that he always regretted, but a sign of the concern about the prospect of violence.

Finally, on March 4, storm clouds over the capitol literally gave way to sunshine as Lincoln took the oath of office from Taney and delivered an inaugural address intended to reassure skeptics in both sections. He announced that "all the protection which, consistently with the Constitution and the laws, can be given, will be cheerfully given to all the States when lawfully demanded, for whatever cause," thereby reassuring the South of its rights but declaring secession "legally void" and "insurrectionary and revolutionary." He hoped to avoid "bloodshed or violence" unless they were "forced upon the national authority," which warned the South against action but seemed to proclaim the region safe. Although he appealed to "the mystic chords of memory" and "the better angels of our nature" in concluding, the previous paragraph declared, "In your hands, my dissatisfied fellow countrymen, and not in mine, is the momentous issue of civil war. The government will not assail you. You can have no conflict, without being yourselves the aggressor."[28]

Predictably, reactions to the inaugural address depended on who was reacting. Most Republicans praised Lincoln, although radicals wished for more fire and conservatives for a more soothing approach. Stephen Douglas, sitting near the new president as he spoke, said, "I defend the inaugural if it is as I understand it, namely, an emanation from the brain and heart of a patriot, and as I mean . . . to act the part of a patriot, I indorse it." *The New York Times* warned, "If the Union cannot be saved on this basis and consistently with these principles, then it is better that it should not be saved at all." But the *Richmond Enquirer,* in still loyal Virginia, called it "the cool, unimpassioned, deliberate language of the fanatic, with the purpose of pursuing the promptings of fanaticism even to the dismemberment of the Government with the horrors of civil war."[29]

Those horrors proved to be near. Before his first full day as president was over, Lincoln learned of the need to provision Fort Sumter, in the harbor of Charleston, South Carolina, and Fort Pickens in Florida. His cabinet split over what to do and at which fort to do it, with Blair determined to send in supplies, Chase mostly in favor, and Seward secretly dickering with Confederate commissioners and trying to manipulate Lincoln and the rest of the secretaries. On April 6, Lincoln finally notified South Carolina's governor that a ship would arrive only with supplies—nothing military or, for that matter, provocative. But, from his perspective and that of many southerners, Davis could allow no other country to enter Confederate waters and aid its own troops, even on a humanitarian mission. Fire-eater Edmund Ruffin reasoned, "The shedding of blood will serve to change many voters in the hesitating states, from the submission or procrastinating ranks, to the zealous for immediate secession." Davis ordered P. G. T. Beauregard, the first brigadier general of the Provisional Army of the Confederate States of America, to demand Fort Sumter's surrender and, if not heeded, attack. On the morning of April 12, that is what Beauregard did. In response, Lincoln called out troops, four more southern states seceded, and over the next four years the dead would include 620,000 Americans and slavery itself—the institution that southerners had seceded to protect.[30]

THE END OF THE BEGINNING

In a decade-and-a-half since the Mexican-American War began, the North and the South had both changed and remained the same. The major changes included a greatly expanded northern population, thanks partly to immigration from Ireland and central Europe, and a new political system that had evolved from two national parties trying to avoid slavery to two substantially sectional parties either unable to avoid the issue or eager to take it on. A subtler but no less important change was that northerners wearied of conceding to southerners, and southerners became convinced that northerners wished to remake their society by eliminating slavery. Indeed, that was the ultimate Republican goal, whether or not most Republicans even realized it: to isolate slavery where it existed and keep it from expanding in the hope of choking it. Southerners demanded that northerners accept slavery where the country would expand, and northerners worried that that meant slavery not only in all newly acquired territory, but also where it was no longer permitted: in their midst. Whether out of a sense of moral outrage, a fear of the competition for free labor from slave labor, racism, concern about political power, or a variety of other issues, more northerners found it unacceptable that southerners demanded the right to take their slaves into previously unorganized territory. The battle had preceded the Mexican-American

War, but that war and the territory it made part of the United States set the country on the path to an irreconcilable debate over the spread of slavery.

The debate snowballed beyond whether slavery could expand into territory acquired in the Mexican-American War. The question became which region—and who within each region—would control the federal government and its ability to protect that territory from slavery or for slavery. Other issues were involved, including the rise of sectional political parties, one rooted entirely in the North, the other claiming to be national but ultimately southern-dominated, and the inability of national parties to avoid the question of slavery; the differences between the economies of the two regions, and whether they were compatible; different interpretations of the Constitution, and whether it was a document of slavery or of freedom; and sociocultural differences both between and within the North and the South. While these provoked debate and, at times, violence, slavery proved to be the pivot on which each of these topics turned. Thus, four years after the war began, Lincoln could rightly say, as he did in his Second Inaugural Address, "These slaves constituted a peculiar and powerful interest. All knew that this interest was, somehow, the cause of the war."[31]

But at the heart of the debate lay whether slavery could grow and be protected, first in the Mexican Cession, then in Kansas, and perhaps even in places not yet part of American soil. Slavery and its growth had been controversial throughout the American past, became a more divisive issue in the 1840s and 1850s, and finally had divided the country so completely that whether the republic the Founding Fathers saw as a beacon to the world even had a future had become open to question. Nearly a quarter of a millennium after the first Africans arrived in Virginia, 85 years after the Declaration of Independence, just under three quarters of a century after the Founding Fathers had met to write a Constitution and agreed to a series of compromises that allowed slavery to survive and the United States to grow, the North and the South went to war for the future of their regions, and for the West. The country would never be the same again.

NOTES

PROLOGUE

1. Stanley M. Elkins and Eric L. McKitrick, *The Age of Federalism: The Early American Republic, 1788–1800* (New York: Oxford University Press, 1993), 754.

2. Daniel Walker Howe, *What Hath God Wrought: The Transformation of America, 1815–1848* (New York: Oxford University Press, 2008), 157.

3. David M. Potter, *The Impending Crisis, 1848–1861* (New York: Harper and Row, 1976), 98.

4. Ibid.

5. Sean Wilentz, *The Rise of American Democracy: Jefferson to Lincoln* (New York: W.W. Norton, 2005), 568.

6. Ibid., 574.

7. Thomas M. Leonard, *James K. Polk: A Clear and Unquestionable Destiny* (Wilmington: Scholarly Resources, 2001), 42.

8. Geoffrey C. Ward, Ken Burns, and Ric Burns, *The Civil War: An Illustrated History* (New York: Alfred A. Knopf, 1990), 264.

CHAPTER ONE

1. *Congressional Globe*, 29th Congress, 1st session, August 8, 1846, 1214–17.

2. "Handbill Replying to Charges of Infidelity," July 31, 1846, in *Illinois Gazette*, August 15, 1846, in Roy P. Basler, ed., *The Collected Works of Abraham Lincoln* (9 volumes,

New Brunswick: Rutgers University Press, 1953–55), I, 382; David Herbert Donald, *Lincoln* (New York: Simon and Schuster, 1995), 113–15.

3. Leonard, *Polk*, 120.

4. Ibid., 136–37.

5. James K. Polk, Saturday, May 9, 1846, in Allan Nevins, ed., *Polk: The Diary of a President, 1845–1849* (New York: Longmans, Green & Co., 1929), 81.

6. James D. Richardson, ed., *A Compilation of the Messages and Papers of the Presidents, 1789–1897* (10 volumes, Washington, D.C.: Government Printing Office, 1896–99), IV, 449–50

7. Donald, *Lincoln*, 126.

8. Joshua R. Giddings, *Speeches in Congress* (Boston: John P. Jewett, 1853), 171–200.

9. Merrill D. Peterson, *The Great Triumvirate: Webster, Clay, and Calhoun* (New York: Oxford University Press, 1987), 422–23.

10. Sean Wilentz, *The Rise of Democracy: Jefferson to Lincoln* (New York: W.W. Norton, 2005), 583; Eric Foner, "The Wilmot Proviso Revisited," *Journal of American History* 56, no. 2 (1969): 273.

11. Wilentz, *Rise of Democracy*, 584; Jonathan H. Earle, *Jacksonian Antislavery and the Politics of Free Soil, 1824–1854* (Chapel Hill: University of North Carolina Press, 2004), 66.

12. Earle, *Jacksonian Antislavery*, 66; Wilentz, *Rise of Democracy*, 585; Polk, Saturday, January 23, 1847, in Nevins, ed., *Polk Diary*, 190.

13. Foner, "Wilmot Proviso," 276.

14. Michael F. Holt, *The Rise and Fall of the American Whig Party: Jacksonian Politics and the Onset of the Civil War* (New York: Oxford University Press, 1999), 248–49.

15. Polk, Saturday, November 21, 1846, and Monday, December 14, 1846, *Diary*, 173–74, 175. Polk often vented his displeasure about both generals in his diary.

16. David Herbert Donald, *Charles Sumner and the Coming of the Civil War* (New York: Alfred A. Knopf, 1960), 130–59.

17. *Congressional Globe*, 30th Congress, 1st session, January 12, 1848, 154–56; Donald, *Lincoln*, 125.

18. *Congressional Globe*, 29th Congress, 2d session, January 19, 1848, Appendix, 211; Holt, *Whig Party*, 255, 265–67.

19. William W. Freehling, *The Road to Disunion, Volume 1: Secessionists at Bay: 1776–1854* (New York: Oxford University Press, 1990), 461; Holt, *Whig Party*, 255.

20. Holt, *Whig Party*, 310.

21. Ibid., 312–17.

22. Ibid., 326.

23. Earle, *Jacksonian Antislavery*, 75.

24. Wilentz, *Rise of Democracy*, 616.

25. Ibid., 618.

26. Ibid., 624–25; Eric Foner, *Politics and Ideology in the Age of the Civil War* (New York: Oxford University Press, 1980), 82.

27. "Speech in the U.S. House of Representatives on the Presidential Question," July 27, 1848, in Basler, ed., *Lincoln's Works*, I, 501–16.

CHAPTER TWO

1. Holman Hamilton, *Prologue to Conflict: The Crisis and Compromise of 1850* (New York: W.W. Norton, 1964), 160; Allan Nevins, *Ordeal of the Union*, vol 1, *Fruits of Manifest Destiny, 1847–1852* (New York: Charles Scribner's Sons, 1947), 343.

2. David M. Potter, *The Impending Crisis: 1848–1861* (New York: Harper & Row, 1976), 90–120; Sean Wilentz, *The Rise of American Democracy: Jefferson to Lincoln* (New York: W.W. Norton, 2005), 637. See also Michael A. Morrison, *Slavery and the American West: The Eclipse of Manifest Destiny and the Coming of the Civil War* (Chapel Hill: University of North Carolina Press, 1997), 96–125.

3. Rodman W. Paul, *Mining Frontiers of the Far West, 1848–1880*, rev. ed. (Albuquerque: University of New Mexico Press, 2001), 12; Andrew F. Rolle, *California: A History*, 2nd ed. (New York: Thomas Y. Crowell Company, 1969), 217.

4. Sally Denton, *Passion and Principle: John and Jessie Frémont, the Couple Whose Power, Politics, and Love Shaped Nineteenth-Century America* (New York: Bloomsbury, 2007), 158; Leonard L. Richards, *The California Gold Rush and the Coming of the Civil War* (New York: Vintage Books, 2007), 1–68, especially 67–68.

5. David Alan Johnson, *Founding the Far West: California, Oregon, and Nevada, 1840–1890* (Berkeley: University of California Press, 1992), 101–38.

6. James D. Richardson, ed., *A Compilation of the Messages and Papers of the Presidents, 1789–1897* (10 volumes, Washington: Government Printing Office, 1896–99), 5:4–6; Holman Hamilton, *Zachary Taylor: Soldier in the White House* (2 volumes, Indianapolis: Bobbs-Merrill, 1951), especially 2:149–61; Nevins, *Ordeal of the Union*, 229.

7. Nevins, *Ordeal of the Union*, 229; Michael F. Holt, *The Rise and Fall of the American Whig Party: Jacksonian Politics and the Onset of Civil War* (New York: Oxford University Press, 1999), 410; George Ticknor Curtis, *Life of Daniel Webster* (2 volumes, New York: D. Appleton and Company, 1870), 2:358–59.

8. Merrill D. Peterson, *The Great Triumvirate: Webster, Clay, and Calhoun* (New York: Oxford University Press, 1987), 450.

9. Nevins, *Ordeal of the Union*, 231; Holt, *Whig Party*, 397–98.

10. Abraham Lincoln to John M. Clayton, Springfield, Illinois, July 28, 1849, in Roy P. Basler, ed., *The Collected Works of Abraham Lincoln* (9 volumes, New Brunswick: Rutgers University Press, 1953–55), 2:60; Holt, *Whig Party*, 426.

11. Holt, *Whig Party*, 406–30.

12. Ibid., 436.

13. Holt, *Whig Party*, 436–38; William W. Freehling, *The Road to Disunion*, vol. 1, *Secessionists at Bay, 1776–1854* (New York: Oxford University Press, 1990), 492; Richards, *Gold Rush*, 69–70.

14. Richards, *Gold Rush*, 73; Holt, *Whig Party*, 438–39; Wilentz, *Rise of American Democracy*, 637–38; Morrison, *Slavery and the American West*, 104–05.

15. Hamilton, *Taylor*, 225; Richard H. Sewell, *A House Divided: Sectionalism and Civil War, 1848–1865* (Baltimore: Johns Hopkins University Press, 1988), 31.

16. *Congressional Globe*, 31st Congress, 1st session, December 13, 1849, 27–28; Nevins, *Ordeal of the Union*, 250–58.

17. Richardson, ed., *Messages and Papers*, 5:9–24.

18. Ibid.

19. George E. Baker, ed., *The Works of William H. Seward* (5 volumes, Boston: Houghton Mifflin, 1887–90), 3:301.

20. Hamilton, *Prologue to Conflict*, 45; Nevins, *Ordeal of the Union*, 261.

21. Hamilton, *Prologue to Conflict*, 53–54; *Congressional Globe*, 31st Congress, 1st session, January 29, 1850, 244–52; Nevins, *Ordeal of the Union*, 266.

22. *Congressional Globe*, 31st Congress, 1st session, February 5–6, 1850, Appendix, 115–27; Hamilton, *Prologue to Conflict*, 52–59; Nevins, *Ordeal of the Union*, 267.

23. Hamilton, *Prologue to Conflict*, 60–62; Nevins, *Ordeal of the Union*, 1:268; Potter, *Impending Crisis*, 100; Peterson, *The Great Triumvirate*, 458–59.

24. Hamilton, *Prologue to Conflict*, 70–71.

25. Harriet Martineau, *Retrospect of Western Travel* (3 volumes, London: Saunders and Otley, 1838), 1:243; Nathan Sargent, *Public Men and Events from the Commencement of Mr. Monroe's Administration, in 1817, to the Close of Mr. Fillmore's Administration, in 1853* (2 volumes, Philadelphia: J.B. Lippincott, 1874), 2:363–65; *Congressional Globe*, 31st Congress, 1st session, March 4, 1850, 451–55; Hamilton, *Prologue to Conflict*, 71–74.

26. Hamilton, *Prologue to Conflict*, 74–75; *Congressional Globe*, 31st Congress, 1st session, March 5, 1850, 461–64 (Foote) and Appendix, 242–48 (Hamlin).

27. *Congressional Globe*, 31st Congress, 1st session, March 7, 1850, Appendix, 269–76.

28. Hamilton, *Prologue to Conflict*, 81–83.

29. *Congressional Globe*, 31st Congress, 2nd session, March 11, 1850, 262–76.

30. Ibid., 84–86; Holt, *Whig Party*, 489–93.

31. Hamilton, *Prologue to Conflict*, 64–65, 86–87.

32. John C. Waugh, *On the Brink of Civil War: The Compromise of 1850 and How It Changed the Course of American History* (Wilmington: Scholarly Resources, 2003), 129–30; Freehling, *Road to Disunion*, 481–86.

33. Hamilton, *Prologue to Conflict*, 105–07.

34. Hamilton, *Prologue to Conflict*, 84–117, details the intricacies of Senate action that led to the Omnibus bill's defeat. See *Congressional Globe*, 31st Congress, 1st session, August 1, 1850, Appendix, 1486–88; Robert W. Johannsen, *Stephen A. Douglas* (New York: Oxford University Press, 1973), 294.

35. *Congressional Globe*, 31st Congress, 1st Session, August 1, 1850, Appendix, 1486–88; Hamilton, *Prologue to Conflict*, 146–47. Davis's comment appears in *Congressional Globe*, 31st Congress, 1st session, September 16, 1850, 1830.

36. *Congressional Globe*, 31st Congress, 1st session, August 12, 1850, Appendix, 1520, 1533.

37. Potter, *Impending Crisis*, 97; Hamilton, *Prologue to Conflict*, 151–65; *Congressional Globe*, 31st Congress, 1st session, August 28, 1850, 1682–87, 1695–1704.

38. Potter, *Impending Crisis*, 110.

39. *Congressional Globe*, 31st Congress, 1st session, September 18, 1850, 1859 (Chase); September 16, 1850, 1830 (Douglas).

CHAPTER THREE

1. Michael F. Holt, *The Rise of the American Whig Party: Jacksonian Politics and the Onset of Civil War* (New York: Oxford University Press, 1999), 754–62; Allan Nevins, *Ordeal of the Union*, vol. 2, *A House Dividing, 1852–1857* (New York: Charles Scribner's Sons, 1947), 36; Tyler Anbinder, *Nativism and Slavery: The Northern Know Nothings and the Politics of the 1850s* (New York: Oxford University Press, 1992), 16; William E. Gienapp, *The Origins of the Republican Party, 1852–1856* (New York: Oxford University Press, 1987), 32.

2. Richard H. Sewell, *Ballots for Freedom: Antislavery Politics in the United States, 1837–1860* (New York: Oxford University Press, 1976), 250.

3. Holt, *Whig Party*, 558–79.

4. Holt, *Whig Party*, 581–83; David Herbert Donald, *Charles Sumner and the Coming of the Civil War* (New York: Alfred A. Knopf, 1960), 183–204, at 187.

5. Holt, *Whig Party*, 583–96, 654.

6. Gienapp, *Origins of the Republican Party*, 41; Glyndon G. Van Deusen, *Thurlow Weed: Wizard of the Lobby* (Boston: Little, Brown, 1947), 171–88.

7. Nevins, *Ordeal of the Union*, 2:402.

8. William J. Cooper, Jr., *Liberty and Slavery: Southern Politics to 1860* (New York: Alfred A. Knopf, 1983), 233; David M. Potter, *The Impending Crisis: 1848–1861* (New York: Harper & Row, 1976), 128.

9. William W. Freehling, *The Road to Disunion*, vol. 1, *Secessionists at Bay, 1776–1854* (New York: Oxford University Press, 1990), 520.

10. Potter, *Impending Crisis*, 130.

11. Don E. Fehrenbacher and Ward M. McAfee, *The Slaveholding Republic: An Account of the United States Government's Relations to Slavery* (New York: Oxford University Press, 2001), especially 205–30; Henry Steele Commager, *Theodore Parker* (Boston: Little, Brown, 1936), 197; Nevins, *Ordeal of the Union*, 2:379; Potter, *Impending Crisis*, 130–32.

12. Gilbert Muller, *William Cullen Bryant: Author of America* (Albany: State University of New York Press, 2008), 223; Potter, *Impending Crisis*, 132; Frederick J. Blue, *The Free-Soilers: Third Party Politics, 1848–1854* (Urbana: University of Illinois Press, 1973), 204; Fehrenbacher and McAfee, *The Slaveholding Republic*, 233.

13. Sean Wilentz, *The Rise of American Democracy: Jefferson to Lincoln* (New York: W.W. Norton, 2005), 645–46, 650; Commager, *Parker*, 197–247; Nevins, *Ordeal of the Union*, 2:388; Philip S. Foner, *History of Black Americans from the Compromise of 1850 to the End of the Civil War* (Westport: Greenwood Press, 1983), 19.

14. Nevins, *Ordeal of the Union*, 2:388; Robert V. Remini, *Daniel Webster: The Man and His Time* (New York: W.W. Norton, 1997), 695–97; Fergus M. Bordewich, *Bound for Canaan: The Epic Story of the Underground Railroad, America's First Civil Rights Movement* (New York: HarperCollins, 2005), 320–23; Robert W. Johannsen, *Stephen A. Douglas* (New York: Oxford University Press, 1973), 340.

15. Bordewich, *Bound for Canaan*, 325–33; Hans L. Trefousse, *Thaddeus Stevens: Nineteenth-Century Egalitarian* (Chapel Hill: University of North Carolina Press, 1997), 84–85.

16. Bordewich, *Bound for Canaan*, 323, 333–40.

17. *Congressional Globe*, 31st Congress, 2nd session, February 24, 1851, Appendix, 322; Ibid., Appendix, 1–5.

18. Fehrenbacher and McAfee, *The Slaveholding Republic*, 233; Gienapp, *Origins of the Republican Party*, 14.

19. "A Word about Ourselves," *The New-York Daily Times*, September 18, 1851; Francis Brown, *Raymond of "The Times"* (New York: W.W. Norton, 1951); Nevins, *Ordeal of the Union*, 2:87–91.

20. Potter, *Impending Crisis*, 140.

21. Thomas F. Gossett, *Uncle Tom's Cabin and American Culture* (Dallas: Southern Methodist University Press, 1985), 185–211; McPherson, *Battle Cry of Freedom*, 90; Carl N. Degler, *The Other South: Southern Dissenters in the Nineteenth Century* (New York: Harper & Row, 1974), 149–50.

22. Arthur M. Schlesinger, Jr., *The Age of Jackson* (Boston: Little, Brown, 1946), 370–90; Wilentz, *Democracy*, 653–54.

23. Nevins, *Ordeal of the Union*, 2:13–14.

24. Larry Gara, *The Presidency of Franklin Pierce* (Lawrence: University Press of Kansas, 1991), 24.

25. Johannsen, *Douglas*, 339–73.

26. Johannsen, *Douglas*, 339–73.

27. Gara, *Pierce*, 35; Nevins, *Ordeal of the Union*, 2:23.

28. Holt, *Whig Party*, 673; Nevins, *Ordeal of the Union*, 2:26; Van Deusen, *Weed*, 191.

29. *Congressional Globe*, 32nd Congress, 1st session, March 31, 1852, Appendix, 371–73.

30. Gara, *Pierce*, 38.

31. Holt, *Whig Party*, 745–46; Gienapp, *Origins of the Republican Party*, 20–25.

32. Holt, *Whig Party*, 770–71, 794–95; Nevins, *Ordeal of the Union*, 2:37; Gara, *Pierce*, 40.

33. Holt, *Whig Party*, 772.

34. John A. Garraty, ed., *Interpreting American History: Conversations with Historians* (2 volumes, New York: The Macmillan Company, 1970), 1:286–87. See also Roy Franklin Nichols, *Franklin Pierce: Young Hickory of the Granite Hills*, 2nd ed. (Philadelphia: University of Pennsylvania Press, 1958).

35. Ibid.; Gara, *Pierce*, 54; Nichols, *Pierce*, 279–84.

36. Gara, *Pierce*, 51–52.

37. Gara, *Pierce*, 51–52; Nichols, *Pierce*, 247–58; Gienapp, *Origins of the Republican Party*, 41–42.

38. Gara, *Pierce*, 47–48.

39. *Congressional Globe*, 33rd Congress, 1st session, March 16, 1854, 417; Potter, *Impending Crisis*, 190.

40. James M. McPherson, *Battle Cry of Freedom: The Civil War Era* (New York: Oxford University Press, 1988), 109; Gara, *Pierce*, 150–55.

41. Gara, *Pierce*, 90; Potter, *Impending Crisis*, 152–54.

42. Nevins, *Ordeal of the Union*, 2:92.

43. Gienapp, *Origins of the Republican Party*, 70.

44. Eric Foner, *Free Soil, Free Labor, Free Men: The Ideology of the Republican Party Before the Civil War*, 2nd ed. (New York: Oxford University Press, 1995), 94.

45. *Congressional Globe*, 33rd Congress, 1st session, January 23, 1854, 239–40, 281–82; Gara, *Pierce*, 92.

46. Nevins, *Ordeal of the Union*, 2:118, 135; *Congressional Globe*, 33rd Congress, 1st session, February 17, 1854, Appendix, 150; *Congressional Globe*, 33rd Congress, 1st session, March 28, 1854, 447; Johannsen, *Douglas*, 422.

47. *Congressional Globe*, 33rd Congress, 1st session, March 3, 1854, 532; *Congressional Globe*, 33rd Congress, 1st session, March 21, 1854, 701–03, Appendix; *Congressional Globe*, 33rd Congress, 1st session, February 24, 1854, 226; Gara, *Pierce*, 95; Gienapp, *Origins of the Republican Party*, 73.

48. "Renewal of the Slavery Agitation—The Nebraska Bill," *The New York Times*, January 24, 1854; *Congressional Globe*, 33rd Congress, 1st session, May 22, 1854, 1254; Freehling, *Road to Disunion*, 560.

49. Potter, *Impending Crisis*, 171–72; *Congressional Globe*, 31st Congress, 1st session, March 13, 1850, Appendix, 371.

CHAPTER FOUR

1. Edward J. Renehan, Jr., *The Secret Six: The True Tale of the Men Who Conspired with John Brown* (Columbia: University of South Carolina Press, 1997), 64–65; James M. McPherson, *Battle Cry of Freedom: The Civil War Era* (New York: Oxford University Press, 1988), 119–20; Sean Wilentz, *The Rise of American Democracy: Jefferson to Lincoln* (New York: W.W. Norton, 2005), 677.

2. Louis Filler, *The Crusade Against Slavery: 1830–1860* (New York: Harper & Row, 1960), 213–16; Lewis Hyde, ed., *The Selected Essays of Henry David Thoreau* (New York: North Point Press, 2002), 179–94.

3. Robert W. Johannsen, *Stephen A. Douglas* (New York: Oxford University Press, 1973), 451.

4. Eric Foner, *Free Soil, Free Labor, Free Men: The Ideology of the Republican Party Before the Civil War*, 2nd ed. (New York: Oxford University Press, 1995), 189–95.

5. Foner, *Free Soil*, 40–72, 194.

6. William E. Gienapp, *The Origins of the Republican Party: 1852–1856* (New York: Oxford University Press, 1987), 82–83.

7. Gienapp, *Origins*, 85–87; Foner, *Free Soil*, 193; Wilentz, *Democracy*, 675.

8. Michael F. Holt, *The Rise and Fall of the American Whig Party: Jacksonian Politics and the Onset of Civil War* (New York: Oxford University Press, 1999), 821.

9. Foner, *Free Soil*, 157; Gienapp, *Origins of the Republican Party*, 79–80.

10. Wilentz, *Democracy*, 675; Foner, *Free Soil*, 158–59.

11. Michael F. Holt, *The Political Crisis of the 1850s* (New York: Wiley and Sons, 1978), 23; *Congressional Globe*, 33rd Congress, 2nd session, February 23, 1855, Appendix, 216.

12. Tyler G. Anbinder, *Nativism and Slavery: The Northern Know-Nothings and the Politics of Antislavery in the 1850s* (New York: Oxford University Press, 1992), 3–8; Wilentz, *Rise of American Democracy*, 682–83.

13. Anbinder, *Nativism and Slavery*, 20–43.

14. Ibid., 43–45.

15. Gienapp, *Origins of the Republican Party*, 91.

16. Don E. Fehrenbacher, *Prelude to Greatness: Lincoln in the 1850's* (Stanford: Stanford University Press, 1962), 25; Gienapp, *Origins of the Republican Party*, 89–106.

17. "Speech at Peoria, Illinois," October 16, 1854, in Roy P. Basler, ed., *The Collected Works of Abraham Lincoln* (9 volumes, New Brunswick: Rutgers University Press, 1953–55), 2:247–83, at 282; David Herbert Donald, *Lincoln* (New York: Simon and Schuster, 1995), 168–71.

18. Donald, *Lincoln*, 184.

19. Gienapp, *Origins of the Republican Party*, 158; Anbinder, *Nativism and Slavery*, 149.

20. Gienapp, *Origins of the Republican Party*, 172–73.

21. John Niven, *Salmon P. Chase: A Biography* (New York: Oxford University Press, 1995), 169–70; Gienapp, *Origins of the Republican Party*, 105–13.

22. Foner, *Free Soil*, 231–32; Abraham Lincoln to Joshua Speed, Springfield, Illinois, August 24, 1855, in Basler, ed., *Lincoln's Works*, 2:322–23.

23. Anbinder, *Nativism & Slavery*, 167.

24. Gienapp, *Origins of the Republican Party*, 243–47.

25. Ibid., 249.

26. Ibid., 255–59.

27. *Congressional Globe*, 33rd Congress, 1st session, May 25, 1854, Appendix, 769; James A. Rawley, *Race and Politics: "Bleeding Kansas" and the Coming of the Civil War* (Philadelphia: J.B. Lippincott, 1969), 78; Wilentz, *Democracy*, 677.

28. Rawley, *Race and Politics*, 81, 85; Wilentz, *Democracy*, 678; Nicole Etcheson, *Bleeding Kansas: Contested Liberty in the Civil War Era* (Lawrence: University Press of Kansas, 2004), 31–32, 47; McPherson, *Battle Cry of Freedom*, 145–46.

29. Etcheson, *Bleeding Kansas*, 38–39.

30. Wilentz, *Democracy*, 686; Etcheson, *Bleeding Kansas*, 53, 59; William W. Freehling, *The Road to Disunion*, vol. 2, *Secessionists Triumphant, 1854–1861* (New York: Oxford University Press, 2007), 63–64.

31. Etcheson, *Bleeding Kansas*, 63; Rawley, *Race and Politics*, 91–92.

32. Rawley, *Race and Politics*, 96; Etcheson, *Bleeding Kansas*, 78, 91.

33. Etcheson, *Bleeding Kansas*, 97; *Congressional Globe*, 34th Congress, 1st session, April 9, 1856, Appendix, 399.

34. Stephen B. Oates, *To Purge This Land with Blood: A Biography of John Brown* (New York: Harper & Row, 1970), 129; Etcheson, *Bleeding Kansas*, 109–11.

35. Etcheson, *Bleeding Kansas*, 137; Gienapp, *Origins of the Republican Party*, 169.

36. David Herbert Donald, *Charles Sumner and the Coming of the Civil War* (New York: Alfred A. Knopf, 1960), 208; *Congressional Globe*, 32nd Congress, 1st session, August 26, 1852, Appendix, 1102.

37. *Congressional Globe*, 32nd Congress, 1st session, August 26, 1852, Appendix, 1113–15.

38. Donald, *Sumner*, 277–78.

39. Donald, *Sumner*, 285; *Congressional Globe*, 34th Congress, 1st session, May 19–20, 1856, Appendix, 529–44.

40. *Congressional Globe*, 34th Congress, 1st session, May 19–20, 1856, Appendix, 529–47.

41. *Congressional Globe*, 34th Congress, 1st session, May 20, 1856, Appendix, 545; Johannsen, *Douglas*, 503.

42. Donald, *Sumner*, 289–93.

43. Ibid., 294–95.

44. Ibid., 295–97; Johannsen, *Douglas*, 504; Anna Laurens Dawes, *Charles Sumner* (New York: Dodd, Mead, and Company, 1892), 113.

45. Freehling, *Secessionists Triumphant*, 84; William C. Davis, *The Union That Shaped the Confederacy: Robert Toombs and Alexander H. Stephens* (Lawrence: University Press of Kansas, 2001), 68–69; Donald, *Sumner*, 307.

46. *New York Evening Post*, February 27, 1854, in William Cullen Bryant, II, ed., *Power for Sanity: Selected Editorials of William Cullen Bryant, 1829–1861* (New York: Fordham University Press, 1994), 273; May 23, 1856, (Ibid., 289); Donald, *Sumner*, 300–01.

47. Foner, *Free Soil*, 55–56.

CHAPTER FIVE

1. Allan Nevins, *Ordeal of the Union*, vol. 2, *A House Dividing, 1852–1857* (New York: Charles Scribner's Sons, 1947), 498–99.

2. William E. Gienapp, *The Origins of the Republican Party: 1852–1856* (New York: Oxford University Press, 1987), 305.

3. Robert W. Johannsen, *Stephen A. Douglas* (New York: Oxford University Press, 1973), 506–07.

4. Nevins, *Ordeal of the Union*, 2:459.

5. Johannsen, *Douglas*, 516–18.

6. Gienapp, *Origins of the Republican Party*, 306–07; Johannsen, *Douglas*, 523.

7. Eric Foner, *Free Soil, Free Labor, Free Men: The Ideology of the Republican Party Before the Civil War*, 2nd ed. (New York: Oxford University Press, 1995), 249; Gienapp, *Origins of the Republican Party*, 279, 286, 307.

8. "Presidential," *The New-York Times*, April 18, 1856; Gienapp, *Origins of the Republican Party*, 311.

9. Gienapp, *Origins of the Republican Party*, 311–16.

10. Sally Denton, *Passion and Principle: John and Jessie Frémont, The Couple Whose Power, Politics, and Love Shaped Nineteenth-Century America* (New York: Bloomsbury, 2007), 234–42.

11. Gienapp, *Origins of the Republican Party*, 323–24.

12. Ibid., 334–38.

13. Ibid., 355–59.

14. Ibid., 366; Foner, *Free Soil*, 250.

15. Tyler G. Anbinder, *Nativism & Slavery: The Northern Know Nothings and the Politics of the 1850s* (New York: Oxford University Press, 1992), 210, 215, 235–36.

16. Anbinder, *Nativism & Slavery*, 216–23.

17. William W. Freehling, *The Road to Disunion, Volume II: Secessionists Triumphant, 1854–1861* (New York: Oxford University Press, 2007), 94–95.

18. Anbinder, *Nativism & Slavery*, 244–46; Foner, *Free Soil*, 255.

19. Kenneth M. Stampp, *America in 1857: A Nation on the Brink* (New York: Oxford University Press, 1992), 6–7.

20. *Ibid.*, 62.

21. *Ibid.*, 64–67.

22. Unless otherwise indicated, the details of the case appeared originally in Don E. Fehrenbacher, *Slavery, Law, & Politics: The Dred Scott Case in Historical Perspective* (New York: Oxford University Press, 1981). This is an abridgment of Fehrenbacher's 1978, Pulitzer Prize-winning *The Dred Scott Case: Its Significance in American Law and Politics.* Quotations from the opinions are from *Dred Scott v. Sandford,* 60 U.S. (19 How.) 393 (1857). For the opinions and other relevant documents, see Paul A. Finkelman, *Dred Scott v. Sandford: A Brief History with Documents* (Boston: Bedford Books, 1997).

23. Fehrenbacher, *Slavery, Law & Politics*, 152.

24. Stampp, *1857*, 89.

25. *McCulloch v. Maryland*, 17 U.S. 316 (1819).

26. Fehrenbacher, *Slavery, Law & Politics*, 167–68; Stampp, *1857*, 92.

27. Fehrenbacher, *Slavery, Law & Politics*, 169–99; *Dred Scott v. Sandford*, 60 U.S. (19 How.) 393 (1857).

28. Fehrenbacher, *Slavery, Law & Politics*, 199–213.

29. Finkelman, *Dred Scott*, 92.

30. Fehrenbacher, *Slavery, Law & Politics*, 228–29.

31. *Ibid.*, 239.

32. *Ibid.*, 230–31; Stampp, *1857*, 101.

33. Fehrenbacher, *Slavery, Law & Politics*, 230; Stampp, *1857*, 104; *New York Evening Post*, March 9, 1857.

34. Stampp, *1857*, 105–06; *Illinois State Journal*, June 18, 1858, in Roy P. Basler, ed., *The Collected Works of Abraham Lincoln* (9 volumes, New Brunswick: Rutgers University Press, 1953–55), 2:465–67.

35. Foner, *Free Soil*, 97; *Illinois State Journal*, June 18, 1858, in Basler, ed., *Lincoln's Works*, II, 465–67.

36. *Congressional Globe*, 35 Congress, 1 Session, March 3, 1858, 941.

37. Johannsen, *Douglas*, 569.

38. *The New-York Times*, July 7, 1857; *Illinois State Journal*, June 29, 1857, in Basler, ed., *Lincoln's Works*, II, 398–410.

CHAPTER SIX

1. George E. Baker, ed., *The Works of William Seward* (5 volumes, Boston: Houghton Mifflin, 1884), 4:292.

2. *Congressional Globe*, 35th Congress, 1st session, May 24, 1858, Appendix, 401; Foner, *Free Soil*, 69–70; *Illinois State Journal*, June 18, 1858, and *Chicago Daily Tribune*, June 19, 1858, in Roy P. Basler, ed., *The Collected Works of Abraham Lincoln* (9 volumes, New Brunswick: Rutgers University Press, 1953–55), 2:461–62.

3. Kenneth M. Stampp, *America in 1857: A Nation on the Brink* (New York: Oxford University Press, 1992), 231–32.

4. *Congressional Globe*, 35th Congress, 1st session, March 4, 1858, 961–62.

5. Ibid.; Sean Wilentz, *The Rise of American Democracy: Jefferson to Lincoln* (New York: W.W. Norton, 2005), 725; "The Southern Monarchy," *The New-York Times*, March 18, 1858.

6. "Laboring Men but Mud Sills," *Chicago Daily Tribune*, March 16, 1858.

7. *Congressional Globe*, 35th Congress, 1st session, "Message of the President of the United States," Appendix, 5.

8. Wilentz, *Rise of American Democracy*, 732–34.

9. Allan Nevins, *Ordeal of the Union: The Emergence of Lincoln*, vol. 1, *Douglas, Buchanan, and Party Chaos, 1857–1859* (New York: Charles Scribner's Sons, 1950), 152–53, 168; William W. Freehling, *The Road to Disunion*, vol. 2, *Secessionists Triumphant, 1854–1861* (New York: Oxford University Press, 2007), 128–29.

10. Freehling, *Secessionists Triumphant*, 130–31.

11. Nevins, *The Emergence of Lincoln*, 170–72, 175.

12. Ibid., 233–34.

13. *Congressional Globe*, 35th Congress, 1st session, "Message of the President of the United States," Appendix, 1–5.

14. Nevins, *The Emergence of Lincoln*, 1:250.

15. Ibid.; Robert W. Johannsen, *Stephen A. Douglas* (New York: Oxford University Press, 1973), 521–613, details their already poor relationship and the collapse of it.

16. See especially Harry V. Jaffa, *Crisis of the House Divided: An Interpretation of the Issues in the Lincoln-Douglas Debates* (Garden City: Doubleday, 1959), and Allen C. Guelzo, *Lincoln and Douglas: The Debates That Defined America* (New York: Simon & Schuster, 2008).

17. *Congressional Globe*, 35th Congress, 1st session, December 8, 1857, 5–8.

18. Ibid.; *Congressional Globe*, 35th Congress, 1st session, December 9, 1857, 14–18.

19. Ibid., 18–19.

20. Abraham Lincoln to Lyman Trumbull, Bloomington, Illinois, December 28, 1857, in Basler, ed., *Lincoln's Works*, 2:430; Jaffa, *Crisis of the House Divided*.

21. "A House Divided," Speech at Springfield, Illinois, June 16, 1858, in Basler, ed., *Lincoln's Works*, 2:467–68.

22. Guelzo, *Lincoln and Douglas*, 75.

23. Ibid., 99.

24. Ibid., 120–21; Basler, ed., *Lincoln's Works*. The debates appear in the third volume. All quotations from the debates, unless otherwise stated, are from Guelzo or Basler.

25. Guelzo, *Lincoln and Douglas*, 191–92.

26. Ibid., 163.

27. Lincoln to Anson G. Henry, Springfield, Illinois, November 19, 1858, in Basler, ed., *Lincoln's Works*, 3:339–40.

28. "First Debate with Stephen A. Douglas at Ottawa, Illinois," August 21, 1858, in Basler, ed., *Lincoln's Works*, 3:29; David Herbert Donald, *Lincoln* (New York: Simon and Schuster, 1995), 235. At the time Lincoln spoke, Illinoisans referred to themselves as "suckers," so his comment may have been less self-deprecating than it appears.

CHAPTER SEVEN

1. Michael Burlingame, *Abraham Lincoln: A Life* (2 volumes, Baltimore: Johns Hopkins University Press, 2008), 1:275; Abraham Lincoln to William Herndon, Washington, D.C.,

February 2, 1848, in Roy P. Basler, ed., *The Collected Works of Abraham Lincoln* (9 volumes, New Brunswick: Rutgers University Press, 1953–55), 1:448.

2. Lincoln to Alexander Stephens, Springfield, Illinois, December 22, 1860 and Myrta L. Avary, *Recollections of Alexander H. Stephens* (New York: Doubleday, Page, and Company, 1910), 60, in Basler, ed., *Lincoln's Works*, 4:160–61. The quotation from Stephens refers to Proverbs 25:11 in the King James Version of The Bible.

3. Truman Smith to Lincoln, Stamford, Connecticut, November 7, 1860, and Lincoln to Smith, Springfield, Illinois, November 10, 1860, in Basler, ed., *Lincoln's Works*, 4:138–39.

4. *New Orleans Daily Crescent*, November 28, 1860, *The Editorials on Secession Project*, http://mason.gmu.edu/~rtownsen/Hist615_Maps/Final/Editorials/NO_DCrescent_11_28 _60.htm (accessed April 1, 2008); *Charleston Mercury*, December 3, 1860, http://mason .gmu.edu/~rtownsen/Hist615_Maps/Final/Editorials/CharlestonMerc_12_3_60.htm (accessed April 1, 2009).

5. *Ableman v. Booth*, 62 U.S. 506 (Howard) (1859). See also Harold M. Hyman and William C. Wiecek, *Equal Justice Under Law: Constitutional Development, 1835–1875* (New York: Harper & Row, 1982), 198–201.

6. *Ableman v. Booth*, 62 U.S. 506 (Howard) (1859).

7. Hyman and Wiecek, *Constitutional Development*, 198–201.

8. Leonard L. Richards, *The California Gold Rush and the Coming of the Civil War* (New York: Vintage Books, 2007), 219–21.

9. Stephen B. Oates, *To Purge This Land with Blood: A Biography of John Brown* (New York: Harper & Row, 1970), 351.

10. "Cooper Union Speech," February 27, 1860, in Basler, ed., *Lincoln's Works*, 3:541; David M. Potter, *The Impending Crisis: 1848–1861* (New York: Harper & Row, 1976), 379–80; William W. Freehling, *The Road to Disunion*, vol 2, *Secessionists Triumphant, 1854–1861* (New York: Oxford University Press, 2007), 220; Eric Foner, *Free Soil, Free Labor, Free Men: The Ideology of the Republican Party Before the Civil War*, 2nd ed. (New York: Oxford University Press, 1995), 210.

11. Oates, *To Purge This Land*, 352; Potter, *Impending Crisis*, 383–84; *Congressional Globe*, 36th Congress, 1st session, January 24, 1860, Appendix, 88–93.

12. John Sherman, *John Sherman's Recollections of Forty Years in the House, Senate, and Cabinet: An Autobiography* (2 volumes, Chicago: Werner, 1895), 1:168–80; Allan Nevins, *The Emergence of Lincoln: Prologue to Civil War, 1859–1861* (New York: Charles Scribner's Sons, 1950), 121.

13. *Congressional Globe*, 36th Congress, 1st session, January 18, 1860, 494; February 2, 1860, 658; March 1, 1860, 935.

14. Freehling, *The Road to Disunion*, 2:271–308.

15. Sean Wilentz, *The Rise of American Democracy: Jefferson to Lincoln* (New York: W.W. Norton, 2005), 758.

16. Lincoln to Chase, Springfield, Illinois, April 30, 1859, in Basler, ed., *Lincoln's Works*, 3:378; "Speech at Columbus, Ohio," September 16, 1859, in *Illinois State Journal*, September 24, 1859, (Ibid., 405).

17. Harold Holzer, *Lincoln at Cooper Union: The Speech That Made Abraham Lincoln President* (New York: Simon & Schuster, 2004), 283. As Holzer notes, Lincoln spoke in a hall built by and named for industrialist Peter Cooper, but it was not yet called the Cooper Union.

18. Holzer, *Lincoln at Cooper Union*, 167; Glyndon G. Van Deusen, *Thurlow Weed: Wizard of the Lobby* (Boston: Little, Brown, 1947), 251.

19. David Herbert Donald, *Lincoln* (New York: Simon & Schuster, 1995), 246–51.

20. George Hochfield, ed., *Henry Adams: The Great Secession Winter of 1860–61 and Other Essays* (New York: Sagamore Press, 1958).

21. Lincoln to Trumbull, Springfield, Illinois, November 20, 1860, in Basler, ed., *Lincoln's Works*, 4:141–42; Lincoln to Raymond, Springfield, Illinois, November 28, 1860, (Ibid., 145–46); *Illinois State Journal*, December 12, 1860, (Ibid., 150); Lincoln to John A. Gilmer, Springfield, Illinois, December 15, 1860, (Ibid., 151–52).

22. Lincoln to Trumbull, Springfield, Illinois, December 10, 1860, in Basler, ed., *Lincoln's Works*, 4:149–50; Henry J. Raymond, "Memorandum of a Private Note From Hon. A. Lincoln," in Raymond to Lincoln, New York, November 14, 1860, *Lincoln Papers*, Library of Congress, Series 1, General Correspondence, 1833–1916, http://memory.loc.gov/cgi-bin/ampage?collId=mal&fileName=mal1/044/0449700/malpage.db&recNum=4&temp-File=./temp/~ammem_bYxN&filecode=mal&next_filecode=mal&itemnum=1&ndocs=100 (accessed April 24, 2009); "The Disunion Movement," *Chicago Tribune*, November 8, 1860; Justin S. Morrill to Ruth Morrill, Washington, D.C., December 29, 1860, and January 13, 1861, Justin S. Morrill ms, Microfilm Reel 6, Library of Congress.

23. Michael S. Green, *Freedom, Union, and Power: Lincoln and His Party during the Civil War* (New York: Fordham University Press, 2004), 72. *The Charles Francis Adams Papers*, Series II, Reel 164, in the Massachusetts Historical Society includes numerous examples of Adams's thoughts on how to respond to the South.

24. Freehling, *Road to Disunion*, 2:345.

25. Wilentz, *Rise of Democracy*, 769.

26. *Congressional Globe*, 36th Congress, 2nd session, February 9, 1861, Appendix, 199.

27. Wilentz, *Rise of Democracy*, 775.

28. "First Inaugural Address," in Basler, ed., *Lincoln's Works*, 4:262–71.

29. Robert W. Johannsen, *Stephen A. Douglas* (New York: Oxford University Press, 1973), 844; "The Inaugural," *The New-York Times*, March 5, 1861; "The Declaration of War," *Richmond Enquirer*, March 5, 1861, http://mason.gmu.edu/~rtownsen/Hist615_Maps/Final/Newspapers/RichmondEnq.htm (accessed April 24, 2009).

30. Wilentz, *Rise of Democracy*, 786.

31. "Second Inaugural Address," March 4, 1865, in Basler, ed., *Lincoln's Works*, 8:332–33.

BIBLIOGRAPHICAL ESSAY

The literature on the decade-and-a-half leading up to the Civil War is vast and rich; an even more extensive bibliographic essay than this one would only skim the surface. Several general works are important to understanding how those years would unfold. Arthur M. Schlesinger, Jr., *The Age of Jackson* (1946), remains the starting point for any study of mid-nineteenth-century America, along with three magisterial books with decidedly different approaches to the period: Charles G. Sellers, *The Market Revolution: Jacksonian America, 1815–1846* (1991), Walter A. McDougall, *Throes of Democracy: The American Civil War Era, 1829–1877* (2008), and Daniel Walker Howe, *What Hath God Wrought: The Transformation of America, 1815–1848* (2008). More focused but no less important are Sean Wilentz, *The Rise of American Democracy: Jefferson to Lincoln* (2005), and Don E. Fehrenbacher with Ward McAfee, *The Slaveholding Republic: An Account of the United States Government's Relations to Slavery* (2001). Works not dedicated to this era have also informed my thinking, and I am not alone in citing these: Richard Hofstadter, *The American Political Tradition and the Men Who Made It* (1948) and *The Idea of a Party System: The Rise of Legitimate Opposition in the United States, 1780–1840* (1969), and Eric Foner, *The Story of American Freedom* (1998).

Many works have focused on the years from the Mexican-American War to the Civil War. Earlier classics such as Avery O. Craven's *The Repressible Conflict* (1939), James G. Randall's *The Civil War and Reconstruction* (1937, revised several times since by David Herbert Donald and recently with Jean H. Baker and Michael F. Holt), and

Roy F. Nichols's *The Disruption of American Democracy* (1948) remain important interpretations. David M. Potter, *The Impending Crisis: 1848–1861* (1976) provides a wealth of information and interpretation. Half of Allan Nevins's eight-volume set on the Civil War era, generally referred to by the umbrella title *Ordeal of the Union* (1947–71), address this period with rich detail, but, like Potter, with a slightly more conservative bent than some recent historical approaches. James M. McPherson's *Ordeal By Fire: The Civil War and Reconstruction* (1982) and *Battle Cry of Freedom: The Civil War Era* (1988) are less interpretive but both informative and beautifully written. The American Presidency Series by the University Press of Kansas offers solid surveys of the era's administrations: Paul H. Bergeron, *The Presidency of James K. Polk* (1987), Elbert B. Smith, *The Presidencies of Zachary Taylor and Millard Fillmore* (1988), Larry Gara, *The Presidency of Franklin Pierce* (1991), and Elbert B. Smith, *The Presidency of James Buchanan* (1975). Arthur M. Schlesinger, Jr., and Fred L. Israel, eds., *The History of American Presidential Elections* (1971) provide useful background and documents.

Surveys of the politics of the mid-nineteenth century—parties, ideologies, and regions—demonstrate the vast array of possible interpretations and approaches. Michael F. Holt's *The Rise and Fall of the American Whig Party: Jacksonian Politics and the Onset of the Civil War* (1999) is awe-inspiring, but Daniel Walker Howe's *The Political Culture of the American Whigs* (1979) still offers profitable reading. Eric Foner, *Free Soil, Free Labor, Free Men: The Ideology of the Republican Party Before the Civil War* (1970, 1995) remains the key interpretation of the mindset of the members of that party before and after they created that organization. The opposing school on antebellum politics, stressing local and ethnic issues and placing less emphasis than Foner does on ideology in general and free labor ideology in particular, has champions in Michael F. Holt, *The Political Crisis of the 1850s* (1978) and *The Fate of Their Country: Politicians, Slavery Extension, and the Coming of the Civil War* (2004); Joel H. Silbey, *The American Political Nation, 1838–1893* (1991), and *The Partisan Imperative: The Dynamics of American Politics Before the Civil War* (1985), among other of his works; and William E. Gienapp, *The Origins of the Republican Party, 1852–1856* (1987). Other valuable studies Jonathan H. Earle, *Jacksonian Antislavery and the Politics of Free Soil, 1824–1854* (2004), and Jean H. Baker, *Affairs of Party: The Political Culture of Northern Democrats in the Mid-Nineteenth Century* (1983). On the American Party, see Tyler G. Anbinder, *Nativism and Slavery: The Northern Know-Nothings and the Politics of Antislavery* (1992); W. Darrell Overdyke's *The Know-Nothing Party in the South* (1950) needs updating. David Brion Davis's *The Slave Power Conspiracy and the Paranoid Style* (1969) offers important food for thought, as does Bruce Levine, *Half Slave and Half Free: The Roots of Civil War* (2005).

Few historians have pigeonholed "the antebellum North" or even "antebellum New England," but the South and West have never suffered for lack of attention. On the South, I have found especially valuable William W. Freehling's two volumes, *The Road* to *Disunion: Secessionists at Bay, 1776–1854* (1990), and *Secessionists Triumphant, 1854–1861* (2007). William J. Cooper's studies are especially worth considering: *The South and the Politics of Slavery, 1828–1856* (1978), and *Liberty and Slavery: Southern Politics to 1860* (1983). See also Joseph A. Fry, *Dixie Looks Abroad: The South and U.S. Foreign Relations, 1789–1973* (2002), which puts the South's actions in the 1840s and 1850s into a broader perspective. On the West, particularly helpful to this study were Eugene H. Berwanger, *The Frontier Against Slavery: Western Anti-Negro Prejudice and the Slavery Extension Controversy* (1967); Michael A. Morrison, *Slavery and the American West: The Eclipse of Manifest Destiny and the Coming of the Civil War* (1997); and Eugene P. Moehring, *Urbanism and Empire in the Far West, 1840–1890* (2004). See also David M. Pletcher, *The Diplomacy of Annexation: Texas, Oregon, and the Mexican War* (1973) and Walter T.K. Nugent, *Habits of Empire: A History of American Expansion* (2008). Two approaches to groups defining themselves as "Young America" are addressed in Yonatan Eyal, *The Young America Movement and the Transformation of the Democratic Party, 1828–61* (2007), and Mark A. Lause, *Young America: Land, Labor, and the Republican Community* (2005).

Studies of the principal figures in this period vary in quality. Most have been blessed in their biographers—indeed, the authors often have been far better at their trade than their subjects were at theirs. Charles G. Sellers's *James K. Polk: Jacksonian, 1795–1843* and *James K. Polk: Continentalist, 1843–1846* (1957–) offer insight and are worth supplementing with William Dusinberre, *Slavemaster President: The Double Career of James Polk* (2003), Sam W. Haynes, *James K. Polk and the Expansionist Impulse* (1997), and Thomas M. Leonard, *James K. Polk: A Clear and Unquestionable Destiny* (2001). Holman Hamilton's two-volume *Zachary Taylor* (1941–51) is carefully researched and extensive. Robert J. Rayback, *Millard Fillmore: Biography of a President* (1959) is well-researched but its subject merits another evaluation. Roy F. Nichols, *Franklin Pierce: Young Hickory of the Granite Hills* (1931) is sympathetic without being overly admiring and masterfully thorough. James Buchanan might or might not benefit from an extensive modern biography to supplement Philip S. Klein *President James Buchanan, A Biography* (1962) or Jean Baker, *James Buchanan* (2004).

Prominent politicians of the time have received ample attention. Whigs are fortunate that Robert Remini decided to write about not only Andrew Jackson, but also them: *Henry Clay: Statesman for the Union* (1991) and *Daniel Webster: The Man and His Time* (1997), which can be supplemented with Maurice G. Baxter, *One and Inseparable: Daniel Webster and the Union* (1984). Merrill D. Peterson, *The Great Triumvirate: Webster, Clay, and Calhoun* (1987) is superb, as is John Niven, *John C. Calhoun and the Price of Union: A Biography* (1987), one of many good biographies of "the cast-iron man." Joel H. Silbey, *Martin Van Buren and the Emergence of American Popular Politics* (2002), is one of many fine works on that underrated nineteenth-century figure. Elbert B. Smith, *Francis Preston Blair* (1980) is well done but the Blairs cry out for more attention.

To select biographies of Abraham Lincoln for mention is daunting in itself, but the unsurpassed one-volume biography is David Herbert Donald, *Lincoln* (1995), while Michael Burlingame's two-volume *Abraham Lincoln: A Life* (2008) offers an incredible amount of new discoveries and food for thought. Three helpful works on Lincoln in this era are Don E. Fehrenbacher, *Prelude to Greatness: Lincoln in the 1850's* (1962); John S. Wright, *Lincoln and the Politics of Slavery* (1970); and Gabor S. Boritt, *Lincoln and the Economics of the American Dream* (1978). Glyndon Van Deusen's trilogy on New York's Whig triumvirate—*Thurlow Weed: Wizard of the Lobby* (1947), *Horace Greeley: Nineteenth-Century Crusader* (1953), and *William Henry Seward* (1967)—remains unsurpassed, which is surprising, given the need for a modern scholarly biography of Seward; several other excellent works have assessed Greeley. Frederick J. Blue, *Salmon P. Chase: A Life in Politics* (1987) and John Niven, *Salmon P. Chase: A Biography* (1995) both analyze their subject sympathetically but fairly. Robert W. Johannsen's *Stephen A. Douglas* (1973) has been admirably supplemented but not replaced. Ralph J. Roske, *His Own Counsel: The Life and Times of Lyman Trumbull* (1979) is the best on its subject, who deserves much more. John C. Frémont remains elusive and controversial even after such outstanding works as Allan Nevins, *Frémont, Pathmarker of the West* (several editions) and Sally Denton, *Passion and Principle: John and Jessie Frémont, the Couple Whose Power, Politics, and Love Shaped Nineteenth-Century America* (2007). David Donald, *Charles Sumner and the Coming of the American Civil War* (1960) is outstanding for understanding both its subject and the role of abolitionists and presumed idealists in politics.

On southern leaders, Jefferson Davis has been the subject of William J. Cooper, *Jefferson Davis, American* (2000), and an interesting comparative study, Brian R. Dirck's *Lincoln & Davis: Imagining America, 1809–1865* (2001). The prolific William C. Davis's *The Union That Shaped the Confederacy: Robert Toombs and Alexander H. Stephens* (2001) admirably assesses two parallel lives, and Davis wrote fine biographies of other key southerners: *Breckinridge: Statesman, Soldier, Symbol* (1974), and *Rhett: The Turbulent Life and Times of a Fire-Eater* (2001). Howell Cobb and John Slidell have been the subject of several books but still await the biographies they need. Eric Walther, *William Lowndes Yancey and the Coming of the Civil War* (2006) rectified the omission in that fire-eater's case. See also Kenneth S. Greenberg, *Masters and Statesmen: The Political Culture of American Slavery* (1985), and Richard H. Abbott, *The Republican Party and the South, 1855–1877: The First Southern Strategy* (1986).

Turning points and key events in this era have been the subject of a number of important and often excellent books. On the Mexican-American War, Bernard De Voto's *The Year of Decision, 1846* (1943), which remains a literary tour de force, and Robert W. Johannsen's *To the Halls of the Montezumas: The Mexican War in the American Imagination* (1985); a complete modern history of the war remains to be written. Literature on the Gold Rush is plentiful, but fine examples are H.W. Brands,

The Age of Gold: The California Gold Rush and the New American Dream (2002) and Leonard L. Richards's exceptional *The California Gold Rush and the Coming of the Civil War*. The two key books on their subject are Holman Hamilton, *Prologue to Conflict: The Compromise of 1850* (1964), and Mark J. Stegmaier, *Texas, New Mexico, and the Compromise of 1850: Boundary Dispute and Sectional Crisis* (1996). The two major books on the Kansas issue are James A. Rawley, *Race and Politics: "Bleeding Kansas" and the Coming of the Civil War* (1969), and Nicole Etcheson, *Bleeding Kansas: Contested Liberty in the Civil War Era* (2004). On the Panic of 1857, see Kenneth M. Stampp, *America in 1857: A Nation on the Brink* (1992) and James L. Huston, *The Panic of 1857 and the Coming of the Civil War* (1987). Unmatched on the Dred Scott decision, including its background and aftermath, is Don E. Fehrenbacher, *The Dred Scott Case: Its Significance in American Law and Politics* (1978); see also Harold M. Hyman and William Wiecek, *Equal Justice Under Law: Constitutional Development, 1835–1875* (1982) for additional perspective on the Taney Court. On the Lincoln-Douglas debates and their importance, the best places to start are Harry V. Jaffa, *Crisis of the House Divided: An Interpretation of the Issues in the Lincoln-Douglas Debates* (1959) and Allen C. Guelzo, *Lincoln and Douglas: The Debates That Defined America* (2008). John Brown has received his due as an important figure in such works as Stephen B. Oates, *To Purge This Land with Blood: A Biography of John Brown* (1970), and David S. Reynolds, *John Brown, Abolitionist: The Man Who Killed Slavery, Sparked the Civil War, and Seeded Civil Rights* (2005).

The culmination of this period has generated surprises. Considering that the latest full-length, in-depth study of the 1860 election is Reinhard Luthin, *The First Lincoln Campaign* (1944), Harold Holzer's *Lincoln at Cooper Union: The Speech That Made Abraham Lincoln President* (2004) is especially welcome. On the secession winter, joining David M. Potter, *Lincoln and His Party in the Secession Crisis* (1942) and Kenneth M. Stampp, *And the War Came* (1950) have been two fine recent additions: Russell McClintock, *Lincoln and the Decision for War: The Northern Response to Secession* (2008), and Harold Holzer, *Lincoln, President-Elect: Abraham Lincoln and the Great Secession Winter, 1860–1861* (2008).

INDEX

Ableman, Stephen, 141
Ableman v. Booth, 141–142
Abolitionism, xvi
  Harpers Ferry, 144–145
  literature about, xviii
  The Secret Six, 144
Adams, Charles Francis, 17
African Americans
  citizenship of, 112, 113
  rights of, xvii, 49, 113, 115
Alabama, 156
Alcohol, 79
Alien and Sedition Acts of 1798, xiv
Allen, Charles, 80
American Party. *See* Know-Nothings
Anna, Santa, 66
Anti-Masons, 79
Antislavery
  Barnburners, 7
  Republicans, 84
  uniting the movement of, 86
Arizona, 21, 65

Atchison, David Rice, 23, 67–68, 87

Bancroft, George, 4
Banks, Nathaniel, 105
Barnburner Manifesto, 16
Barnburners, 7, 15–16
Bates, Edward, 153
Beauregard, P.G.T., 158
Beecher, Henry, 54
Bell, John, 149
Benton, Thomas Hart, 4, 23, 48, 67
Birney, James, xx
Black, Jeremiah, 109
Black citizenship, 112, 113, 115
Blair, Francis Preston, 77
Blair, Montgomery, 110, 153
Blow, Taylor, 110
Booth, Sherman, 141
Border Ruffians, 88
Broderick, 143–144
Brooks, Preston, 94–95
Brown, Aaron, 108

Brown, Albert Gallatin, 147
Brown, John, 90
Brown, William Wells, 56
Browns, John, 144–145
Bryant, William Cullen, 55
Buchanan, James, 56
  Cabinet of, 108–109
  Douglas defying, 131–132
  economic downturn, 121
  election of 1856, 99–100, 107
  inaugural address, 109
  Kansas, 125, 128
  Lecompton Constitution, 131–132
  Mormons, 123–124
  secession, 156
Burns, Anthony, 73, 141
Butler, Benjamin, 16, 67

Calhoun, John C., xviii, 12, 19
  Compromise of 1850, 35–36, 42
  death of, 38
  Southern Address, 24
  territorial expansion, 6
California, 4–5, 14
  annexation of, 21
  constitutional convention, 28
  government, 22
  political categorization of, 143
  rush to, 20
  slavery, 22, 28
  state constitution, 22
  statehood of, 36, 42
Cameron, Simon, 83–84, 154
Canada, 52
Canals, 78
Cass, Lewis, 16, 56–57, 108
Catholics, 80
Chase, Salmon, 43
  Barnburners and, 16,
  Lincoln's Cabinet, 153
  Ohio governorship, 84, 150
  Republican nomination in 1856,
    101–102
  reputation of, 38, 68

slavery, 78
Citizenship, 113
Civil Disobedience, 74
Clark, Myron, 83
Clay, Henry, xxi, 19
  career of, 45–46
  Compromise of 1850, 42
  death of, 45–46
  fugitive slave law, 52–53
  Omnibus, 39–40
  preserving the Union, 33–34 (*see also*
    Compromise of 1850)
  slavery, 33
  and Webster, 32
  Whig nomination of 1848, 13, 14–15
Clayton, John, 25, 48
Clotel; or, The President's Daughter: A
  Narrative of Slave Life in the United
  States, 56
Cobb, Howell, 108
  Clay and, 34
  economic downturn, 121
  speaker of the House, 30
  views of, 29
Colfax, Schuyler, 45
Colorado, 21
Compromise of 1820, xvii, 33, 68
Compromise of 1850, 19–20
  Clay and, 33–34
  effects of, 43, 46
  fugitive slave law, 41
  measures of, 41
  passing, 39–41
  Pierce on, 65
  Seward on, 37–38
  significance of, 41–43
  stands on, 34–35
  subsequent elections, 46–47
Compromise Tariff of 1833, 33
Confederate States of America, 157
Constitution
  interpretations of, 113
  and race, 114, 115
  slavery and, xiv–xv, 78

state sovereignty, 142
Taney and, 113
Three-Fifths Clause, 30
Constitutional Unionists, 148–149, 153
Cooper, James Fenimore, 55
Corwin, Thomas, 12
Craft, Ellen, 51
Craft, William, 51
Crittenden, John, 25–26
Cuba, 65–66
Cumming, Alfred, 124
Curtis, Benjamin, 111, 114, 115
Cushing, Caleb, 63, 64

Davis, Jefferson, 38, 43, 63, 64
attack on Fort Sumter, 158
Confederate States of America, 157
Missouri Compromise, 68
slavery, 147
Dayton, William, 104
Democratic Party, xv
anti-Lecompton Democrats, 130
Charleston convention, 148
Compromise of 1850, 20
divisions in, 7–9
Douglas and, 132–133
economic downturn, 122
election of 1848, 15–17
election of 1852, 58–59
election of 1856, 98, 99, 107
electoral disaster of 1858, 130
gaining seats, 127
ideology, 46
Illinois, 132
local elections, 27
loyalty, 46
problems within, 77
rights of African Americans, 115
slavery, 27, 115, 147
in the south, 147, 148
Dickinson, Daniel, 64
Dix, John, 64
Doctrine of nullification, xviii
Donelson, Andrew Jackson, 105

Doughfaces, 41
Douglas, Stephen, 20, 38, 74
and Buchanan, 129–130
Compromise of 1850, 42
election of 1856, 99–100
election of 1860, 153
Freeport Doctrine, 136
Kansas-Nebraska Act, 74
Lecompton Constitution, 131–132
Missouri Compromise, 68, 70
Omnibus, 40
party affiliation, 132–133
railroad, 67
running for president, 57–58
slavery, 70, 132
Supreme Court decisions, 117–118
views of, 38
Douglass, Frederick, 144
Dred Scott v. Sandford, 109–113
Duer, William, 29

Economy, 121
Elections
1848 presidential, 13–17
1852 presidential, 57, 59–62
1856 presidential, 98
1860 presidential, 150–153
issues in, xvi
nominations of candidates, 14
personalities of candidates, xvi
Emancipation, gradual implementation of,
xvii
Emerson, Irene, 110
Emerson, John, 109
Everett, Edward, 55, 149

Farming, 123
Federal law
nullifying, xviii
overturning, 109–115
Federalists, xiv, xv, 78
Fillmore, Millard, 26, 105
Compromise of 1850, 41, 42, 53
election of 1852, 60

Fillmore, Millard (*continued*)
  as presidential candidate in 1856, 106
  results of election of 1856, 107
  Whig Party, 46, 47
Fire-eaters, 49
Fish, Hamilton, 47
Florida, 156
Floyd, John, 108
Foote, Henry, 39, 49
Forney, John, 128
Fort Pickens, 158
Fort Sumter, 158
Forty-niners, 21
Founding Fathers, xiv
Free labor ideology, xvi–xvii, 123
Free Soil Party, 16–17, 34
  anti-alcohol regulation, 79
  growth of, 46
  Kansas, 89
Frémont, Jessie, 102, 105
Frémont, John Charles
  and California, 4, 42, 43
  candidacy of, 105
  Republican nomination of, 102–103,
    104
  results of election of 1856, 107
  vice-presidential candidate for, 104
Fugitive Slave Act, xv, 46, 49–50
  benefits to the South, 52
  circumventing, 141
  Dred Scott v. Sandford, 110–111
  effects of, 43
  enforcement of, 50
  fighting over, 73
  northern rebellion against, 51–52
  northerners, 50
  problems with, 50

Gadsden, James, 65
Gag Rule, xviii
Gardner, Henry, 83
Garrison, William Lloyd, xvii, 74
Geary, John, 90
Geography, 30

Georgia, 156
Geyer, Henry, 110
Gilmer, John, 154
Gold rush, 20
Great Britain, 3, 4
Greeley, Horace P., 11, 15
  criticism of Seward, 152
  Taylor and, 10
  views of, 53
  Whig Party, 152
Grier, Robert, 111, 114
Guadalupe-Hidalgo, Treaty of, 14, 65
Guthrie, James, 63–64
Gwin, William, 22, 42, 143

Hale, John P., 7, 84
Halleck, Henry, 22
Hamilton, Alexander, xiv
Hamlin, Hannibal, 152
Hammond, James Henry, 122–123
Harrison, William Henry, xix
Hastings, Lansford, 22
Hawaii, 65
Hawthorne, Nathaniel, 55
Helper, Hinton, 124
Hemings, Sally, 56
Henry, William, 52
Higginson, Thomas Wentworth, 144
Houston, Sam, 57, 149, 156
Howe, Samuel Gridley, 144
Hunkers, 15
Hunt, Washington, 47
Hunter, R.M.T., 58, 67

Illinois, 82, 132
Immigrants
  bias against, 80, 84–85
  influx of, 80
  Know-Nothings, 84
  political affiliations of, 84
Impending Crisis of the South, The, 124
Indian removal, xviii
Industrial development, 43
Industrial Revolution, xvi

Jackson, Andrew, xviii
Jackson, Thomas Jonathan, 145
Jefferson, Thomas, xiv, 56
Jeffersonian Party. *See* Republican Party
Johnson, Reverdy, 25
Julian, George, 46

Kansas, 68
  Buchanan and, 124, 128–129
  constitutional convention for, 126–127
  disputes over, 87
  Lecompton Constitution, 127, 129 (*see also* Lecompton Constitution)
  significance of, 90
  slavery and, 87–88, 127, 129
  southerners in, 88
  statehood, 156
  violence in, 90
Kansas-Nebraska Act of 1854, 45
  divisions over, 46
  impact of, 74–77
  introducing, 68
  issues related to, 67
King, Preston, 16
King, Thomas Butler, 28
Know-Nothings, 80–81
  attack on, 85
  declining influence of, 130–131
  divisions between, 86–87
  election of 1855, 84
  election of 1856, 101, 105–107
  and immigrants, 84–85
  popularity of, 81
  slavery, 85, 106
Know-Somethings, 84
Kossuth, Louis, 59–60

Laws
  anti-alcohol, 79
  federal, xviii
  fugitive slave, 41, 73 (*see also* Fugitive Slave Act)
  overturning federal, 109–115
  personal liberty, 49, 141

social liberty, 79
state sovereignty, 142
Leaves of Grass, 55
Lecompton Constitution, 127, 129, 131–132
Liberty Party, xx
Lincoln, Abraham, 17, 26, 43, 101
  Cabinet of, 64, 153–154
  chance of victory for, 152–153
  on civil war, 157
  debates with Douglas, 134–138
  and Douglas, 133, 134–135
  Dred Scott v. Sandford, 116
  Fort Sumter, 158
  "House Divided" speech, 134
  inaugural address, 157–158
  Mexican-American War, 11
  nomination for U.S. senator, 120, 133
  party nomination for, 150–151
  political affiliation of, 82, 85
  on race, 118
  and religion, 2
  senate race of 1858, 133, 138
  slavery, 154
  speech at the Cooper Union, 150–151
  Spot Resolutions, 11
  and Stephens, 139–140
  strengths of, 151
  taking office, 157
  threat of secession, 154–155
  views of, 2
Lincoln-Douglas debates, 134–138
Literature
  antislavery, 124–125, 155
  classic, 54–56
Little Giant. *See* Douglas, Stephen
Louisiana, 156
Louisiana Purchase, xiv
Lovejoy, Elijah, xvii

Madison, James, xiv
Maine, 79
Marcy, William, 56, 63, 64, 65
Marshall, John, xv

Mason, James, 31, 67, 132
Masonic lodges, 79
May, Samuel, 52
McLean, John, 102, 111, 114
Meade, Richard, 29
Melville, Herman, 55
Mexican-American War, 3
  concerns about, 6–7
  cost of, 21
  end of, 14, 21
  Lincoln and, 11
  provocation of, 5
  results of, 21
Mexico, xix–xx
  buying territory from, 65
  Polk and, 5–6
Mining rushes, 20
Mississippi, 156
Missouri, xvii
Missouri Compromise, xvii
  debate over, 68–70
  legality of, 112, 113
  passing, 70
  significance of, 68, 70
  voting on, 39
Missouri line, 68
Moby Dick; or The Whale (Melville) 55
Monroe, James, xiv, xv
Mormon War, 123–124
Mormons, 22–23
  and Buchanan, 123–124
  statehood, 28
Mountain Meadows Massacre, 124

National Free Soil Convention, 16
National Intelligencer, 97–98
National Reform Association, 81–82
Nebraska, 68
Nelson, Samuel, 111, 114
Nevada, 21
New Mexico, 21, 28, 40, 43, 65
New York, 82–83
New York Times, The, 53
Nicaragua, 66

No Territory, 12
North
  Compromise of 1850, 43
  differences within, 49
  farming in, 123
  population growth, 30–31, 35
Northeners
  fugitive slave law, 50–51
  in rural areas, 9
  slavery, xvii
Northwest Ordinance of 1787, xiv

Omnibus, 39, 40
Order of the Star-Spangled Banner, 80
Oregon, xxi, 3, 4
Ostend Manifesto, 66

Panic of 1819, xv
Parker, Theodore, 50, 144
Party system
  antislavery and, 78–79
  evolution of, xiv, 78
  first, 78
  Founding Fathers, xiv
  issues driving, 83
  and region, 31
  second, xv, 79
  slavery, 83
  third, 79
  two-, 31
Pearce, James, 39, 40
Pennsylvania, 104
Pierce, Bennie, 63
Pierce, Franklin, 45, 58
  Cabinet of, 63–64
  Compromise of 1850, 65
  death of son, 63
  election of 1856, 98
  first annual message, 108
  inaugural address, 65
  liabilities of, 98–99
  Missouri Compromise, 68
  problems of, 63
  wife of, 63 (*see also* Pierce, Jane)

Pierce, Jane, 58, 63
Polk, James K., xxi, 3
  death of, 31
  Mexican-American War, 3, 21
  and Mexico, 5–6
  northerners and, 8
  and Taylor, 10
  territorial expansion and, 3–5, 8
Popular sovereignty, 136
Population
  demographics and slavery, 12
  growth, 30–31, 35
Presidential elections
  issues of 1848, 13
  nominations for, 14
  results of 1848, 17
Prigg v. Pennsylvania, 49–50
Prohibition, 79
Prosperity, 121

Quitman, John, 66–67

Railroad
  building, 78
  transcontinental, 65, 67
Raymond, Henry Jarvis, 53
Reeder, Andrew, 88–89
Religion
  in 1852, 62
  California, 4
  instruction of, 80
  in the North, xvi
  politics, xvi
  revival movement (*see* Second Great
    Awakening)
  in the South, xvi
Republic
  birth of, xiv, 81
  slavery, 81–82
Republican Party, xiv
  attack at Harpers Ferry, 145
  campaigning, 105
  candidate nomination in 1856, 104
  candidate nomination in 1860, 151–152

division of, xv
and Douglas, 132–133
Dred Scott v. Sanford, 115
economic downturn, 122
election of 1860, 149
gains in, 131, 133
growth of, 85, 86
issues, 101
and Lincoln, 133–134, 151
nativism, 107
platform of 1856 election, 103
rights of African Americans, 116
slavery, 103, 115
Rights, xvii, 49, 113, 115
Ruffin, Edmund, 158

Sack of Lawrence, 90
Sandwich Islands, 65
Sanford, John F.A., 109, 110
Scott, Dred, 109, 115
Scott, Harriet, 109, 115
Scott, Winfield, 45, 60–62
Secession
  call for, 48
  constitution, 157
  convention, 156
  discouraging, 49
  efforts to stop, 156
  Lincoln and the threat of, 154–155
  planning for, 155–156
  states participating in, 156
  Yancey and, 148
Second Continental Congress, xiv
Second Great Awakening, the, xvi, 10, 79
Secret Six, The, 144
Seward, William Henry, 20
  and Buchanan, 117
  Compromise of 1850, 37–38
  Confederate States of America, 158
  controversial address, 119–120
  criticism of, 152
  election of 1855, 82–83, 104
  Fillmore and, 26
  immigration and, 80

Seward, William Henry (*continued*)
  Lincoln's Cabinet, 153
  Republican nomination in 1856, 101
  slavery, 42, 87
  Taylor and, 27, 31, 47
  Whig Party, 75
Shadrach, 51
Shields, James, 82
Silver Greys, 11, 47
Slave Power, xx, 116
Slave trade
  in the District of Columbia, 41, 43
  under Taylor, 24
Slavery
  Barnburners and, 16
  in California, 28
  in the Constitution, xiv, 78
  divisions over, xiii, 147
  election of 1844, xx–xxi
  elections of 1849, 27
  Industrial Revolution, xvi
  Kansas voting on, 127
  Know-Nothings and, 85
  literature, 54–56
  northern farmers and, 9
  northerners and, xvii
  party system, 83
  political parties and, 115
  states deciding on, 40–41
  Taylor, 27–28
  territorial expansion, 9, 12
  Texas and, xx–xxi
  in the West, 28, 29, 67–68
Slaves
  fugitive, 51, 52, 73 (*see also* Fugitive
    Slave Act)
  rebellions, xvi
Smith, Caleb, 153
Smith, Joseph, 22, 23
Smith, Truman, 76, 140
Soulé, Pierre, 64, 65
South
  differences within, 49
  distrust for the North, 52
  divisions within, 129
  expansion, 129
  federal supremacy, 142–143
  Lincoln's election, 155
  population growth, 30–31, 35
South Carolina, xviii, 156
Southern Address, 24
Southerners
  antislavery literature, 124–125
  Brown and, 145–146
  concerns about Lincoln, 155
  divisions between, 78, 147, 148
  economic downturn, 122
  in Kansas, 88
  Wilmot Proviso, 12
Sovereignty, 142
Spot Resolutions, 11
States
  admission of Kansas, 156
  Jacksonian view of, 142
  Missouri's admission, xvii
  secessionist, 156
Stearns, George, 144
Stephens, Alexander, 43
  Confederate States of America, 157
  and Lincoln, 139–140
  Missouri Compromise, 70
  territorial expansion, 12
Stowe, Harriet Beecher, 54–55
Sumner, Charles, 47
  altercation with Brooks, 94
  Senate speeches, 91
Supreme Court
  Douglas and, 117–118
  Dred Scott v. Sandford, 115 (see also
    Dred Scott v. Sandford)
  respect for, 115
  rights of African Americans, 109–115
Sutter, John, 20
Suttle, Charles, 73

Taney, Roger Brooke, 109, 111, 113,
  141–142, 157
Taylor, Zachary, 10, 31, 47

annual message of 1850, 30
Cabinet, 25
Compromise of 1850, 42
death of, 39
inauguration of, 23–24
issues, 26–27
Mexican-American War, 5
presidency of, 24–29
as presidential candidate, 14
Wilmot Proviso, 27
Territorial expansion
California, 3
Cuba, 65–66
Great Britain and, 3, 4
Mexico, 1–2, 65
Nicaragua, 66
Pierce and, 65
Polk and, 3–5, 8
population demographics, 12
slavery, 9, 12
and the South, 13, 129
Treaty of Guadalupe-Hidalgo, 14 (*see also* Guadalupe-Hidalgo, Treaty of)
westward, 67–68
Wilmot and, 1–2
Terry, David, 143–144
Texas, 43, 156
annexation of, xx, 3, 4
boundaries of, 31, 41
debts of, 41
independence of, xix
and New Mexico, 39
Thompson, Jacob, 108
Thoreau, Henry David, 74
Toombs, Robert, 29
Toucey, Isaac, 108
Trail of Tears, xviii
Trist, Nicholas, 14, 21
Trumbull, Lyman, 133
Turner, Nat, xvi

Uncle Tom's Cabin; Or, Life Among the Lowly (Stowe), 53
Unionism, 49

United States, in the mid-1840s, xiii
Utah, 21, 40
Buchanan and, 123–124
slavery, 43

Van Buren, Martin, xv, xx–xxi, 7, 15, 16, 17
annexation of Texas, 7
election of 1844, xx–xxi
election of 1848, 15, 16, 17
Jacksonian Democrats and, xv

Wade, Benjamin, 47
Walden (Thoreau), 74
Walker, Robert J., 125–126
Walker, William, 66
War of 1812, xiv, 6
Webb, James Watson, 53
Webster, Daniel, 11, 13, 19
career of, 45–46
and Clay, 32
death of, 45–46
election of 1852, 59
preserving the Union, 36–37
Whig Party, 47
Weed, Thurlow, 10
Fillmore and, 26
Taylor and, 15, 27, 47
Weller, John, 43
Welles, Gideon, 153
West, significance of, 96
Whig Party, xv
Conscience, 11
Cotton, 11
difficulties faced by, 46–47
dissolution of, 45, 76
divisions in, 9, 49, 59
election of 1840, xix
election of 1848, 13–15
election of 1852, 59–61
ideology of, 46
Kansas-Nebraska Act, 74–77
leadership problem, 13
migrating to a new party, 82–83
New York, 47

Whig Party (*continued*)
  newspaper, 97–98
  northern, 10–12
  and the presidency, 25
  and the religious movement, xix
  slavery, 75–76
  in the south, 12–13, 76
Whitman, Walt, 55
Wilmot, David, 1–3, 29
Wilmot Proviso, 9, 12–13, 27

Wilson, Henry, 81, 83
Winthrop, Robert, 11, 29, 34
Wisconsin, 141, 142
Woodbury, Levi, 57
Wright, Silas, 8–9
Wyoming, 21

Yancey, William Lowndes, 148
Yates, Richard, 69
Young, Brigham, 22, 23, 123–124

About the Author

MICHAEL S. GREEN is a professor of history at the College of Southern Nevada. He is the author of *Freedom, Union, and Power: Lincoln and His Party during the Civil War* (2004) and the forthcoming *Lincoln and the Election of 1860*. In addition, he is the editor of the forthcoming *Blackwell Companion to Abraham Lincoln*.